# The Culture of Inequality

# The Culture of Inequality

### MICHAEL LEWIS

*Second Edition, with a New Introduction*

University of Massachusetts Press    AMHERST

22.95

Copyright © 1978 by Michael Lewis
Introduction to the second edition © 1993 by Michael Lewis
All rights reserved
Library of Congress Catalog Card Number: 77-24214
ISBN 0-87023-857-4
Printed in the United States of America
Designed by Mary Mendell
Library of Congress Cataloging in Publication Data
appear on the last printed page of the book.

# Contents

# Introduction to the Second Edition

Written in the late seventies, this book houses a pessimistic argument about American culture, an argument I unfortunately find no reason to modify. If anything, in the years since its first publication, *The Culture of Inequality*'s speculative fears about American life have become matters of awful fact. It is as though payment on our Faustian bargain has come due. The *individual-as-central sensibility*, the cultural element most responsible for our great (primarily economic) successes during the twentieth century, has revealed itself, fully and finally, to be our culture's heart of darkness as well. As the century draws to a close, the meanest moralism appears to have triumphed and the estrangement predicted in the final chapter of *The Culture of Inequality* seems even more profound than expected.

Driven by culturally induced self-doubt, by a sense that even though we live in the best of all possible societies, we have, nevertheless, not fully seized our opportunities, we war against those whose apparent failure to meet even minimum standards of achievement and decency curiously reassures us by emphasizing the human lapses and moral infirmities that, if nothing else, we have avoided. This need for reassurance is not new. As I argued in these pages, it is as old as the individual-as-central sensibility that took root in North America during the eighteenth century.[1] What is new is the intensity of the need and the willingness of those burdened by its trauma to wage their reassuring war against the disinherited with pitiless determination.

As recently as the seventies it was possible to identify two views of the disinherited that framed mainstream opinion and the policy space it defines.[2]

---

[1]Liberated personal aspiration was (and is) the sensibility's siren song even as it rendered (and continues to render) individuals vulnerable to self-excoriation for any perceived failure to realize their dreams.

[2]Policy space is a metaphoric evocation of the range of social and economic initiatives that, irrespective of their potential for effect, are likely to become matters of law and regulation.

The first and older of these held the miserable among us to be slackers and miscreants whose condition was justly deserved. Having forsworn the effort and self-restraint necessary for a productive and estimable existence, they had consigned themselves to an underclass—and as such had forfeited any claim upon the charity and forbearance of decent, hard-working people.

The second of these views—influenced by the work of social scientists such as E. Franklin Frazier, Oscar Lewis, Daniel Patrick Moynihan, Talcott Parsons, and Walter Miller, as well as by developmental psychology's establishment as professional social work's intellectual beacon—rejected the demonization of the disinherited. In this view they were not slugs and miscreants, but rather incompetents who by virtue of faulty socialization and constant exposure to maladaptive subcultures simply lacked the attitudes and life skills necessary to achieve a decent existence.

Although each of these characterizations emphasized the individual's role in the purchase of his or her misery, the first view (favored by conservatives) was, by far, the crueler of the two. The second (espoused more often than not by liberals) held out the possibility of redemption through resocialization and subcultural transformation, but the first held that only punishment had any chance of moving the self-consigned bottom feeders to a redeeming repentance.

Today, the crueler view prevails, the more generous and hopeful view having all but disappeared. Estrangement between the disinherited and the rest of us has proceeded to a point where attributions of incompetence and cultural maladaption have themselves become moral judgments. Now in the last decade of the twentieth century, few explain the miserable poverty of the disinherited without resorting to a rhetoric worthy of Hester Prynne's accusers. Americans of every station (including in some cases the self-loathing among the disinherited themselves), struggling to hold intimations of personal inadequacy at bay, cast the poor as willful transgressors against common decency—so that, by comparison, the accusers may claim a righteousness which, momentarily at least, allows them to deny their self-doubts.

Its scarlet accusations everywhere, the opprobrium is inescapable. Candidates for public office, from town clerk to president of the United States, vie with one another for the political gains that "getting tough" with the poor can bring. For example, there is little different between George Bush and Bill Clinton (who at this writing are seeking the presidency) on the issue of welfare reform. At a time when the economy threatens to permanently pauperize millions of Americans previously able to scrape by, Bush makes a great show of advocating welfare reductions while Clinton would limit welfare recipients to no more than two years of assistance. The former seeks votes by voicing his indignation at the temerity of those scoundrels who actually go from state to state seeking extra welfare dollars that will facilitate their indolence. The latter seeks those same votes by demanding that welfare recipients be responsible, that they make use of the "second chance" which his proposed limited welfare system will provide; that they clean up their acts, realizing welfare will no longer entitle them to wile away their days guzzling beer, having sex, and watching soap operas. (Clearly there is only one subtext in these pronouncements and it is hardly subtextual.)

Much of what contemporary politicians say about the disinherited has been drafted by a coterie of intellectuals—once barely respectable because they insisted upon policies that would abandon the poor to their own devices but now given an appreciative and, in some precincts, almost worshipful hearing for that very same reason. Where once the likes of George Gilder, Lawrence Mead, and Charles Murray would have been ignored by mainstream media, they are today interviewed on network news programs, their pronouncements have become a staple of the Public Broadcasting System, and their books are prominently reviewed in the pages of the *New York Times*, the *Washington Post*, *Time*, and *Newsweek*. If there is a riot such as the one that occurred on the streets of South Central Los Angeles, these champions of not-so-benign neglect will be heard from, explaining it all, and worrying that the violence may, contrary to good sense, stimulate a round of spending on wasteful and futile social programs; and when welfare reform becomes the inevitable C-Span miniseries, these pundits and their ideas will figure prominently in its dramaturgy. No longer marginal, they have elevated harshness toward the disinherited poor to a first principle of antipoverty policy—and they have done so to cascading applause from the gallery.[3]

Without the slightest hesitation, otherwise decent people add the burden of their contempt and mistrust to the economic misery of the disinherited poor. Women alone, struggling against great odds to provide their children with loving care, find themselves (unless they have been widowed) the objects of scorn because of what others perceive as their affront to that most publicly and officially revered of American institutions—the family. If the conservatives among us are explicit in condemning the threat to family values posed by what they see as the irresponsible behavior of women and teenage girls whose pregnancies have occurred because they refuse to control their voracious sexual appetites, the liberals' moralistic exasperation and loathing are nevertheless clear enough. The problems of poor women in the liberal view are basically too many children born to mothers too willing to accept welfare as a

---

[3] I am indebted to Timothy Black for drawing my attention to the increasing prominence of these and other intellectual proponents of punitive antipoverty policies. See Timothy Black, "The Longest of Odds" (Ph.D. diss., University of Massachusetts/ Amherst, 1993).

way of life. This, so the argument goes, leads directly to the twin horrors of child abuse and child neglect. Irresponsible pregnancy, they piously assert, is the sad prelude to irresponsible parenting.

In the last decade of the twentieth century, poverty itself has been criminalized. The poor, simply because of their poverty, are routinely denied the presumption of innocence. Unless they can prove otherwise, the disinherited, it seems, must be guilty of something. What else can be made of news programs that harp on welfare fraud and facilely cite unfounded estimates that suggest upwards of 50 percent of welfare recipients actively engage in ripping off tax-supported public assistance?[4] What else can be made of the millions of dollars the federal government spends annually to intensify surveillance activities in public housing projects on the assumption that since these projects house the poor they must also house drug traffickers and their retinue of petty criminals (e.g., pimps and prostitutes)?[5] And what else can be made of the fact that some Americans now seriously entertain proposals for cordoning off certain neighborhoods—the inner-city slum-ghettoes—so that the police can proceed with house-to-house searches for drugs and other contraband? That the disinherited are not universally viewed with such contemptuous distrust is, of course, true. Those who demur, however, seem increasingly to do so sotto voce.

I live in a state where local communities regularly confront fiscal problems generated by a legally mandated property-tax limitation. The only way to transcend this limitation is by a referendum in which voters are asked to give their assent to a proposed suspension of its required imposition. Characteristically there are several such referenda on the ballot in any given fiscal year, each pegged to a specific municipal function. Thus voters have the option of choosing among the various overrides being proposed. Last year in a community neighboring the one in which I reside, voters were asked to approve two overrides, one to pay for garbage collection and the other to rescue a bankrupt school system. The first of these initiatives passed; the second was rejected despite the fact that such a rejection meant that teachers would be fired, schools would be closed, and even those remaining open would be on reduced schedules with larger classes and fewer course offerings.

On the face of it, these results would appear perplexing indeed. Americans make a great show of valuing children and being willing to invest in them. They are, after all, the American future. So how is it that these voters chose to

---

[4]See, for example, ABC News Prime Time Live, "Welfare Fraud" (September 17, 1992).
[5]See Public Housing Drug Elimination Program, Department of Housing and Urban Development (HUD). This is not to say that drug trafficking does not occur in public housing. It does. The surveillance, however, is not based upon any evidence that criminal behavior is occurring but merely upon the *assumption* that it is.

injure the interests of their community's children even as they were willing to spring for publicly financed garbage collection? The answer, I believe, has to do with just who these children are. Increasingly, the children in this community's public schools are poor and Hispanic. During the period leading up to the vote, much was made of the fact that more than 50 percent of the community's school-age population lived in families receiving public assistance. Thus the referendum on the school override was actually transformed into a referendum on the presence of the poor and particularly the minority poor within the community. When the votes were counted, the contempt that many in the community held for the poor was given official recognition in a decision that in effect said "You can raise our taxes to deal with garbage, but you cannot do so to deal with the children of the lazy, cheating, crime-ridden, non-English-speaking interlopers."[6] The vote leaves very little to the imagination. The poor in this community are not merely an aggregate of individuals with insufficient resources, they are not merely people injured by life's precarious fortunes. To be sure, they are that, but they are as well an imagined company of scavenging malefactors. And when the voters turned down the school override they intended to do precisely what they did: hurt the poor. In the privacy of the polling booth, they no doubt registered their "no" vote as though they were striking a blow for embattled decency: their "decency"—that quality which above all else signals the moral chasm separating the us, the good decent people, from the them, those ruled by sulphurous urgencies.[7]

If you are poor in this last decade of the twentieth century, opprobrium is indeed inescapable. You are who you know yourself to be, but you are as well an imagined accusation—an alien presence more injurious to yourself than the conditions of material deprivation traditionally associated with poverty. So, in this last decade of the century if you are poor you are likely to spend as much or more time fending off the you whom others so cruelly imagine as you do struggling to overcome the material deprivations of your station. The following letter appeared in the daily newspaper published in a small city that is arguably among the most tolerant communities in the United States, a community aggressive in its ostensible affirmation of equal rights and protections for all. It

---

[6]Some may object that other communities without such a school population profile also regularly reject education overrides, thus indicating that the minority poor were really not the issue in this instance. To such an objection, I can only respond that the gravity of the situation was such—the school system was literally bankrupt—that the voters' rejection of the override must be seen as a judgment on the school population.

[7]The symbolic status enhancement function of political behavior has been thoroughly analyzed by contemporary social scientists. See, for example, Joseph Gusfield, *Symbolic Crusade* (Urbana: University of Illinois Press, 1986) and Murray Edelman, *The Symbolic Uses of Politics* (Urbana: University of Illinois Press, 1964).

was written by a woman who may or may not be poor but who, as the text indicates, certainly knows the accusations summoned by the use of that troubled designation:

> *To the Editor:*
>
> *In one of your front-page articles . . . you use the word "poor" in a headline—"Poor Parents Decry Loss of Buses"—under a picture of several . . . residents. Some of us were in that picture, and we are angry and embarrassed.*
>
> *Some of [our] children . . . were worried about what their friends are going to think and say; are they going to pick on them and make fun of them and their parents? . . . "Poor" also suggests "poor" weather, or that was a "poor" test score. . . . [As] you can see, the word "poor" has many different definitions and because of that, if you refer to someone as being "poor," it leaves them open to discrimination. . . .*
>
> *We acknowledge that the [paper] printed another article that brings out . . . that people featured in that article strongly object to being called "poor." We hope that it will never happen again. . . .*
>
> *Nydia Hernandez on behalf of the Pre-GED class of [the] Adult Education Co-operative*[8]

In the course of writing *The Culture of Inequality*, I worried a great deal about being misunderstood. In particular, I was concerned that I might be read as dichotomizing the social world I was seeking to explain into guiltless victims (the disinherited) and driven tormentors (the rest of us). I still worry about such a misunderstanding, perhaps even more than I did previously because I am so deeply troubled by what I believe has happened to us—*all* of us. As this century rushes toward its conclusion, the disinherited poor are no doubt being made to suffer more than the rest of us because of moralism's hegemony. But the rest of us do suffer. The triumph of moralism is, as explained and predicted in this book's final chapter, the result of a process by which estrangement between, on the one hand, the "have-nots" and, on the other, the "have-some-things" and the "have-a-lots" proceeds inexorably. In the course of this intensified mutual estrangement, American culture is regressively transformed, so that only a moralistic version of the individual-as-central sensibility remains. In the years since this book was first published, I believe this calculus has indeed played itself out and we are now—all of us—confronting its awful consequences: the disinherited poor as objects of a terrible contempt; the rest of us as prisoners of the hectoring morality (look at yourself—why, with all the chances in the world, have you not achieved more than you have?), requiring that contempt.

---

[8]Published July 27, 1992.

Given the cultural emphasis upon the individual, it is very difficult for any American—even an impoverished American—not to believe that success (usually defined in economic terms) is there for the taking, provided you are sufficiently tenacious in its pursuit. Even an economic slowdown in the late 1980s and early 1990s has not cast this tenet of American belief into significant doubt. While Americans worry about the economy in general, opinion polls suggest they remain confident that should they do what is required of them, it will only be a matter of time before they grasp the brass ring. Although this has been the characteristic instruction of the individual-as-central sensibility throughout the twentieth century, since the 1960s its apparent truth has seemed increasingly, if speciously, self-evident. In what has seemed like progress, women, for example, have routinely joined men in daring to dream of the big score earned by the quality of their talents and the quantity of their efforts. Affirmative action, more rhetoric than reality, has nevertheless made it appear that the last remaining barriers to a true meritocracy are collapsing. In 1978 William Julius Wilson judged race to be of declining significance as an impediment to achieved personal success.[9] And although he is too canny an observer of American life to serenade us with hosannas celebrating the complete realization of equalitarianism, he has remained steadfast in his view. Since the 1960s, the possibility of higher education, once out of reach of the masses, has become a staple of the guidance counselor's motivational talk even in inner-city schools. The Reverend Jesse Jackson regularly exhorts poor black students to overcome the only barriers to education that count, the ones, he says, within themselves.[10] If you cannot attend the University of Chicago or Harvard, there are always the state schools, and if for some reason you cannot attend a state university or college, well then, there are always the community colleges. With the availability of all these schools and financial aid to boot, it is hard for contemporary Americans not to believe that, as far as higher education is concerned, where there's a will, there's a way. And because everyone "knows" that education is the key to getting ahead, the brass ring, it must be concluded, is within reach of anyone sufficiently disciplined to make the required effort.

In reality, of course, there are impediments to "getting ahead" that remain well beyond the individual's control. The absence of a tax-supported family allowance and universal public funding for day care—both unexceptional in western Europe—seriously restrict women's vocational options. Affirmative action often appears little more than the application of a cosmetic that covers

[9]See William J. Wilson, *The Declining Significance of Race* (Chicago: University of Chicago Press, 1978).
[10]See, for example, transcripts of Jackson's "I am somebody" speech regularly given in inner-city schools on behalf of Operation PUSH.

but really does little to heal he scars of systematic exclusion. Surely, since the 1960s, race has declined in its power to impede *some* African Americans and other minority people as they try for the brass ring; before 1960 there were no Michael Jordans, Eddie Murphys, and Spike Lees. But no one who has recently walked the streets of inner-city slum-ghettoes or found his or her way into the unemployment offices of urban America would give much credence to any view that holds race to be little more than a trivial impediment to economic success. Educational opportunity surely does exist, but it is not equal opportunity. The best predictor of where you go to school, and thus the quality of the education you receive is, as it always has been, not your talent and your motivation, but rather the socioeconomic characteristics of your parents.

The brass ring thus continues to elude the grasp of many people through no fault of their own. But the American cultural emphasis on the individual does not allow us to see it that way. Caught up in the calliope's triumphant anthems, we keep grasping for the ring, never noticing the mechanism that pulls it just beyond our reach with every revolution of the carousel. Believing more than ever in the reality of equal opportunity and in the imperative requiring all individuals to make the most of their chances, Americans now take any indication of failed aspiration to signal incipient moral bankruptcy. It was bad enough when failure was taken to signify personal incompetence, but now, in the midst of the century's endgame, all of us live in terror of a failure that will mean that we are at odds with the American conception of a good human being.

The same moralism that drives our punitiveness toward the disinherited poor constitutes a constant threat to ourselves. If they are irresponsible, we may be as well. If they lack the work ethic perhaps we do too. If their failures have earned our contempt, what should we make of our own failures? Ironically, in order for the disinherited poor to be held in thrall as psychic hostages to our well-being, their apparent failures must constitute failures we are capable of as well. They have failed to honor the American success imperative—and their failure is gross and impossible to miss. It is the failure that might have been ours, but because of our efforts we do not share their fate. We salvage our self-esteem by this contrast. But every act of contempt toward the disinherited is also a reminder of our own burdens and traumas. Savaging the disinherited poor has become an American addiction because each time such savaging occurs it fires our anxieties anew, so we must save ourselves from our own moralism by engaging in the bashing yet one more time. Do the poor suffer? Yes, terribly. But the rest of us do as well. In the last decade of the twentieth century there may be pleasure—sex, drugs . . . rock and roll—but it seems to me that happiness has become a concept whose meaning we have misplaced, perhaps never again to rediscover. And contentment . . . ?

We, all of us, now live in a society where fearing the other has become routine. It is rare to visit someone who doesn't have a minimum of two locks (one invariably a deadbolt) on any door that opens on a public way. In most cities three or four such devices are de rigueur. T.V. cameras scan the lobbies of apartment buildings, elevators are equipped with mirrors to allow passengers to see if any undesirables are skulking in wait, taxi cabs have bullet-proof screens to isolate drivers from passengers, who are thereby deemed potential assailants. The loud, high-pitched chirp of the automotive security system is alive in the land. There are neighborhoods in our cities where whites dare not go and neighborhoods which blacks and other visibly identifiable minorities must avoid. Whole cities are off-limits to many suburbanites because they believe that they will be set upon should they so much as walk a single city block.

Fear is ubiquitous in American society. It would be foolhardy, however, to attribute its hold upon us solely to the estrangement that is the necessary correlate of the need to cast the disinherited poor as immoral and even dangerous. That estrangement is, nevertheless, a not insignificant element in its genesis.

Most of the despised poor have suffered the injuries done them with more sorrow than anger—a tribute, no doubt, to the importance of religious faith and, in particular, Christian stoicism in their lives. Some, however, have harbored for years a rage just barely held in check. From time to time that rage has found expression in what, at some remove, seems to be senseless violence in which only the poor themselves are harmed. Even the urban riots of the 1960s, widespread though they were, did not characteristically spill over into areas populated and used by the middle class. Recently, however, there has been a change; the pariahs' violent rejection of their stigma has begun to focus upon those they blame for the insults they suffer. The riots in South Central Los Angeles spread into areas of the city that in the past would have escaped unscathed. Mobs of impoverished black and Hispanic youths felt justified in their aggression by a verdict that had exonerated four police officers in the brutal beating of a black man. These young people turned on anyone and anything that represented the world in which they counted for so little that even a videotaped record of some eighty blows and kicks raining down upon one of their own could not convince a jury that anyone had done anything wrong. Buildings were burned, stores plundered, and people beaten in a paroxysm of fury. Street crime, while still very much a problem for the disinherited themselves, has come to the neighborhoods of the middle class, and in a manner that seems to put a premium on violence. Hold-ups, which once used the threat of violence to intimidate a victim into docilely giving up cash and jewelry, have been transformed into muggings in which the perpetrator hits or maims first and steals second. Car theft, best and most easily accomplished when no one is around, has of late been recast as a public act calculated to terrorize motorists. From New York to California, stopping for a light or because of an apparent accident can now leave you vulnerable to an armed attack in which you will be deprived of both your senses and your automobile. That violence against the "haves" seems to be the primary purpose of these ambushes would appear to be clearly established by the fact that automobiles taken in this manner are soon abandoned, thus ruling out pecuniary gain as the underlying motive. And then there is the *wilding* in which groups of teenagers commit mayhem as they maraud through neighborhoods once assumed to be reasonably safe. In a frenzy ordinarily associated with the behavior of undisciplined troops entering a city populated by their most hated enemies, the youths beat, rape, and otherwise physically humiliate those crossing their path who represent a world in which they are the objects of scorn.

There are two basic tragedies in all of this. First, as might be expected, the increasing incidence of violent acts committed by the disinherited against "respectable citizens" confirms, for those who wish it to, the disrepute of the "rabble" and stimulates popular support for a crackdown which, when it occurs, is likely to be both repressive and indiscriminate.[11] Second, the violence, which in some measure may be traced ultimately to our need for denigrating comparisons, endows our fears with a reality-based sense of urgency that imprisons us all. None of us is free, not the disinherited poor imprisoned by the contempt of their fellow citizens, and not the rest of us who, having made the violent response of the disinherited increasingly likely, now must recognize that we have lost our freedom to go where we want, when we want, as well as our freedom from pervasive worry about threats to person and property in the sanctum of our own homes.

I still believe the arguments made in *The Culture of Inequality* can be instructive and, if taken seriously, can help us make choices that will change the course of our experience. That is why I am pleased the University of Massachusetts Press has chosen to reissue these pages. I hope enough readers will come to the same conclusion, so that their life-enhancing rejection of our cultural straitjacket will attract the notice that must precede any effort at serious reform. I hope—and thus I continue to write—but if asked whether I am sanguine about this hope, I would have to answer I am not. I thought it was too late in 1978 and I have experienced nothing since then that would lead me to abandon my pessimism. My children, whom I acknowledged in the original edition of this book, are now adults. It is their turn, but I am afraid they are about to inherit the fire this time.

*September 1992*

[11]At this writing Congress is considering an anticrime package containing provisions that many civil libertarians consider a threat to the fundamental protections contained in the Bill of Rights.

# Foreword

A novel idea about human social life appeared in the writings of eighteenth-century philosophers and political theorists—the idea that society is a system established among equals. Although for some time this idea was little more than a curiosity, it has since become so fascinating that now most people of the world regard it as the only respectable account of social arrangements. Since World War II, few societies have remained untouched or unchanged by this idea, and it remains the crucial issue underlying social change and political conflict in capitalist, socialist, and third-world societies. It is especially prominent in the history of American society. Ours was among the very first to make the idea of equality a defining term of its existence.

In 1776, American society officially adopted a curious story about itself. It was to be a society defined not by its land, language, or traditional culture, nor by its continuity with the legitimate past, but by an unprecedented act of self-creation as a *political* arrangement. This arrangement was based from the very beginning on the denial of inequality.

This announcement, of course, like other human proclamations, was more of a pious hope than a description of the prevailing pattern of life. We may safely believe that the proclaimers of the American doctrine of equality did not envision the various conclusions that members of later generations would reach from their original, noble premises. We have no reason to believe that they specifically had in mind claims to equality by persons of diverse sexual preferences, grammatical habits, stages in the life cycle, or moral codes. Still less can we credit such farsightedness to the great mass of Americans in whose name those proclamations were made.

Nevertheless, they established the language, the terms of discourse, and the standards of reasonable argument for the future discussion of social issues in America. From then on, any program of social conservation or change that was being promoted would have to be justified in terms of the premise of human equality. In particular, no assertion of the rightness of an inequality in American life could be taken for granted, and no existing inequality in fact could be sustained without an elaborate apology, once it had been brought to public attention.

When equality became the orthodox theory of citizenship, inequality became a social embarrassment that could call into question the legitimacy of the social system itself.

Yet, such rules of talk did not eliminate inequality from American society then or now. Indeed, no human society has yet succeeded in constructing the system of equality called for in the story. A large number of acknowledged experts on human affairs have concluded that equality can never be achieved, even in theory; and these experts include righteous people who are just as sentimentally attached to the ideal as are other modern disciples of equality. Neither Michael Lewis nor I am convinced by this theoretical pessimism, but we share with the skeptics a grim appreciation of the fact of social inequality in the contemporary world, in general, and in America, in particular. We know that the theory of equality did not preclude a legal system of slavery that defined the most extreme inequality of social participation, nor an industrial factory system that virtually incarcerated workers, nor the invention and construction of custodial institutions that deprived inmates of the universal citizenship just created, nor the expropriation of native Americans long established in the land. Since America, like other societies, continued to display deeply rooted institutions of inequality, our cultural history had to revolve around our attempts to rationalize the discrepancy between our announced premises and our actual lives. By committing ourselves to a social life based on equality, we condemned ourselves to creating and maintaining a culture of inequality, that is, an elaborate apology for the existence of living inequalities.

Equality was not the only pillar on which the American edifice was built. Of comparable importance were the ideas of liberty and opportunity—and with good reason. The theory of equality not only outlawed inequalities of station, but also denied the principle of station itself. It made literally absurd all notions that a person's place in society was defined by *who* he or she was, since only one sort of who existed. There was no one here but us citizens. American society was not conceived to be a long-standing institutional order whose enjoyment could be made the content of equality. Instead, it was thought either to be under construction or to be characterized by institutions that were themselves emerging in the European world, the institutions of liberal capitalism. Thus Americans would have to be equal in their activities rather than in their identities. The official structures of the society, in accordance with this mythical picture, could take no notice of distinctions not rationalized by the theory. This did not prevent such distinctions from continuing and arising in ways significant to practical social life. Wealth, political and military power, and even family honor had serious effects on the emerging patterns of American life. These effects were even more pronounced because America plunged immediately into two centuries of economic, technological, territorial, and population change. By the post-World War II period, this prolonged spasm had produced a large, complicated nation inhabited for the most part by people who only recently had arrived at positions in society that had themselves been newly created. Important features of this system were beyond the control or comprehension of most individuals. Americans were left with few cultural resources for constructing a sophisticated picture of the scheme of things or of their own places in it. Very few places were secure over the generations; all had to be renewed or redefined almost on a daily basis. People did work that did not resemble their parents' work, lived far from their native ground, and faced unprecedented problems and opportunities.

These massive social changes deepened old inequalities and produced new ones. At the same time, many individuals experienced the breaking up of existing patterns of inequality. It was a rare person who had a clear idea, wrong or right, of the developing structure of economic and political control. The American culture gave these embattled citizens this legacy: a small and unstable set of collective loyalties and identities, an idea that official inequality was unacceptable, and a sense that survival depended on the shrewd use of opportunities. These were not resources rich enough to handle an American reality that included concentration in industry, finance, and corporate organization, metropolitanization of the population, national consolidation of government, and the emergence of regional and national elites. As many observers of American society from Tocqueville on had predicted, the efficacy of local organizations, human in scale, to deal with these realities had declined. Many Americans had been "liberated" from loyalties to family, region, and traditional culture to face modern life as unorganized individuals.

In this postwar scene there suddenly appeared a new incarnation of the old national myth of equality. Beginning with the Civil Rights movement, American culture became preoccupied with unequal social structures in national life. We witnessed the revival of dormant movements like Feminism, and the birth of new movements like the Youth Revolution and Gay Rights. Whatever the impact of these movements on American social structure, they profoundly shook our ordinary ways of thinking and talking, our picture of America. Most Americans, daily engaged in finding their way through an awesome and uncharted social universe, were challenged by these movements in the few principles they could safely claim.

This climactic scene is the occasion for Michael Lewis's daring attempt to unravel the ideological knots that bind millions of ordinary Americans to a structure of inequality built in the name of equality.

Periods of social turmoil are particularly fruitful for students of social structure because they usually illuminate important features of ordinary life that are taken for granted and remain unchallenged in quieter times. In fact, since many of the regularities we depend on rest primarily on our common willingness to accept them automatically, they usually work best when they are least questioned. When times are stormy, we find ourselves working hard and in public to renegotiate those regularities. This gives the social scientist an opportunity to see what underlying values we rely on, and how we make them serviceable in practical affairs.

The postwar period, especially the episode conventionally known as "the Sixties," provided just such an opportunity to students of American society. It generated a large volume of studies and commentaries that expanded our common knowledge of the life situations of people who were poor, oppressed, unorthodox, socially distant or hidden. It also produced a new wave of studies of the large-scale workings of our society, and how concentrated social power was being used in circles that were even more obscure. In short, the ideological attack on inequality created the conditions and the motives for a detailed inspection of the forms of inequality in our society.

For some decades before the Sixties, social science had dealt only occasionally with inequality in American life. The subject appeared under two headings that were too often kept distinct from each other, Social Stratification and Intergroup Relations. These were usually conceived as questions of personal attitude, that is, as personal responses to social life rather than as objective characteristics of our institutional arrangements. This approach had some sociological validity, since social structures are essentially dependent on shared beliefs and attitudes. It resulted even more from the assumption by social scientists of the American premises of political equality, as discussed convincingly by Michael Lewis in terms of the "individual-as-central sensibility." If there were problems of inequality, they were thought to require a change of attitude, a reduction of suspicion and hostility through contact and

communication among different social strata and subcultural groups.
The recent revision of sociological thinking focused more on the rigid
limits to equality imposed by our entrenched systems of distributing
property, power, social recognition, jobs, education, housing, health
care, and legal representation. The constraints on individual life that
derived from our economic and political structure, our dependence on
the policy of the United States in international relations, and the routine role of patterns of inequality in maintaining American business
as usual, came to be seen as the fundamental sources of problems of
inequality.

Nevertheless, the basic insight that a pervasive system of inequality
would not be possible in America without the tacit compliance of the
mass of ordinary people remained persuasive. It is necessary to sub-
stantiate this insight by discovering and revealing the role played by
so many ordinary citizens in preserving patterns so opposed to their
announced principles. It is even more important to explain why they
assume this role.

Michael Lewis has undertaken the necessary task of facing this
refractory problem. He has rightly refused to be satisfied with the superficial and tendentious accounts that rely on moral exhortations and
generalities about human nature. He has taken seriously the need to
analyze a culture in which ordinary people could resort to rationaliza-
tions of inequality to fulfill the peculiar life plans that culture specifies
for them.

Lewis's approach has been properly empirical. He has sought an answer through a long, thorough study of the ways an American community deals with the challenge of equality in its day-to-day handling
of specific issues. For it is only through close acquaintance with these
practices that we can understand and address their practitioners, and
not merely feed our own self-righteousness by exorcising them.

The account he has written is addressed not only to his fellow sociologists but to all concerned citizens who will grant him an audience.
The book has avoided the detail and comprehensiveness typical of a
research report. It has not been limited to conclusions that can be firmly
established by incontrovertible evidence. In the general sections in
which he presents his conception of the basic view of human action
built into American culture, Lewis has leaped past the limits of safe
inference. Not everyone will agree with his interpretation of the cen-
trality of individual achievement as the fruit of an equalitarian premise,
or with his assertion of the near universality of a deficit between aspira-

tions and achievements. Many will have reasons more personal than scientific skepticism to resist his unflattering depiction of Americans in flight from their fear of failure, or his warnings about our probable future.

But every reader will have to admire Lewis's scrupulous honesty in calling attention to parts of his argument that are open to question, hypotheses that lack conclusive evidence, and points where other interpretations might be made. He has come to us on a serious matter, and he has not flinched from taking risky positions in order to avoid criticism. Nor has he tried to conquer our good sense with salesmanship when his theories outrun his available evidence.

Many of the components of his case are facts and arguments familiar to specialists on sociology and social problems. Lewis is not the first to remark on the desperate pursuit of self-esteem by respectable Americans. Nor is he the first to find that our efforts to "eradicate" social problems turn out to be ways to preserve those problems. The originality of his argument comes in weaving these and other elements of sociological knowledge into a coherent picture presented for the enlightenment of a large public, not merely for the consumption of his colleagues. He is submitting his case to a very large jury that is, in his analysis, uniquely competent to render a verdict. For his readers possess the very evidence needed to test his ideas. That evidence is their own knowledge of the lives they lead. Lewis offers us an extended description of people and events in a community he calls Middle City. But these data are not presented to prove his theories. They are presented as an example of how he applies his ideas to the ordinary facts we all have about our own corners of society. With this example before us, we should be able to apply his thesis to our lives. He invites us to do this and to judge for ourselves whether he has discovered something about us.

Although Michael Lewis is a skilled, judicious social scientist, he does not hold himself above the process he describes, nor does he exempt himself from its tragic conclusions. Much of his confidence in his own argument comes not from a cynical derogation of the lives of others but from a self-conscious honesty about his own life. I know that he has illuminated disturbing aspects of my life and the lives of people around me. I suspect that a very large part of his jury of readers will recognize their lives as well.

The harsh picture of how our personal goals and highest ideals are implicated in our views and actions toward our fellow citizens on the low end of the system of inequality should be disturbing to the precious opinion we hold of ourselves as good people. If we read Lewis as honestly as he writes, we must become aware that the problems of inequality are not attributable to some mischievous "others." We must face a cruel dilemma: it is our striving to be good that recruits us into the army that fights to preserve inequality in American culture. But Lewis hopes that by making us conscious of how these themes fit together, we might free ourselves from automatic participation in that humiliating and dangerous system.

In spite of the anger and pessimism that sometimes characterizes his thinking, Lewis writes from the peculiar position of optimism that informs all applied social analysis. If people are made aware of how their social world is constructed, they can make real choices about how they want it to run. To the driven individuals who inhabit America now, the social commentator hopes to offer a larger, more detailed map, one that reveals several alternate routes. There is nothing to prove that this sociological myth is more serviceable than any other article of faith about social practice. But in its paradoxical union of passion and dispassion, it represents the best we have to offer to our fellows.

The pages that follow are not comfortable, and they offer no new trick solution to the problems of the culture of inequality. In some ways, they imply a situation more gloomy than they themselves disclose. For there are many weighty reasons beyond ignorance or stubbornness that explain why we maintain inequalities that we supposedly abhor but have come to depend upon. These reasons arise from a large social system that we have little power to change as individuals and few resources to use in addressing it collectively. The culture of inequality grew as a response to those realities, and it will take more than individual resolve to dissipate their constraining effect on us. The structure of inequality does not rest on the accepted culture of inequality alone. But it is the part of the problem most within our sphere of experience, the one most accessible to our efforts for change. When we free ourselves from our dependence on inequality, we are attacking inequality itself. And if we cannot through words alone free the most oppressed victims of inequality, we might at least excuse them from the terrible tribute we force them to pay for the sake of our self-esteem. As Michael Lewis shows us, it is poor comfort we get from it, anyway.

Bernard Beck
Northwestern University

Because I believe
that the society created by our fathers
should not be the society
inherited by our children . . .

## Acknowledgments for the Second Edition

In writing this book I accumulated a number of intellectual and personal debts. I hope that what follows in these pages has proven worthy of the support I was so fortunate to receive; that what I wrote honors the faith and generosity of those to whom I am still in considerable debt.

Beyond this general acknowledgment of appreciation I would like to identify and publicly thank a number of people for their efforts in behalf of my work: Peter Rose of Smith College encouraged me to write *The Culture of Inequality* and there isn't a page in this book which has not benefited from his considerable editorial acumen. The late Charles Page, then Emeritus MacIver Professor of Sociology at the University of Massachusetts, as he did so often for so many scholars and writers, provided an extensive critical commentary that contributed immeasurably to whatever cogency these pages possess. Jon Simpson of the University of Massachusetts read an early draft and on the basis of that reading engaged me in a dialogue which stimulated important revisions in my thinking. Other friends and colleagues—Louise and Sanford Bloomberg, Mickey and Penina Glazer, Lewis Killian, Gordon and Dee Sutton—contributed suggestions and offered the kind of support which made the lonely task of writing endurable.

In the years since their first publication, the ideas in *The Culture of Inequality* have drawn me into critically useful exchanges with a number of people I esteem. I should like to thank Howard Altstein, Bernard Beck, Tim Black, Robert Cook, Ethan Lewis, Rachel Lewis, Jo Ann L. Miller, John O'Connor, Alice Rossi, and Peter Rossi for asking those questions that have moved me to sharpen my understanding of both American culture and American inequality. Fortunately for me they are implicated in the continuing life of these pages.

Michael Lewis
*Northampton,* 1992

## A Very Few Words about These Pages

This book is about the manner in which
many Americans interpret the existence of
social and economic inequality. It is about
their beliefs concerning such inequality
and the consequences of these beliefs for
the human serviceability of the American
experience.

# PART ONE

# THE CULTURE OF INEQUALITY EXPLAINED

# 1

## Inequality and Equalitarianism:
## The Individualization of Success and Failure

As a matter of historical fact *unequal* access to the means of personal well-being and prestige has been taken for granted in most societies, by both those who have benefited from the inequality and those who have been deprived by it. In most societies of record, inequality has been fairly well institutionalized, in that it has not been a source of those moral dilemmas which occur when there is a departure in actual behavior from values that are widely if not universally endorsed. For centuries the English gentry took a leisured existence as their just due, while yeomen farmers toiled patiently at their daily labors and the urban poor suffered their station. While the Russian nobility played the games of Western European cosmopolitanism in their daschas, the Russian peasants in their thrall turned the earth, oblivious to all save the rhythms of seasonal change and the meanings of their Orthodox religion-cum-superstition. For centuries neither nobleman nor peasant thought that it could, would, or should be any other way. Until the Kuomintang led by Sun Yat Sen and later the Communists led by Mao Tse-Tung revolutionized the Chinese consciousness, gross inequalities among that ancient people were graced with an assumption of divinely inspired legitimacy. Inequality was simply in the order of things. Until Mahatma Gandhi created a new truth for the Indian subcontinent, what "untouchable" dared challenge the justice of his abject destiny, what Brahman felt constrained to justify the prerogatives of his august estate?

It is not that the impoverished masses bore no animus toward those whose access to the means of well-being and prestige far surpassed theirs. It is simply that until recently in most societies there existed few cultural justifications for questioning the persistence of inequalities in individual life circumstances—few widely held rationales emphasizing equalitarianism in any manifestation. Unequal distribution of opportunity and of the means to well-being was normatively sanctioned while equalitarianism, whether of outcome or of opportunity, was the aspiration of but a small minority of progressive thinkers and visionaries.

In the United States, however, the situation has been quite different. Even as social and economic inequality has marked the American experience, Americans have felt constrained to justify its existence in what are essentially equalitarian and ultimately individualistic terms. If in other societies inequality has, historically, been taken for granted, in American society its existence has been a source of concern. From the time of the earliest colonies, Americans have subscribed to the belief that since all men are equal in the eyes of their creator, none should be inhibited by external social or political constraints from exercising their ambitions to the fullest extent of their talents. Individual opportunity—equal freedom to desire and aspire—has been presumed the birthright of every individual American.[1] While having to recognize the existence of unequal outcomes—inequalities in the possession of wealth, power, and prestige—Americans have characteristically emphasized the *equal chance*: in reality, the equal chance for individuals to wind up unequal.

Although real inequality of opportunity in the American experience confounds this presumption, conditions peculiar to the development of American society—its geo-political expansiveness, its relative newness, and the consequent relative absence of revered tradition—have indeed resulted in circumstances which have made it easy to negate unequal opportunity and to assume the behavioral reality of the normative ideal.

The open frontier provided many opportunities for those individuals hardy enough to brave the physical threat of an untamed environment and the hostility of Indians. New settlements emerged rapidly, virtually guaranteeing the expansion of opportunity. If a man found that he could not realize his dreams in one community he could always move on to another. Success, he could always believe, was awaiting him just over the next hill or across the next river. The frontier community in its struggle for survival was "forced . . . to seize upon whatever talent it

[1] See the discussion of ideological equalitarianism in S. M. Lipset and Reinhard Bendix, *Social Mobility in Industrial Society* (Berkeley-Los Angeles: University of California Press, 1959), pp. 78–79. Of course, in the ante-bellum south and to a considerable extent in the post-bellum south as well, blacks were beyond the pale of this ideology. See Gunner Myrdal et al., *An American Dilemma* (New York: Harper and Brothers, 1946).

could find," creating "unfettered opportunity for all. . . ." [2] In this context of openness, this milieu of imminent success, illiterate yeomen farmers became plantation masters, religious dissenters like the Mormons established themselves in communities where they could implement their own vision of personal well-being, and immigrant Jewish peddlers did indeed become merchant kings. [3]

In the late nineteenth century and the first quarter of the twentieth century industrialization contributed significantly to the developing ethos of equal personal opportunity. Men of humble origins became financial barons through personal inventiveness, business acumen, and, so it seemed, the sheer will to succeed. Carnegie, Frick, Morgan, Rockefeller, Ford and others began with little and yet amassed extraordinary fortunes. They achieved their overwhelming successes by recognizing that opportunities were made available by the revolutionary economic development of the nation precisely because that development was revolutionary and consequently without established rules for participation. And if exceptional success was relatively infrequent, modest achievements were not. In the relatively undeveloped economy, most men could put an increment of distance between their origins and their achievements if they were willing to take initiative and work hard. The peddler became the modestly endowed but respected merchant. The average workingman at the very least earned enough, usually by toiling long hours at more than one job, to give his children a better start in life. In the big city ghettos and the rural hamlets there were few who did not know of someone who had risen above humble origins. The ethos of equalitarian access to the means of self-realization was thus kept alive both by the spectacular successes of the newly risen entrepreneurial elites and by the more modest achievements of "just plain folks."

Life seemed full of chances to be taken, and for many Americans trying and succeeding through individual effort became a moral imperative. If in other societies fealty to tradition or obedience to divine will marked the good or moral man, in the United States it was the successful ex-

---

[2] Stanley Elkins and Eric McKitrick, "A Meaning for Turner's Frontier," *Political Science Quarterly* 69 (September 1964): 1–353, particularly pp. 346–49.

[3] The rise of the yeoman farmer in the south is documented in Francis B. Simkins, *A History of the South* (New York: Alfred A. Knopf, 1956), and in William B. Hesseltine, *A History of the South* (New York: Prentice-Hall, 1936). An excellent account of the Mormon experience can be found in Thomas F. O'Dea, *The Mormons* (Chicago: University of Chicago Press, 1957). Anecdotal accounts of the Jews can be found in Stephen Birmingham, *Our Crowd: The Great Jewish Families of New York* (New York: Harper and Row, 1967).

ercise of individual effort in pursuit of economic and social mobility which elicited encomiums; conversely, apparent failure in the pursuit of one's economic and social chances drew censure.

While economic and social success was not of itself the mark of moral superiority, its achievement was taken as an indicator that the successful person had, given his chances, exerted his talents to the fullest; and such productive exertion in its assumed contribution to the commonweal was considered proof of moral elevation. William Graham Sumner, the influential champion of individualism as the active agent of evolutionary social progress, articulated the matter: "If a chance," he wrote in 1890, "is used one way it results in gain or advantage; if it is used the other way it issues in loss or disadvantage. A chance, therefore, has no moral quality or value; the moral question is: *what will be done with it?*" [4] And some years later Thomas Nixon Carver, a respected political economist of his day, went to the heart of this moral sensibility when he wrote, "He who does less than he can *does ill*." [5]

That success was taken as an indicator of socially productive exertion and, consequently, moral elevation can also be seen in reactions to its obverse, personal failure. Disadvantage (poverty, unemployment, and ill health) can be understood in a number of different ways. It can be interpreted as the result of hard luck; it can be interpreted as an inherited destiny, as in those societies which have known extensive poverty as a tradition; it can be interpreted as a function of structural inequities and the propensity of the economically strong to exploit the economically weak; or it can be interpreted as the result of morally censurable individual mis- or malfeasance.

During the late nineteenth and early twentieth centuries, in what appeared (with some justification) to be an America of opportunities, there were a few who perceived the existence of disadvantage as a traditional destiny, some who accounted for its presence by bad luck, and

---

[4] William Graham Sumner, "Liberty and Responsibility," *Independent*, November 1889 and July 1890; reprinted in *Essays of William Graham Sumner*, vol. 1, ed. Albert Galloway Keller and Maurice R. Davie (New Haven: Yale University Press, 1934), pp. 310–57 (quotation from pp. 330–31 [emphasis mine]).
[5] Thomas Nixon Carver, *Essays in Social Justice* (Cambridge: Harvard University Press, 1915), p. 129 (emphasis mine). This characterization of personal destiny is, in some measure, suggestive of Max Weber's characterization of economic success among the early Protestants, in which economic success is taken as an indicator of divine election. In a sense the characterization offered above is a secular version of this "Protestant Ethic," with *moral elevation* replacing *divine election* as the quality symbolized by personal success.

others—trade unionists, agrarian populists, settlement house reformers, socialists, and the like—who saw disadvantage as a function of structured inequity and exploitation. The dominant interpretation of disadvantage, however, held it the result of personal ineptness or misbehavior and therefore a sign of moral inferiority. Again we have the words of the highly influential Sumner: ". . . the weak [meaning the disadvantaged] . . . are the shiftless, the imprudent, the negligent, the impractical and the inefficient, or they are the idle, the intemperate, the extravagant and the vicious." [6] And, it was not just the hardheaded philosopher of success who could voice such sentiments; even those who sought to help the disadvantaged often saw them as burdened by morally censurable personal misbehavior. Mary Richmond, a pioneer of American social work, in 1890 exhorted friendly visitors (early social workers) to "put out the fires . . . of intemperance, of wrong relations of man to man and plant God's sunlight there in place of them." [7] Some years later Porter R. Lee, a luminary of the burgeoning social work movement, suggested to his fellow professional altruists that "inefficiency, ill-health, waywardness, unemployment and unstable character have a way of intertwining . . . and [in] the atmosphere in which they develop are found also, many attendant evils like . . . ignorance and immorality." [8] To be poor, to have suffered disadvantage, was taken to mean failure to make the most of an abundance of chances; through sloth, venality, or simple ineptitude, one had not exerted sufficient productive effort, and having done less than one might, one had done ill.

In a society experiencing rapid expansion and development, whose major resource problem was a scarcity of human energy and whose traditions did not include institutionalized exclusion (except for Indians and the slaves and their descendants), it is not difficult to see how such a moral sensibility might become dominant. The received collective experience, as we have seen, was replete with successes apparently based upon individual effort, successes which appeared to benefit the community and indeed the society. And, to many of those who thought about it, the massive immigration of that time from southern and

[6] William Graham Sumner, "The Forgotten Man," 1883; reprinted in Keller and Davie, Essays, pp. 466–96 (quotation from p. 476).
[7] Mary Richmond, "The Friendly Visitor" (1890), in The Long View: Papers and Addresses (New York: Russell Sage Foundation, 1930), p. 42.
[8] Porter R. Lee, "Social Work with Families and Individuals: A Brief Manual for Investigators" (1915), in Porter R. Lee, Social Work As Cause and Function (New York: Columbia University Press, 1937), p. 52.

eastern Europe could only have been taken as proof that there were more opportunities than there were individuals to take advantage of them. Economic and social success, so it must have appeared, might not be easy to achieve, but in some measure it awaited those who exerted productive effort which contributed to the common good. Conversely, because productive effort appeared to be all that was necessary for at least some personal success, it was easy to associate the signs of visible disadvantage with the morally culpable failure to do one's best.

☆

The emergence of this individualistic moral sensibility is of considerable significance,[9] for as we shall see it has become central to the existence of the American *culture of inequality*—an interpretation of unequal outcomes given the assumption of equal chances. It is a sensibility that virtually ignores the impact of social structure upon personal achievement and mobility. According to this sensibility, it is the individual alone who is socially significant, who determines what his or her contribution to the commonweal will be, and who is therefore responsible for the degree of personal success achieved. Society is seen as benign, offering up opportunities and waiting to be enriched by those who have the will and the capacity to make productive use of them. This sensibility therefore removes inequality of personal perquisites from the category of social conditions in need of reform. If such inequality is seen as the product of traditional restrictions on opportunity it becomes a target for social reformers to whom it is the arbitrary and unjust outcome of a reactionary system. If, however, such inequality is simply an indication of differentials in the productive exertion of individuals, free to exercise their ambitions and talents to the fullest, then the presumption of social arbitrariness cannot be sustained and only the individual can be held accountable for the state of his or her well-being. If inequality exists it is nothing more than a reflection of different personal qualities.

Since its first flowering this *individual-as-central* sensibility has demonstrated considerable resiliency, although some of its manifestations have undergone some change, primarily in response to presumptions of sophistication about human behavior which have been the products of American social science and the emergence of such "helping professions" as social work, psychotherapy, and special education. While it is still easy enough to locate widespread subscription to this sensibility in what

[9] For an extended treatment of this phenomenon see Richard Hofstadter, *Social Darwinism in American Thought*, rev. ed. (Boston, Beacon Press, 1955).

might be termed its pure *moralistic* manifestation (that is, individuals succeed or fail because of the presence or absence of a commitment to do their personal best),[10] there is also widespread adherence to a modified form of the sensibility which still sees individual effort as central to success or failure, but explains the presence or absence of this effort with such morally neutral qualities as *psychodynamic makeup, cultural commitments* ("mainstream" or the hindering "poverty" cultures), *family background and contingent socialization, degree of cognitive (educational) competence,* and *extent of interpersonal competence.*

American social scientists, most prominently psychologists and sociologists, as well as "helping professionals," have produced *deficiency explanations* for the absence of expected productive effort and its concomitant—the absence of personal success. These explanations suggest that, because of inadequate personality structures, some people are self-defeating and therefore incapable of making the most of the opportunities which society (once again benign) proffers. Because they subscribe to poverty or lower-class subcultural world-views, some are inadequately motivated to make their way in a middle-class-dominated urban-industrial world. Because of the absence of a strong paternal model of conventional masculine competence, some boys grow up in families which ill-prepare them to participate fully and successfully in the economic mainstream. Because they lack sufficient cognitive skills to read at expected levels or reason adequately with figures, some people simply do not qualify for vocational opportunities which hold out real promise of personal success. Because of insufficient knowledge of what it takes to get along and work well with others (interpersonal competence), some are unable to make the best use of whatever productive talent they possess.[11]

---

[10] See Joe R. Feagin, *Subordinating the Poor: Welfare and American Beliefs* (Englewood Cliffs, N. J.: Prentice-Hall, 1975).

[11] It is important to understand that there have been significant dissents from those social science approaches which have emphasized deficiency explanation. Among the more important critiques and disavowels of deficiency explanation in its many forms are: Charles A. Valentine, *Culture and Poverty: Critique and Counter-Proposals* (Chicago: University of Chicago Press, 1968); William Ryan, *Blaming the Victim* (New York: Random House, 1971); Frances Fox Piven and Richard A. Cloward, *Regulating the Poor: The Function of Public Welfare* (New York: Pantheon Books, 1971); Ernest Drucker, "Cognitive Styles and Class Stereotypes," in *The Culture of Poverty: A Critique,* ed. E. B. Leacock (New York: Simon and Schuster, 1971), pp. 41–62; Eleanor Burke Leacock, "Introduction," in ibid., pp. 9–37; Bernard Farber, *Mental Retardation: Its Social Content and Social Consequences* (Boston: Houghton

The focus of deficiency explanations on individuals and their personal characteristics is similar to the focus of the moralistic form of the individual-as-central sensibility; deficiency explanations depart from the moralistic form by holding that, while the individual fails to succeed because of personal characteristics and experiences, these personal inadequacies are not volitional. Implicit and, as we shall see, sometimes explicit in the use of deficiency explanations is the assumption that if those who are inadequate to the demands of life in our modern society could do something about their inadequacies, they would almost invariably choose to do it. Personal success and personal failure in this modified manifestation of the individual-as-central sensibility are matters not of moral superiority and inferiority, but rather of capacity and incapacity. Failure is not a sign of immorality, but it does signify inability or incompetence; success is not a sign of moral superiority but does signify superior talent or capacity: an effective mobilization of the individual's sufficiencies.

Whether in its pure or in its modified form, the sensibility has at least one major interpretive implication: as success honors those who have achieved it, failure, and economic failure in particular, stigmatizes those who suffer it. Such failure, meaning in the first instance moral inferiority, can only make those who have "failed" the objects of criticism or scorn. Because in the second instance it is taken to mean inadequacy based upon deficiency, failure evokes pity or concern. And if it is better to be pitied than scorned, in either case one is the object of an attitude reserved for those whose behaviors are deemed unacceptable or deviant. One is seen as an outcast or as an incompetent—an objectionable about whom some corrective measures must be taken.

These corrective measures (and the debates which often surround them) are themselves very instructive in indicating the influence of the individual-as-central sensibility on the manner in which inequality is explained and justified in American society.

In the conventional political parlance of our time, much is made of the conflicts between liberals and conservatives about the existence of

Mifflin, 1968); Thomas Scheff, *Being Mentally Ill* (New York: Aldine Atherton, 1966).

A reading of this literature of dissent is quite instructive, not only because of the substantive criticisms leveled but also because these and other commentators make it abundantly clear that the deficiency explanation they are criticizing and dissenting from represents a dominant conventional wisdom in the social sciences and the "helping professions."

disadvantage or benighted economic circumstance and the question what, if anything, should be done. Liberals are perceived as sanguine proponents of "doing good" for the unsuccessful—those who suffer poverty and its myriad disadvantages—and as activists convinced of the necessity and rectitude of massive public expenditures for programs which have the intention of relieving (if not obliterating) disadvantage. Conservatives are viewed as committed individualists who, interpreting disadvantage as a product of moral infirmity, can find no value in the expensive do-gooding efforts of the liberals. In their view, as commonly understood, it is sheer folly to spend money to help people whose circumstances are proof that they are unwilling to help themselves—better to make the wages of sloth intolerable, to make malingering a censurable offense, to punish the unsuccessful poor for their failure to do the best that they can do.

It would of course be an error to disregard the differences separating liberals from conservatives. The differences are real; they characterize much of the debate over the role of government in dealing with the persistence of inequality, and their differing programmatic consequences are not insignificant. When the liberals have the upper hand politically, as in the Kennedy-Johnson years, we are likely to witness an acceleration in the development of welfare, educational, and medical programs, each intended to ameliorate those deficiencies which lead to disadvantage. It would be difficult to gainsay that in an immediate sense the disadvantaged are better off as a result of this liberally inspired acceleration. When the conservatives are in power, as in the Eisenhower or the Nixon-Ford years, we are likely to witness a corresponding deceleration in the development of such programs—perhaps indeed an absolute decline in the number of such programs. And whatever our reservations about their potency, I think we would be hard-pressed to deny the negative impact of such retrenchment upon the immediate circumstances of the disadvantaged (or, to use a more apposite term, the disinherited).

Despite the existence and significance of these differences, there is more similarity between the standard liberal and conservative positions on poverty and disadvantage than is commonly recognized. Irrespective of the differences between them, both liberals and conservatives appear to view poverty and disadvantage as a function of qualities characteristic of the disadvantaged poor; the two political positions are both derivatives of the individual-as-central sensibility. For the conservative it is the sensibility in its pure moralistic form, according to which each individual is responsible for his or her destiny without regard for the impact of structural circumstance, which leads to a jaundiced view of ameliorative programs. For the liberal it is the modified form of the sensibility, with its focus on the individualized misfortunes of incompetence and incapacity, which together with an emphasis on deficiency explanations leads to an espousal of the necessity and efficacy of such programs. While some liberal spokesmen may on occasion flirt with the notion that it is the circumstances of poverty and disadvantage which are in need of reform (as in those instances where liberals have initiated and supported income maintenance proposals, or where they have initiated and supported proposals for upgrading urban environments, such as the New Towns legislation), instead of the poor and the disadvantaged themselves, the major emphasis of the liberal position has been the funding of such programs as Head Start, Upward Bound, the Careers Opportunity Program, Job Corps, welfare, increased psychological services, nutritional counseling, and birth control—programs intended to upgrade the competencies and change the behaviors of the disadvantaged so that they will presumably be better able to compete for a fair share of society's bounty. The liberals appear ready to help—they are appalled by the existence of disadvantage—but like their conservative opponents they often seem incapable of understanding disadvantage as a product of social and economic circumstances over which the disadvantaged poor have no real control. Like those conservatives with whom they are locked in what often appears mortal political combat, the liberals hold society to be essentially benign.

That both liberal and conservative opinions on failure and success, disadvantage and advantage, stem from the same source (the individual-as-central sensibility) is, in my view, highly significant. It indicates with undeniable force that the individual-as-central sensibility sets the limits within which widely accepted interpretations of the relationship between individual destiny and what might be termed the morphology of American society develop and are sustained. The sensibility appears to define the range of "respectable" opinion, the universe of discourse within which legitimate differences may occur about the meaning of inequality in American society. It sets the boundaries for "thinkable" ideas about the mitigation of disadvantage, and consequently for "feasible" or "practical" policies concerning inequality. It makes moral and political outcasts of those whose ideas about failure and success—about inequality—in American life persistently run counter to the sensibility's cardinal precept: *the separability of personal destiny from social circumstance*, of biography from history.

To the liberals, the conservatives are pitiless moralizers who are wrong about failure, about poverty and disadvantage, because they mistake unintended deficiency for volitional default; the conservatives are wrong about success because they mistake the expression of competence and talent for the exercise of will. To the conservatives, the liberals are "bleeding hearts," much too ready to explain away malfeasance as mere incompetence and much too ready to spend the taxpayers' hard-earned dollars on those who *refuse* to earn anything; the liberals—ever the "nice guys" bent on doing good for the undeserving—weaken the moral fibre of American life because their explanation of malfeasance as mere incompetence implies that personal success requires not superior effort (a moral characterization) but simply the exercise of "know-how" which some people have the good fortune to possess (a technical characterization). But to both liberals and conservatives the position of the other is a *conceivable* error. While it is wrong, it is wrong because of faulty observation and inaccurate information, not because of some inconceivable and thereby illegitimate presupposition about American life, such as the conception that poverty and disadvantage (and therefore inequality) must more often than not be accounted for by unjust social and economic circumstances imposed upon those who appear to fail (the disadvantaged poor), and that freedom from poverty and disadvantage ("success," in varying degrees) must more often than not be accounted for by social and economic circumstances which at minimum do not impede the realization of ambition and frequently guarantee a modicum of success irrespective of talent or intensity of ambition.

Those who interpret failure and success in this latter manner are beyond the pale; they are the radicals who, depending upon the mood of the times, are considered either muddle-headed, simplistic, inconsequential thinkers or subversives whose extirpation must be given priority if the "American Way" is to be salvaged.[12] In either case, because they dare to challenge the separability of personal destiny and social

[12] Both liberals and conservatives are capable of holding these views, although conservatives are more likely than liberals to embrace the latter stronger position. Generally speaking, conservative elements have been responsible for the creation of the witch-hunt mentality, while all too many liberals have simply followed in step; witness the "red scare" during the twenties and the short-lived but repressive hegemony of Joseph McCarthy and others during the fifties.

circumstance, because their presuppositions have sources other than the individual-as-central sensibility, they are viewed as committing *inconceivable* errors of interpretation, errors which are quite simply illegitimate and abhorrent to the majority who are well versed in the tenets of the "American Way."

The individual-as-central sensibility, in both its pure and its modified manifestations, has a potency in the American present which we should take care not to underestimate. It is the informing presumption, the master theme, of what may justifiably be termed the American *culture of inequality*, wherein advantage and disadvantage (inequalities) are explained and frequently justified. In its hegemony it permeates everyday discourse and shapes the conventional wisdom on the meaning of failure and success in American life; it sets limits for feasible social policy, and its influence is of considerable significance in the issue— relevant areas of social scholarship. Moreover, the individual-as-central sensibility affects our personal biographies and in particular the way we evaluate ourselves.

If "success" (and its attendant perquisites) comes to be understood as being within the grasp of any individual who possesses the will and develops the necessary competence to succeed, if alternatively "failure" (or visible disadvantage) comes to be understood as the price an individual must pay for personal dissolution and/or incompetence—then in order to maintain one's sense of personal worth, it is necessary (absolutely, with no equivocation) to believe that one has been personally successful. The individualization of success and failure, a progressive cultural development in that it insists upon the freedom of all Americans to make what they will and can of themselves, and in that it refuses to legitimate a tradition of poverty and exclusion for some and a tradition of privilege for others, is thus not affirmed without significant psychological cost. If its existence allows and indeed encourages us all to lay claim to the possibility of "the good life," if it insures our right to dream big dreams and imagine that the best of everything is within our reach or that of our children, it simultaneously makes any perceived failure to "reach," any inability to "grasp," a threat of significant psychological force to our self-esteem. If we see ourselves as living in a society where all individuals are presumed equally free to achieve and to be socially mobile, then there appears to be no legitimate limit to the aspirations of any individual, and our sense of self-respect is likely to depend upon the extent to which we aspire and our ability to convince ourselves that we have in fact realized our dreams.

While aspiration is of itself relatively unproblematic (even the poorest and least advantaged among us can and often do find reasons to hope for the big success),[13] convincing ourselves that we have indeed been successful—that our dreams have been realized and that consequently we may respect ourselves—is extremely problematic. In a situation which makes great or near great expectations a moral and therefore a psychological imperative, all adults must confront the need to reconcile their actual achievements or success with their personal expectations. If our quest for self-respect leads us to high aspirations, the chances are very great that in the overwhelming majority of cases there will be a considerable difference between what we think we are capable of and what it is we actually seem to be achieving. And if the maintenance of self-respect depends upon not only great expectations but great expectations realized, then such disparities are likely to pose a major threat to the self-esteem of many Americans.[14]

Modern American capitalism is a complex economic system characterized by an extensive and hierarchical division of labor. In reality such a system limits the success most of us can achieve, even as the individual-as-central sensibility encourages us to believe otherwise. Irre-

---

[13] See Robert K. Merton, "Social Structure and Anomie," in Merton, *Social Structure and Social Theory* (Glencoe: Free Press, 1957). Also see Elliot Liebow, *Tally's Corner* (Boston: Little Brown and Co., 1967), and Ely Chinoy, *Automobile Workers and the American Dream* (New York: Doubleday and Co., 1955).

[14] It is of course true that the lower one's aspirations are the more likely they are to be realized in full. However, embarking on the course of easily realized modest aspirations is itself likely to be costly to one's self-image. The man who hopes to become an automobile mechanic is probably more likely to fulfill his ambition than the man who hopes to become a physician, but, having succeeded, the mechanic must live with the knowledge that he has realized an aspiration which in the American scheme of things counts for relatively little. He is far less likely than the aspiring physician to suffer from the implications of the deficit between aspiration and achievement, but given the American culture of inequality, he is likely to have considerable difficulty in justifying the modest level of his realized aspiration.

It may be true that not everyone has high aspirations. Perhaps, for example, working-class people frequently want less than do middle-class people; but if they choose modest goals they do so not without believing that they could and probably should have done otherwise. Even if they escape the threat to self posed by the aspiration-achievement disparity, they are unlikely to escape a very similar threat emanating from the difference between what their aspirations were and what, deep down, they believe their aspirations *should have been*.

spective of what we believe, there simply is not much room at the top. "Most people," observes Jules Henry, "do the job they have to do regardless of what they want to do. . . . The young worker enters the occupational system not where he would but where he can; and his job dream, so often an expression of his dearest self, is pushed down with all his other unmet needs to churn among them for the rest of his life." [15]

Were this experience consistent with what we have learned to expect —if we understood that our individual destinies depend in great measure upon economic circumstances and system imperatives beyond our personal control—we would, no doubt, be frustrated and angered by this externally imposed renunciation of our dreams. But troubling as that circumstance might be, far more troubling is what results from the existing inconsistency between the reality of limited opportunity, which is an effect of the functional imperatives of modern American capitalism, and the belief, inspired by the individual-as-central sensibility, that opportunity is virtually unlimited and that the extent of one's success or failure depends solely upon the quality of one's efforts. Most of us, in fact, do the jobs we have to do, entering the occupational system where we can instead of where we would, and most of us remain within close proximity of this point of entry throughout our working lives. The success we have learned to want frequently eludes us, but because we subscribe to the individual-as-central sensibility we are more likely to be troubled by a sense that we lack the ability or character to succeed than by any sense that we have been victimized by the requisites of American capitalism. Having, out of a commitment to the "American Way," aspired, having desired the perquisites and prestige which we do not and, no doubt, will not possess, our problem is not an opportunity structure which we perceive as constraining, but is rather an insidious intimation of personal inadequacy, a sense that lacking the success we have aspired to we are thereby lacking in worth.

The American culture of inequality has emphasized the necessity for the individuated self to want and achieve, and in so doing it has placed a considerable burden on many of us. To the extent that we embrace this "American Way"—and being Americans we cannot help but embrace it in some measure—we place ourselves in psychological jeopardy. The American culture of inequality, praiseworthy though it may be for its emphasis upon personal possibility and personal account-

---

[15] Jules Henry, *Culture Against Man* (New York: Random House, 1963), p. 25.

ability, is nevertheless misleading in its failure to prepare us to realize that there are indeed very real limitations upon what most of us may achieve—limitations which have very little to do with our willingness to work or the quality of our efforts. The individual-as-central sensibility makes personal aspiration a moral necessity and when such aspiration is to any extent thwarted, it virtually requires us to interpret this circumstance as of our own making. Unless our aspirations are realized in full (and given the moral necessity of high aspiration such achievement is unlikely for most of us), the individual-as-central sensibility—whatever its positive contribution to the American experience—threatens our self-esteem by causing us to doubt our character, our competence, or quite possibly both. Inequality in American society has to a very considerable degree become a personal matter, at least in the way we think about it and interpret its existence. To the extent, therefore, that our aspirations go unrealized (whatever the reason), we are threatened and troubled by personal guilt. Fearing that we have done less than we should, we are all too frequently haunted by a sense that we have done ill.

If the American culture of inequality has as potent an impact upon our lives as I have suggested, there can be no question but that we need to understand it to a far greater extent than we presently do. In spite of its significance in our lives probably few of us are conscious of its existence. When we think about success or failure, the culture's major tenet—the individual-as-central sensibility—establishes the parameters of meaning within which we develop and articulate our views, but few of us sense that what we think and feel is determined by anything other than our own perceptions of fact. When we think about the existence of inequality in American life and what steps, if any, should be taken to mitigate it, the culture of inequality determines the character of our consideration, although few of us are conscious that we are doing anything except making an objective and presumably just assessment of the way things are and ought to be. When, because we believe ourselves less successful than we had hoped to be, we are troubled by a threat to our self-esteem, few of us are able to recognize our difficulties as anything except personal. Few of us in such a circumstance are able to recognize the cultural antecedents of our personal malaise. The hegemony of the culture of inequality is such that we unself-consciously embrace it and internalize its tenets as though no alternatives were conceivable. The beliefs which constitute the culture seem so natural to us, so much a part of who and what we are, that few of us sense that they are anything other than conclusions derived from our personal experience.

But if this unthinking acceptance exists, there is good reason to wish that it did not, to wish that more of us were conscious of the culture of inequality and were capable of understanding its impact, for good and for ill, upon our lives. Without such awareness and understanding our freedom is likely to be limited, our creativity minimized, and our ability to transcend the culture's negative implications for the maintenance of our self-esteem nonexistent. As long as the tenets of the culture of inequality seem so natural and self-justifying that alternatives to them appear inconceivable, we will be bereft of the choice to forego the lonely striving mandated by the individualization of success and failure. As long as the individual-as-central sensibility goes unrecognized for what it is— a cultural product which more often than not misrepresents the character of contemporary opportunity—our responses to the problems of inequality will be limited to conservative moralism and liberal therapeutics. As long as we fail to recognize that our anxiety about "not doing well enough" is a psychological derivative of this sensibility, even at our happiest we shall continue to feel threatened.

Where the culture of inequality is concerned, too many Americans appear unable, as C. Wright Mills put it, to achieve *lucid summations* of what is going on in the world and what may be happening within themselves." [16] And because of this inability, the hegemony of the culture is maintained without the challenge of serious criticism. The culture is for the most part unexamined, because although it is an important component of our thoughts and actions few of us recognize its reality and the precedence it takes over our presumably individual initiatives. This, of course, would not be a problem if we could conclude that the culture of inequality were unequivocally positive in its impact upon us. But given that the impact of the culture is frequently negative, its unexamined and unchallenged hegemony can only minimize the human serviceability of the American experience, present vintage. We need, therefore, to try to make a *lucid summation* of the culture of inequality and its impact upon us. We need to become conscious of the culture of inequality as a culture—a set of beliefs and prescriptions to which there are alternatives if indeed we should wish to embrace them. We need to understand the dynamics of its continuing dominance over the

[16] C. Wright Mills, *The Sociological Imagination* (New York: Oxford University Press, 1959), p. 5.

manner in which many of us construe both personal destiny and social topography. We need, in other words, to make an analysis which will render us disenchanted with the culture and its implications. Without such disenchantment, we have no choice except obedience to dictates which are, to say the least, not always life-enhancing; with it, what is presently unthinkable may very well be thought, to the end of increased personal options in a society characterized by maximized equity and human serviceability.

In what follows my purpose will be to offer analysis and interpretation which I believe makes disenchantment with the culture of inequality possible. Having considered the origins and the influence of the culture in this opening chapter, I consider in depth how its hegemony is maintained, what implications it has for the way we respond to the problems inherent in the persistence of social inequality, and what, given the sustained dominance of the culture, is likely to become of us in the forseeable future. I believe that what follows will ring true for most readers and will, in doing so, provide a basis for disenchantment with what is, disenchantment that must of necessity precede any reconstruction of the culture of inequality along lines maximizing the human serviceability of the American experience. My purpose in these pages is admittedly audacious and I am not sanguine about the probability of its full realization. I am, however, convinced of its importance.

## 2

### Salvaging the Self
### and Perpetuating the Culture

★

The individualization of "success" and "failure" in the American experience and its implications for the way we come to grips (and sometimes to terms) with the facts of inequality may be perceived as a self-
perpetuating phenomenon. To identify and understand it as such is simply
to note that, once established, individualization (or the individual-
as-central sensibility) creates a condition necessary to and sufficient for
its continued existence. This condition is primarily psychological, and
I shall attempt its analysis and explication in this chapter. I shall
endeavor to indicate how it is that the individualization of success and
failure creates a psychological need which only the continuing embrace
of the individual-as-central sensibility itself can assuage with any effectiveness; I shall argue that other attempts to assuage this need are likely
(for reasons which themselves often stem from the dominance of the
individual-as-central sensibility) to fail, and the consequent necessary
and often desperate embrace of the sensibility reinvigorates it and
insures the maintenance of its hegemony.

If, as I suggested at the conclusion of the previous chapter, the individual-as-central sensibility is likely to threaten our self-esteem by
implying that any disparity between culturally mandated high aspirations and actual personal achievement is of our own making, then for
many of us the maintenance of a sense of self-worth is likely to depend
upon our ability to manage such disparities out of existence. Three
stratagems are theoretically available for this purpose. Individuals confronted by such disparities might try to explain them away by convincing
themselves that the disparities are the products of circumstances beyond
their control; they might move to wipe out the disparities by lowering
their personal aspirations to bring them more in line with actual achieve-

ments; or they might attempt to remove the perceived differences by inflating their achievements, by counterfeiting personal success so that the disparities appear to have never really existed after all. In reality, only one of these stratagems—the third—is likely to be used with any effectiveness, and even this effectiveness is usually more apparent than real.

The first stratagem—a claim of situational impediment—is obviously used by many, but its effectiveness is limited by the fact that it really contradicts the individual-as-central sensibility, the existence of which occasions the need to disprove the existence of the disparity between aspiration and achievement in the first place. Its effective use depends upon the individual's ability to claim an impediment whose existence and impact are not called into question by the individualization of success and failure. Serious physical illness is perhaps the only circumstance universally recognized as an impediment over which individuals have little or no control, but even the claim of serious illness is somewhat problematic. Conventional wisdom often celebrates success in the face of serious physical trauma. Wide publicity has been given to athletes who have overcome such illnesses as heart disease (for example, Dave Stallworth in basketball and John Hiller in baseball) and cancer (Jack Pardee in football) to continue their successful careers—not to mention those who, like Sandy Koufax, an extremely successful pitcher with an arthritic arm, or Joe Namath, a quarterback with badly damaged knees, have overcome less serious but nevertheless career-threatening physical problems. And then there is the shining example of Franklin Delano Roosevelt, elected president of the United States for four terms even though he had been severely crippled by infantile paralysis. We have all heard of quadraplegics who complete their college educations and sightless people who rise to positions of prominence in spite of their severe handicaps. These and other accounts of the individual triumphant over even extreme physical hardship render claims to physical impediment less than completely satisfactory as legitimate situational explanations for the failure to realize high aspirations. Given the emphasis upon individual efforts in the pursuit of success, the quest for self-respect often makes physical handicap less an excuse than a challenge which tests the character of the individual.[1] Thus, while physical handicap might in

[1] Other personal characteristics which seem to be beyond the control of those afflicted by them—such as mental retardation or mental illness—cannot, of course, be used to manage the disparity out of existence, because they are socially stigmatized. It is inconceivable that anyone would attempt to maintain self-respect by

some instances excuse the disparity between aspiration and achievement, it would appear that those who claim it must nevertheless acknowledge that in the eyes of many people their failure to overcome imposed physical adversity can itself be a sign of characterological weakness.

Given the existence and cultural strength of the individual-as-central sensibility, attempts to explain away the disparity between aspiration and achievement by resort to a claim of social victimization are likely to be ineffective. Most people will encounter very little support for claims of discrimination ("I tried and I know I have the ability but I never really had a fair chance"). Blacks, Puerto Ricans, Chicanos, and American Indians may claim discrimination or social victimization with some success, if only because those with whom they interact on a sustained and intense basis, their significant others, collectively invoke the existence of discrimination as an explanation for their disadvantaged condition.[2] And, to a certain degree, feminism allows some women to claim sex discrimination. But for the majority of Americans the individual-as-central sensibility virtually rules out recourse to a claim of discrimination. The psychological effectiveness of this claim depends upon its confirmation by significant others, and the existence of the individual-as-central sensibility makes such confirmation extremely unlikely. In fact, an assertion of social victimization is very risky to the maintenance of self-respect. Individuals who publicly make such an assertion, only to have it fall on deaf ears, have to contend with not only the aspiration-achievement disparity but also the shame of knowing that others regard their excuse as illegitimate. It is difficult enough not being as successful as you think you should be, but how in the world can you maintain your self-respect when you know that those around you have written you off as a whiner, a complainer with no real cause for complaint?

There are of course times when claims of social victimization appear more legitimate. Certainly anyone living through the Great Depression years of the 1930s could with some psychological success explain away the disparity between aspiration and achievement by asserting that he

---

claiming that a failure to achieve at the hoped-for level can be ignored because of mental retardation or illness.

[2] The truth of the claim of discrimination or social victimization is not at issue here. In the case of the groups listed, there is of course imposing evidence of the truth of such a claim. What is more significant to the effectiveness of such a claim is the degree to which it receives support from those who are significant to the individual invoking it.

or she had simply been deprived of a fair chance.[3] And the economic
slowdown of the seventies has created a climate of opinion more than
usually receptive to such assertions: we do have Ph.D.'s who have been
forced to work as taxi drivers, engineers on the unemployment lines,
stockbrokers working as door-to-door salesmen, professors who can find
no place to profess. But we do not view such periods as normal, as
characteristic of the American scene. They are, rather, viewed as temporary down-turns, and their presumed abnormality is itself an indication
that claims of victimization cannot, as a general rule, be successfully in-
voked to explain away the aspiration-achievement disparity. If bad times
are abnormal or uncharacteristic, then good times are normal and characteristic. By obvious extension, for most of us, most of the time, opportunity is presumably there for the taking. So much for the situational
impediment strategy!

Recourse to the second strategem—lowering one's aspirations so that
they will be more in line with one's achievements—is likely to be even
more ineffective than a claim of situational impediment in dealing with
the aspiration-achievement disparity. If self-respect depends at least in
part on the vigor and exaltation of one's aspirations, then lowering
aspirations to the level of actual achievements cannot buttress one's
sense of self-worth even though the aspiration-achievement disparity (so
threatening to that sense) is eliminated. Where aspiring to the "big
success" is encouraged and perhaps even mandated, relinquishing such
aspiration will necessarily be costly to the individual's morale. When I
have held out great expectations for myself how can I settle for considerably less without feeling that somehow I have failed? If high aspiration was right or legitimate to begin with, if my grand self-expectations
provided a basis for my positive sense of self, how can I now admit
that I should have been less ambitious without damaging that which I
am striving to protect—my self-esteem?

There is probably only one circumstance which permits an individual
to lower personal aspirations without at the same time damaging the

[3] Indeed, to this day there are people who manage the disparity by citing their depression experiences as its source: the insurance salesman who tells himself and
usually anyone else who will listen, "You know I wanted to be a lawyer. Probably
would have been a good one too if I didn't have to leave school because of the
depression"; or the bookkeeper about to be retired who reminds himself that if he
hadn't had to take a job—any job—to support his family during "those days," he
would have taken the risks involved in setting up his own accounting firm and, who
knows, by this time might have made it to the top.

sense of self. A lowering of aspirations without morale costs could conceivably be combined with a successful claim of situational impediment to provide an apparently successful method of dealing with the disparity. A claim of situational impediment may explain away the disparity—in its confirmation by significant others it relieves the individual of personal responsibility for the fact that the disparity exists—but by itself it does not eliminate the disparity. For some, perhaps for those who have achieved their aspirations to at least a certain extent—for example, the black man who having aspired to become a lawyer has become a police officer, the woman who having aspired to become a journalist has instead become a teacher, the athlete whose physical disability has prevented him from becoming a professional and who instead has become a high school coach—the very existence of the disparity (even with a disclaimer of responsibility for it) is personally painful. Its existence symbolizes the "might have been if only" in their lives, and as such it devalues whatever success they have been able to achieve. For such people the lowering of original high aspirations may occur as they attempt to manage the painful disparity out of existence. It may be possible for them to convince themselves that because they have been disabled or discriminated against, their original high aspirations were in reality nothing more than the dreams of naïve youth. Maturity and the worldly wise sophistication which comes with it (qualities which all adults hope to possess) require them to give up these overblown expectations, because in their circumstances such expectations were foolish to begin with. If their original aspirations can be viewed as foolish and naïve, then of course to cling to them does not profit their self-respect but on the contrary signifies more than a little foolishness and immaturity—the recognition of which can only undermine self-regard. By relinquishing these naïve expectations these individuals are freed to take pride in whatever success has been in fact achieved. Free of the painful recognition that a disparity between aspiration and achievement exists, whatever its source, they can convince themselves that they are persons of some value because the successes they *have* achieved are in line with realistic aspirations for people confronted by impeding circumstance.[4]

Whether this psychological process actually occurs is open to question. I have argued only that it is a possibility. But even if it does occur,

---

[4] The process just described is of course psychological in nature and, if it is to be effective, cannot occur at a conscious level: the individual must *not* be aware that he or she is manipulating the components of self-assessment in the manner described.

it can do so only when individuals have made successful claims of situational impediment in order to neutralize the impact upon their self-respect of the disparity between what they expect of themselves and what they appear to be achieving. As indicated earlier, successful claims of situational impediment are relatively infrequent. Therefore, if the second stratagem is used at all, it too must be quite infrequent—even, it would seem, more infrequent than the successful pleading of situational impediment. The use of the second stratagem therefore appears extremely ineffective as a means of managing out of existence the disparity between our aspirations and our achievements.

We are left with the third stratagem: the attempt to remove the aspiration-achievement disparity by inflating achievements so that the disparity appears not to have existed in the first place—the *counterfeit of success!* The inflation-or-counterfeit stratagem appears to be widely used in the United States at present. You won't have to look very far before signs of it catch your eye.

Perhaps the most obvious evidence of its use is the extent to which Americans lust after goods and services the possession and use of which are difficult to justify or explain by reference to their ostensible functions. For example, although the threat of an energy shortage has now imposed an unwelcome austerity upon many consumers of motorized conveyances, the American motorist has for several decades shown considerable ardor for precisely those automobiles which are the least economical to operate.[5] There is indeed something strange about the purchase of an automobile armed with over three hundred horsepower, particularly when you realize that all that power cannot be used efficiently without violating the traffic laws, and that its inefficient use costs the motorist considerably in high fuel consumption. The purchase of an automobile virtually guaranteed to be mechanically unreliable within five years at best is economically perverse, necessitating as it does the expenditure of several thousands of dollars for one new car after another. We take great pride in the presumption that we are a people whose economic rationality is eclipsed by none—we drive hard bargains and we demand our money's worth—and yet many of us seem downright profligate as soon as we find ourselves within a new-car showroom.

[5] At this writing the Carter administration has proposed a heavy tax on new automobiles deemed wasteful and a stand-by tax increase on gasoline. It remains to be seen whether Congress will support these proposals with appropriate legislation. Moreover, should these taxes be put into effect, it remains to be seen whether there will be any significant change in consumer behavior.

But perhaps this observation is erroneous; perhaps we are getting our money's worth; perhaps our profligacy is more apparent than real, because when we purchase an automobile we are really not just purchasing a machine which takes us from here to there, but more importantly we are purchasing a prop that we employ in the construction of an illusion which allows us to counterfeit personal success.

Viewed in such a manner there is a certain rationality to this otherwise perplexing behavior. The three hundred-plus up front isn't there to be used; it's there to be possessed. Its possession *is* an achievement. Three hundred-plus is a big number and to have bigness is to be big! All that money spent on a rapid succession of new automobiles is not so irrational either. To possess something big and new (a car with its sleek design, plush interior, and impressive horsepower is certainly that) is an achievement. It is exhilarating and no doubt reassuring to gaze upon the big new machine which is yours. When that big new machine starts to get old, when it begins to sputter instead of purr, when it begins to look a bit less sleek and the interior begins to show signs of wear, anxiety begins to threaten—not necessarily anxiety about functional adequacy of the automobile, but anxiety about achievement and success. The big new machine attracts attention. Others admire it and, through it, the owner, whose self-esteem is thereby buttressed. But when the compliments have ceased because the car has become just another machine which takes its owner from here to there, when it no longer elicits the admiration which appears to confirm the owner's claim to success, the time will soon be at hand to "achieve" another big new machine, to convince the others that the owner hasn't settled into an ordinary existence and, through them, to convince him or herself of that fact.

Even spending all that money is more reassuring than problematic. If you can keep spending, and particularly when your spending is visible to others, you must have something going for you, you must be achieving something. If you are paying big, your success is big, because no ordinary man or woman would be able to manage it.

By purchasing and possessing the big and the new, people can counterfeit personal success so that no matter how far short of their aspirations they fall they appear to convince themselves that they have not fallen short at all. For just about anyone who isn't what he or she wants to be, the automobile can become a prop for the "I am more successful than I am because look at what I own" fantasy—which, if it doesn't actually remove the disparity between aspiration and achievement, at the very least serves (as many fantasies and illusions do) to distract the individual from the disparity and the implied threat to self-respect. Its use makes of us Walter Mittys—but with a difference: whereas Walter Mitty merely daydreamed his great success, his distinctive achievements, we play-act our fantasies in the real world, with the help of the automotive dream machine.

It isn't just the automobile that serves as a convenient prop for the counterfeit of success; there are a whole host of goods and services the purchase, possession, and use of which would seem inexplicable except that they are extremely useful in the fabrication of success illusions. In spite of the fact that many imported wines are both overpriced and of poor quality, the market for these French, German, and Italian pretenders, with labels whose visual style and linguistic inaccessibility proclaim their purchaser's aristocratic good taste, is big and getting bigger in the United States. Some women will pay extraordinary prices just so the labels on their apparel will be among those that elicit expressions of admiration (a gown by any other name would simply not be the same!). How high can hi-fidelity get? When I surround myself with a sound system that everyone "knows" is special, am I not special—even if I cannot really distinguish between those bass timbres or those upper range resonances? Then of course there are the interior decorators who bring distinction into our lives by changing the draperies, moving the couch from one wall to another, rearranging those knick-knacks, and charging wonderfully exorbitant fees. We dine in restaurants which make a pretense of distinctive atmosphere (this is a special place, so to eat here is to be special) even while our palates tell us that the food we are ingesting is undercooked and overpriced. We vacation in an ersatz grand style at those resorts which allow and even encourage us to fantasize the realization of an exalted self. The plumber at the Fontainebleau cannot help but see himself as making it big—at least for those two weeks during which he spends and spends—while he basks, wines, and dines amidst a splendor that is all too obvious. The file clerk, having discovered that a BankAmericard can make you king for today (tomorrow? well, that's tomorrow, so why worry about it?), acts out that regal fantasy amidst the moneyed ambience of the fabled Concord where even the price list on the coffee shop menu momentarily convinces him that only the really big spenders frequent that particular scene. Even our addresses are convenient props for the counterfeit illusion of success. There are simply too many Chateau Villas, Elite Arms, Monte Carlo Apartments, and Versailles Manors for us not to notice that those who live in them are hardly likely to own real chateaus, are anything but members of an elite, and are unlikely ever to have been within an ocean's distance of either Monte Carlo or the palace at Versailles—although probably all of them would like to think of themselves as having access to these august precincts. The names on the awnings and the burnished bronze doors make that illusion of access possible, if only momentarily, for those who can cross these decorous portals on their way home from the humdrum routines which mark their daily endeavors.

All of these goods and services—automobiles, wines, clothing, hi-fi components, professional decoration, "classy" restaurants, vacations extraordinary, and the residential masquerade (there are others which I am sure the reader will have no trouble identifying)—whatever their ostensible functions, are used by many Americans to counterfeit personal success, to create an illusion of success, however momentary, which allows them to feel more successful, more important, or more distinguished then they actually are. These goods and services are the stuff of fantasy—of comforting distraction that allows many people to avoid if ever so briefly their aspiration-achievement disparities and the threats to self-respect which such disparities pose.

The use of these props in the construction of what may be termed the success-illusion is, however, not entirely unproblematic, and therefore it is not likely to be completely effective. The problems seem to be two-fold. First, it would appear that success-illusions constructed with such props are very difficult to sustain for more than relatively short periods of time. Economic limitations as well as the demands of daily living severely restrict their scope. Easy credit notwithstanding (and at the time of this writing it's not so easy as it used to be), unless you happen to be very well off, the frequency of your access to such props will be more or less limited. Very few people can afford to buy a big new car every time the models change, and each time the models change the car you possess loses some of its fantasy potential. The plumber may be able to afford the Fontainebleau on occasion, but only on occasion; and if he is going to continue to afford a vacation at this palace of earthly delights he must spend more than just a little time fixing leaky faucets and replacing worn-out toilets. How many times can the interior decorator move the couch? How often can we afford the money and the time to comfort ourselves by ingesting (if not digesting) squab prepared by a Michelin-rated three-star chef and served with the graceful, if studied, obsequiousness of waiters who know that the size of their gratuity depends upon how important they make us feel? The memory may linger on (reinforced perhaps by digestive disturbance), but for how long? Put simply, all too many of the goods and services we purchase as props for our success-illusions fail us after relatively short duration. Try as we might to sustain our illusions by almost incessant purchasing, we are never quite able to disprove the reality of the disparity between our aspirations and our achievements.

The second problem attending the use of goods and services as props for the construction of success-illusions is a function of the extent to which such use actually occurs. If the counterfeit is to be viable, the counterfeiter must avoid or block out any information which confounds the premises of the success-illusion, any signal which might undermine its effectiveness. Unfortunately, given the widespread use of goods and services to maintain such counterfeits, this avoidance becomes difficult. To an individual engaged in creating a success-illusion, the fact that so many other people are doing precisely the same thing must be somewhat disconcerting, especially because many of these others are, in objective terms, relatively undistinguished. Underlying the use of goods and services to create an illusion that counterfeits success is the premise which holds that the consumption of particular goods or the use of particular services is a clear indicator of exalted personal status. If it turns out—as it does—that others whose statuses are obviously not exalted are making use of such goods and services, then this information is likely to undermine the premise which makes the illusion possible. When the experienced drill press operator parks his Mercury Marquis in the company lot he probably puts it between a Chrysler Newport on one side and a Pontiac LeMans on the other—both new and both owned by co-workers who have not been on the job half as long as he has. The plumber expects to find the Fontainebleau populated by the "beautiful people"—and no doubt they are there—but he keeps running into other plumbers, not to mention the hardware store managers, the haberdashers, and the insurance salesmen who are also there expecting to find themselves surrounded by the wealthy and notable. The props you use to construct the illusion which counterfeits success often turn out to be the very same ones used by some very ordinary people, and to the extent that you are aware of this situation, the props—the goods and the services—lose much of their success fantasy potential. The premise that only really successful people can possess and use such goods and services is undermined by the apparent ordinariness of many of those people who do possess and use them. Such disillusionment notwithstanding, you may very well continue to counterfeit personal success by making use of these props, doing so because there is virtually nothing else you can do to avoid confronting the disparity between your aspirations and your achievements—but you are unlikely to do so without persistent doubt and discomfort.

There are other facets of the counterfeit-strategy often put to use to inflate our successes. For example, American society is a virtual clutter of voluntary associations. Many of these have programs focused on some clearly recognized social need, but others seem to exist without such programs or with programs that appear secondary to the simple fact of their existence. Programmatically focused or not, this plethora of associations seems to serve purposes not explicitly recognized in their charters or self-congratulatory pronouncements. One such purpose is obviously sociability and good fellowship. It is clear that these associations provide many people with a reason for going out and getting together with other people, as well as a place to go. Anyone who has ever been in a V. F. W. post hall or an Elks Lodge hall, or who has ever attended a League of Women Voters meeting, will recognize the truth of this observation.

But sociability and good fellowship would not appear to be the only non-explicit purposes served by these associations. If these were the only needs to be met, associations would not require the organizational characteristics they invariably seem to possess. Sociability does not imply a need for a very elaborate organizational structure, replete with offices, degrees, and other honorifics. And while it might be argued that in some instances such offices are necessary to carry out the association's program, such an argument can be countered with the observation that, although some of these offices are undoubtedly necessary, it is surely difficult to justify all of them as functional. Is it really the case that the Exchange Club or the Rotary needs all those vice-presidents, as well as all those chairmen of committees which never seem to transact any business? Moreover, associations minimally or not at all committed to a program characteristically create offices for, it appears, the sheer joy of having them. Indeed, it may not be very wide of the mark to note that the proliferation of offices occurs in inverse proportion to the intensity of an association's commitment to programmatic activities.

It would seem, therefore, that the elaborate organization so characteristic of voluntary associations in the United States cannot be explained by either the need for sociability or the functional needs generated by programmatic commitment. These elaborate structures can be understood, however, if we reflect on what beyond programmatic purpose and the opportunity for sociability the voluntary association offers its members. Those who join such associations are, like so many of the rest of us, in a position of having to contend with the esteem-threatening disparity between their aspirations and their achievements. And, like many of the rest of us, they are unlikely to have found a completely effective strategy for managing this disparity out of existence. It may therefore be the case that at least part of the motivation for membership in such associations stems from the need to deal with the aspiration-achievement disparity.

The association, whatever else it does or accomplishes, creates a universe of meaning at once imitative of that which is characteristic of the society-at-large and divorced from the troubling realities of any given individual's place within the society. The association can, if it has a strong programmatic orientation, give its members a special sense of purpose, a sense which may very well be lacking in their everyday existences. If it does not have such a purposive commitment, it is likely to have selective criteria for membership,[6] and merely by becoming a member an individual can believe that he or she has been judged worthy of a special status. But more important than the special meanings generated by membership alone is the structure of opportunity which the organizational characteristics of such an association generate. The many offices, the membership ranks or degrees, and the awards provide the opportunity for personal advancement and distinction based on a limited range of endeavors and competencies. Achieving personal success in the society-at-large is a complicated and risk-laden process, usually involving more than just a little good fortune, and it is a process which few people are able to manage to their complete satisfaction; achieving success within the voluntary association is much less complicated, involving as it does skills which for the most part are narrowly construed according to the limited purview of the association's purpose. The possession of some general skills, such as the ability to organize and follow through on a task, is an obvious advantage in the limited setting of the association, but even those without such skills are likely to find success within easy reach in the association. Perseverance and fealty to the association are likely to be enough to guarantee some honor among one's peers. The competencies one must master rarely require extended periods of study or apprenticeship, and "outside" (or general societal) creden-

[6] Purposive commitment and selective membership criteria are not necessarily mutually exclusive; nevertheless, associations which exist for the advancement of a cause generally appeal for mass membership on the assumption that a large membership will facilitate their programs.

tials or their absence count for little. The association, in effect, constitutes a small social world in which the opportunities for personal success are many and the requirements for achieving it are something less than demanding.

The elaborate organizational structure of the voluntary association—whatever its ostensible purpose—has, then, a very important latent function: it creates a context in which personal "success" can be achieved—success that is imitative of "real world" success but which is not dependent upon ability to manage the complexities and exigencies which test each of us in our real-world lives. We can therefore understand the characteristic over-organization of voluntary associations, as well as the obvious popularity of these collectivities, as an expression of the familiar need to inflate or counterfeit our successes so that we may neutralize the threat to our self-respect posed by the disparity between our aspirations and our achievements.

One of the more memorable comedic characterizations ever to be presented on American television was Jackie Gleason's evocation of the blowhard bus driver in "The Honeymooners"—Ralph Cramden. One of Gleason's funnier Cramden gambits was parading as the Supreme Raccoon of the Loyal Order of Raccoons. Together with his sewer-cleaning sidekick Norton (played by Art Carney), Cramden dressed up in his lodge regalia—a beribboned and bemedalled nineteenth-century British Admiralty uniform topped off with a coonskin cap—and to the delight of millions of viewers blustered his way through the amnidiversions which characterized the meetings and other activities of the Raccoons. It was all very funny and it had, in exaggeration, the ring of truth. There was Cramden, the bus driver, living in what seemed to be very mortal bliss with his wife in a dingy walk-up apartment, stepping into his exalted role amidst his fellow Raccoons. If the real world was drab, the small world of the Raccoons was aglitter, if only because of the play of the lights on all those medals and high colored sashes. If in the real world Cramden was always being defeated by the traffic, by bus dispatchers who regarded the schedule as holy writ, and even by kitchen sinks which would not stay unclogged—if his many schemes to beat the system and make it big always seemed to land him back in the bus and his walk-up apartment—in the small world of the Raccoons he was always a success, always the Supreme Raccoon no matter what he did. The Loyal Order of Raccoons (or was it the Benevolent Brotherhood of Raccoons?) was Cramden's out. In reality he was always aspiring but never achieving. In reality he was forever being confronted with the disparity between what he wanted for himself and what he actually had. The Loyal Order of Raccoons, however, exalted him just enough so that he could deny, at least from time to time, the threat that the real world posed.

There is, I suspect, a little of Ralph Cramden in many of us. To a greater or lesser extent we are often threatened by the reality of our lives, by aspirations which too easily make what we really are seem inadequate. And like Ralph Cramden many of us often seek to avoid the stinging reality of our existences by committing ourselves to the opportunities for "success" provided by voluntary associations.

The success we find is illusory, however—a counterfeit of the real thing—precisely because it is unappreciated except by those who themselves are members of the association. Ralph Cramden's posturing in uniform may not have been hilarious to him, or to Norton or the other Raccoons, but it was to the rest of us. And if he laid claim to a generalized respect on the basis of his eminence among the Raccoons, he would receive only ridicule in return. The Gleason sketches made this sociological point abundantly clear; there were times when just wearing the Raccoon uniform in public ran Cramden afoul of the law, and his wife never missed a chance to tell Ralph and the audience just how ridiculous she found his play at eminence.

As long as we keep our claims to success within the small world created by the voluntary association and its organizational characteristics, the validity of our claims will not be challenged; but in the real world of everyday experience such claims carry little or no weight. Like the "success" based upon frenetic consumption of goods and services, "success" based upon rank and emolument in the context of the voluntary association is illusory—this time because it cannot receive general confirmation in the world beyond the association, the world which, alas, may be too much with us.

Because such claims to personal distinction cannot be confirmed in everyday life, associational participation is limited as a means of dealing with the aspiration-achievement disparity. Some of us may be able to make participation the reigning experience in our lives; to be sure, many of us try to do just this. Those who are able to lose themselves in the activities of their lodges, their fraternities, or the likes of the League of Women Voters or the Rotary can probably counterfeit success without realizing what they are doing. But for the rest of us the real world—the world of making a living by driving a bus, installing sinks, teaching freshman English, the world of keeping house and tending to the needs

of one's children, the world of dealing with frustration and disappointment—occupies so much of our time and consciousness that the failure
of our voluntary association eminence to engender respect and admiration in that world can only threaten us with the knowledge that we
have not really been successful, that associational accolades and testi-
monials aside, we are after all bus drivers, plumbers, teachers, and house-
wives, just ordinary folks who do not and will not make others stand up
and take notice. To the extent that such an awareness intrudes upon
us, the small world of the voluntary association and our success within
it cannot save us from confronting the aspiration-achievement disparity
and the threat it poses to our self-respect.

Imperfect as the counterfeit strategy may be, it is used over and over
again, perhaps because the multi-faceted complexity characterizing
American life offers us so many opportunities to make use of it. Driven
as we are to prove to ourselves that our personal aspirations have not
been disappointed, we go from one counterfeit to the next, one illusion
to the next, hoping to be convinced that indeed we have been successful. The lengths to which many of us go in search of an effective counterfeit, one that works because it escapes detection by others as well as
ourselves, can finally be seen in the way some of us exploit our children.

We all know of the father who goes to a Little League game and
becomes so involved with his son's (and more recently his daughter's)
athletic achievements and failures that he appears to forget that he is
watching the game of baseball being played, rather inexpertly, by a group
of kids all under the age of thirteen. We likewise know of the "stage
mother" who drags her semi-talented son or daughter from one audition
to the next in the vain hope that the child will be "discovered" and
become a star. More frequently we encounter those parents (middle-
class parents in particular) who insist that their children are cerebrally
gifted and demand that they make use of their "gifts" even when they
are really not very interested in becoming another Einstein or even another Uncle Murray, the pharmaceutical chemist who oversees the work
of three hundred other chemists. Such people as these are often the
objects of slightly chagrined wonderment. We find it difficult to understand why they interfere to such an extent in the lives of their children,
why they fail to see their children for what they are, why they do not
simply leave them alone and let them grow up normally. We sense that
such parents are using their children in the pursuit of ends which have
little or nothing to do with the children themselves—that they want
something and their children are simply the means they are employing

to get it. If we view such parental behavior as a function of the need to counterfeit success, I believe we can better understand what they (perhaps we) are doing, what they (we?) want so desperately that even the welfare of their, or our, children is not too high a price to pay in its pursuit.

If, as has been argued in these pages, we are driven to counterfeit success so that we may avoid the threatening implications of the aspiration-achievement disparity, then for many of us our children can easily become central to the counterfeit process. To begin with, our children are literally ours, we consider them our possessions; we have given them life and we are responsible for them. Without us they would not exist. We are their first and, if the conventional wisdom is to be believed, their most important teachers. As such it is easy for us to see their achievements and successes as reflecting favorably upon us. Certainly to have a successful child elicits admiration from those with whom we interact. "So you're Billy's father—well, he certainly is a great ball-player!" And "That Sarah of yours, she's really something—such grace—what a dancer—she'll be a Margot Fonteyn one these days—you'll see!" No parent can fail to be heartened by accolades such as these. The attention of this sort given to children is almost of necessity as important to their parents as it is to them, if not more so. But the line between taking justifiable pride in the achievements of our children and appropriating those accomplishments (and the kudos which goes with them) for our own is thin and easily crossed.

Much is made of the fact that children identify with their parents as they grow up, but it may also be true that there are conditions under which *parents identify with their children.* When adults are driven to obliterate any recognition of the disparities between their aspirations and their achievements, this condition may very well come to exist. When such a condition exists, parents become their children in a psychological sense, appropriating their children's lives—feeling what their children feel, triumphing as their children triumph—while at the same time directing their children into activities which bear a marked resemblance to their own unrealized aspirations.

It is not simply because our children's lives are easily available for appropriation, however, that they are often made central to our attempts to counterfeit success. There is something about childhood itself particularly predisposing to the psychological appropriation that has been described. Childhood (and adolescence) in American society can be described as a state of becoming. Children are promise; no matter who they are, they appear full of potential, potential which almost always seems to be unforeclosed if only because they are children and have not yet arrived at their place in the scheme of things. In contrast, being an adult soon comes to mean that you have arrived, that barring something unforeseen your place in society has been determined. You may or may not realize fully the possibilities offered by your place in the scheme of things—the professor may or may not become a distinguished professor, the plumber may or may not eventually open his own business, the accountant may or may not become a corporate auditor—but by the time you are thirty who and what you are has usually been decided.[7] The promise of childhood has a special attraction for those of us who, having arrived, do not find our identities consonant with our aspirations. Our access to the lives of our children and the promise which their lives represent can extend the time we have for becoming, the time when all things seem possible. By identifying with our children we can deny to ourselves that we are who we are, that we have ceased to become and now are those persons whose aspirations have not been and will not be fully realized.

When, driven by our need to avoid the aspiration-achievement disparity, we identify with our children and direct them into activities which bear a more than minimal relationship to our own imperfectly realized aspirations, their (our) successes are not merely successes of the moment—they are from our perspective harbingers of the future. Our children's successes reassure us; they give us reason to believe that our aspirations may yet be achieved. And even should they fail, because they are children we can keep hoping that they will eventually realize our aspirations. If childhood's promise (its aura of becoming) makes success a harbinger of the future, it also makes failure unimportant as an indicator of the future. If adults fail at things they desire to achieve, their failures are consequential, because adults really have little time to rectify their failures before the failures have established their identities in the eyes of significant others. If children fail, there is always a next time to look forward to, always time to improve and room for optimism. Learn from your mistakes, we tell our children, thereby making their mistakes useful not only to their development but often to the maintenance of our optimism about the realization of our own aspirations.

[7] This closure of social identity has an important effect on the threat to self-respect posed by the aspiration-achievement disparity. If we could continue to hope past the age of thirty that our highest aspirations might yet be fulfilled, the aspiration-achievement disparity would probably not pose the threat that it does.

Parental identification with children can thus be understood as a means for counterfeiting personal success. By psychologically "becoming" the child, the parent is able to enjoy the child's immediate successes and—ignoring reality—take heart in the supposition that there is still time to realize his or her personal ambitions. But this counterfeit, like all the others discussed here, by its very nature cannot be completely effective.

First, there is the intrusion of everyday reality. The activities one is forced to undertake in order to survive occupy us all much of the time. Our identification with our children simply cannot force those activities and their self-definitional implications from our consciousness, at least not to the extent necessary to a really effective counterfeit. Billy's father, whatever his psychological investment in his son's athletic ability, must spend many of his waking hours as a hardware salesman. And selling hammers and screwdrivers is a lot different from pitching a shutout as the crowd roars its approval. Sarah's mother, visions of an ecstatic opening night audience notwithstanding, must spend her days cooking, marketing, and picking up after Sarah and her siblings—no audience and no Clive Barnes to review the balance and grace with which she accomplishes these tasks! Reality is too demanding, and if we are to maintain a viable presence in our families (as we must if we want to identify with our children), it simply cannot be avoided or ignored.

Second, there is the fact that the "success" counterfeited by an identification with one's children cannot really be confirmed in the reactions of significant others. It is one thing to compliment a parent about a child's achievement, but it is quite another to endorse a parent's appropriation of the child's successes. When we encounter adults who appear to be making such appropriations we express wonder; if we know them well enough we may be explicitly critical. We are unlikely to acquiesce in their claims, and even if we ourselves identify with our children, when others do the same we regard their acts as illegitimate and unfair to their children. It appears, therefore, that appropriated success will not receive the confirmation it needs if it is to be a completely serviceable counterfeit; moreover, it may very well elicit a reaction from significant others which, because it undermines the legitimacy of the identification or appropriation process, is itself a threat to self-esteem.

Third, children quite frequently resist their parents' attempts to identify with them and appropriate their successes. Children often resent parental incursions into their lives, particularly as they grow into adolescence. Because they know their parents so well, they are often able to read the needs underlying such incursions and may resist their parents (consciously or unconsciously) in ways which confound those needs. The more the parent persists the more the child resists, to the end of increasing estrangement between them, estrangement which is doubly devastating to the parent because it means not only the loss of filial affection but also, in the ensuing inability to identify with the child, the increasing ineffectiveness of the all-important counterfeit.

Once again, what first appears to be an effective counterfeit of success turns out to be something less. It may work for some—at great cost to their children—and others, overwhelmed by the need to delude themselves, may attempt its use in spite of the almost inescapable risks and difficulties; but the chances of managing the aspiration-achievement disparity out of existence by resorting to the use of one's children are, it would appear, less than even.

By now it should be abundantly clear that if the counterfeit (or inflation) strategy is the most frequently used of the three strategies employed to deal with the aspiration-achievement deficit (the others being the claim of situational impediment and the lowering of personal aspiration), it is nevertheless problematic and incompletely effective. Symbolic consumption leaves something to be desired, as do the voluntary association gambit and parental appropriation of children's success. While some may utilize such ploys (and other similar ones) effectively, the majority, it seems, will have at best very short-lived success with them.

When we remember that the situational impediment and aspiration reduction strategies are likely to be even more troubling than the counterfeit strategy, we are forced to conclude that many Americans must contend on a sustained basis with a significant threat to their sense of self-worth. If the individual-as-central sensibility creates the conditions in which the aspiration-achievement disparity becomes a reality for many people, the widespread failure to make effective use of the strategies in question must mean that the existence of the disparity is managed out of existence only infrequently and imperfectly. The obvious consequence of this state of affairs is a large number of people in a varied array of personal circumstances who are troubled about themselves, haunted by a sense that they are inadequate no matter what they have actually achieved, dissatisfied with what they are because they believe they should be more than they are, terribly insecure about the meaning and value of the lives they lead.

This *trouble*, itself the product of the individualization of success and failure, is the psychological key to the perpetuation of the culture of inequality and its main tenet, the individual-as-central sensibility as a dominant theme in the American experience.

In this light, let us pose a question: If people need to feel successful in order to be at peace with themselves but in the course of things can neither be as successful as they think they ought to be nor avoid the reality of this disparity, what are they likely to do to minimize their discomfort? Where will they look for reassurance, for something to bolster their diminished senses of self-worth? Sorely discomforted, they might, of course, begin to question the serviceability of a society which places so much emphasis upon the need for personal success. They might reject that society and its values, thereby relieving themselves of the obligation to lust after the bitch goddess of success. Having done so, they might then be in a position to think more positively about themselves—to take a measure of pride in the things they do well regardless of the social value placed on such endeavors in contemporary American society. They might embark upon such a course, and indeed it would appear that some people have done just that—witness the revival of the rural romance among previously citified sophisticates and the attraction of what has been called the counter-culture for some who once seemed highly conventional—but for most Americans, however discontented, the circumstances of existence render such a course highly unlikely. Most simply do not have easy intellectual and emotional access to cultural materials[8] which might inform and justify so robust an alienation from the American mainstream. If, as has been noted in the previous chapter, the individual-as-central sensibility is the stuff of both conservative and liberal opinion, if it establishes the range of *conceivable* interpretation concerning the character of inequality in American society, then the probability that any given person will be able to translate a personal discontent into social and cultural criticism challenging the serviceability of individualized success (conventionally defined) as a moral imperative is likely to be very low.

[8] Phenomenologists refer to such materials as *typifications*, which constitute a kind of collectively held repertoire of meanings used by individuals to construct and/or interpret their life circumstances. See Peter Berger and Thomas Luckmann, *The Social Construction of Reality* (Garden City, N. Y.: Doubleday, 1966), and Alfred Schutz, *Collected Papers* (The Hague: M. Nijhoff, 1964).

Discontent is one thing, but to turn it into a rejection of extant success norms and expectations one would have to find an interpretive mode—an analysis and a rhetoric—which undermines the legitimacy of these expectations. Some form of collectivist ideology would probably serve this function very well. A Marxist or quasi-Marxist interpretation which finds capitalist American society dominated by powerful economic classes bent on interest aggrandizement at the expense of the weaker economic classes, which perceives the individual-as-central sensibility (and the conservative and liberal opinions which serve it) as an ideology of the economic dominators foisted upon the rest of us to blind us to the inequities of their continued domination [9]—such an interpretation, if adopted, would of course undermine the legitimacy of individualized success as a moral imperative. But how many people are likely to have access to such an interpretation of the American condition? If the individual-as-central sensibility defines the conceivable and therefore legitimate range of opinion on matters of social and economic equity in American life, any collectivist interpretation, falling as it must outside this range, will be regarded as deviant and will as such be stigmatized, an anathema to most. Because of their illegitimacy such interpretations cannot be presented to Americans as conceivable alternatives to the mainstream sensibility.

Up until very recently collectivist interpretations of the American condition were rarely if ever presented in "respectable" public forums. As recently as the early sixties, what public school system dared expose its students to "godless communism" or "alien socialism," what schoolbook publisher dared publish a text even hinting that a collectivist interpretation might be illuminating, and how many public universities permitted known communists to lecture on their campuses or—perish the thought—allowed them to be hired as permanent members of the faculty? Even today, in this era of presumed permissiveness, few Americans are exposed to collectivist interpretations in an unbiased manner which allows them to judge such arguments on their merits alone. In some public high schools Marxist and quasi-Marxist ideology is presented for study, but only after it has been identified as the ideology of our international competitors and potential enemies, and only after its study has been justified as a form of intelligence: know what your enemy thinks so that you will be better able to resist him, so that you

[9] In classical Marxist terms, the widespread endorsement of this sensibility by the exploited classes in American society would be understood as a case of false-consciousness.

will be better able to keep ahead of him! Marxists do appear with some regularity on college campuses—some are even faculty members—but more often than not they are characterized as intellectual eccentrics by most of their non-Marxist colleagues, who in spite of their frequent left-of-center political preferences operate within the bounds of the modified form of the individual-as-central sensibility (see above, pp. 9–14).

Under such circumstances few people are likely to find a way of translating their discontent into a coherent rejection of the existing capitalist American society and the individualized success imperative it produces. They simply do not have access to an interpretive mode likely to facilitate such a rejection.[10]

If rejection is unlikely, are we to assume that the discontent, which is the product of the need to be successful beyond realistic possibility, is inevitable, that it really cannot be dealt with and is a condition of existence in America? Unfortunately, it seems that we must answer this question, at least to a considerable degree, in the affirmative. Most people simply have no way of externalizing the discontent born of overweaning and unrealistic aspiration and, as we have seen, no way of effectively hiding the fact that their achievements have fallen (or are falling) short of their ambitions. Whatever their actual achievements they cannot make real peace with themselves. They seem unable to say, "I am what I am and that is enough!" There are too many Willy Lomans in America, too many who have "the only dream you can have—to come out number one man," and who live with the constant if inarticulate fear of being told, "You were never anything but a hardworking drummer who landed in the ash can like all the rest of them!" [11]

Some, like Willy Loman, are driven to despair. Pained beyond the limits of endurance by reality, they seek surcease in narcosis, madness, or the irrevocable self-obliteration of suicide. Most escape such a fate,

[10] It is interesting to note in this vein that even among the poorest and most disadvantaged Americans, collectivist interpretations of the American reality have rarely proved attractive. In the twenties and thirties, for example, when blacks had a choice between the communists and the socialists on the one hand and the individualistic nationalism of Marcus Garvey and his heirs on the other, they appeared more eager to choose the individualistic alternative. See Michael Lewis, "The Negro Protest in the Cities," in *Protest, Reform and Revolt*, ed. Joseph Gusfield (New York: John Wiley and Sons, 1970), pp. 149–90.

[11] Arthur Miller, *Death of a Salesman* (New York: Viking Press, 1949), pp. 139, 132. The play was first presented on Broadway, February 10, 1949.

however, because the complex of beliefs—the individual-as-central sensibility—which underlies their difficulties also provides them with the interpretive means by which they can prevent the descent from discontent into despair.

If the individual-as-central sensibility creates a condition in which individuals must juxtapose their achievements against their aspirations, it also allows them to perceive modest personal achievement in contradistinction to the failures of others to achieve similarly. Indeed, not only does the sensibility allow such perceptions, it actually encourages them. "He who does less than he can does ill," wrote Thomas Nixon Carver; and while the sentiment these words express threatens the individualist's sense of self-worth, it also suggests a means by which this threat might be at least mitigated. Society, the individual-as-central sensibility holds, is benign; no doubt it has problems, but it is basically sound and is still a society of chances. True, people who are not as successful as they hoped to be cannot, in such a circumstance, blame society for this disparity, but the impact of such a deficit can be reduced insofar as the individuals are able to perceive themselves as having avoided, through personal effort and competence, the failures which are the just deserts of those who have done less than they can. If people are not the successes they hoped to be, they may nevertheless take comfort in the belief that they are not the failures that they might have been and that others—for want of effort and competence—are. The individual-as-central sensibility speaks not only to personal credit and responsibility for success but also to personal accountability and culpability for failure. Therefore, as long as individuals are able to separate themselves from those whose "failures" are unequivocal, as long as they are able to distinguish between what they have achieved and what others have failed to achieve, they can count themselves among the worthy—not perhaps the successes they should have been, but "successes" at least in relative terms.

Ironically, the individual-as-central sensibility which authors the threat to the individual's sense of self-worth becomes, in such a circumstance, the only means of psychological succor. Brought to the edge of an abyss by a system of belief which renders almost all personal achievements inadequate before that insatiable goddess of success, by an interpretation of American opportunity which denies inequitous structural restrictions and rarely honors any claim of imposed impediment as an excuse for personal failure, the individual who is about to topple saves him- or herself by recourse to those very same beliefs, and in doing so perpetuates the sensibility and the culture of inequality which has created it. Salvation—if one can call it that—demands that the striking "failure" of others be interpreted as the result of volitional malingering or personal incompetence, so that one's relative "success" can be understood as the result of effort and personal capacity. Society must be perceived as on the whole benign, so that one's success, considered against the failure of others, cannot be written off as a function of one's own relatively advantaged social position. If it were otherwise, relative success could not easily be interpreted as a sign of worthiness, and the individual, left to deal with the disparity between aspiration and achievement, might very well topple into that abyss of despair, that bottomless pit awaiting just beyond illusion.

To make *relative success* personally meaningful—to render it symbolic of self-worth—many Americans, I would argue, find it necessary to espouse those beliefs about individual responsibility for success and failure which threatened their self-esteem to begin with. They have a psychological investment in the individual-as-central sensibility because, once established, it has preempted what might be termed the American cultural consciousness regarding success and failure, regarding the existence of inequality in a society presumed (erroneously) to be equalitarian in opportunity. If they are driven by it to the brink of despair, it is nevertheless the only interpretive system to which they have effective access; and consequently in their struggle against despair it is the interpretive system they are virtually forced to use. The ironic outcome of this state of affairs is an intense (shall we say desperate?) reaffirmation of the cultural sensibility whose very existence may be seen as counter-productive to personal well-being and equanimity: a perpetuation of the individual-as-central sensibility in either its original moralistic form or its modified explanatory form.

Once established in the American experience during the last quarter of the nineteenth and the first quarter of the twentieth centuries (established because it appeared to offer an adequate and, more importantly, an optimistic rendering of the American condition—because it celebrated a society of chances), this sensibility has maintained its veritable hegemony over the American mind. It has created psychological need even as it has provided the cultural means for its *partial* satisfaction. Anxiety and guilt are its issue, but it is also a comforter. It creates the conditions mandating its embrace, and in its embrace by those it has troubled it is strengthened so that it may trouble and comfort again.

It would be a serious error to read what I have just written as a criticism of those Americans who, seeking to salvage their self-esteem, persist in seeing the misfortunes of others as warranted by their mis- or malfeasance. It would be a mistake to condemn them for ignoring the realities of *unequal* opportunity which inhere in American capitalism and which virtually insure the apparent failures of some people. In our desperate need for reassurance, many of us in fact have an investment in those social and economic conditions which insure apparent failure among others—the economic exclusion and social stigmatization of the poor, the racial dichotomy, unequal educational opportunity, unequal justice, and the like [12]—but to see only the wrongness or the immorality of this investment would be to miss the point almost entirely. To do so would be to create a false dichotomy between victim and victimizer, between a class of unfortunate "good guys" on the one hand and more fortunate "bad guys" on the other. In point of ironic fact, the self-perpetuating hegemony of the individual-as-central sensibility makes victims of *all* but the few who have had the good fortune to achieve their high or at least moderately high aspirations in full, and if some people stigmatize others, denying them opportunity and treating them as pariahs, they do so, more often than not, because they are driven to do so.

The victimizers act as they do because they themselves are victims, because their innocent faith in the "American Way" engenders in them a need for reassurance which only the visible and presumably personal failures of others can assuage. They are not free agents acting against others with nefarious intent. They are, rather, men and women whose psychologies have paradoxically been warped by beliefs—the importance of the individual and the necessity of personal aspiration—which in the abstract most of us would applaud. If they cause others to suffer, we should not lose sight of the fact that they do so out of a culturally imposed suffering of their own.

Time and time again I have heard people whom I have regarded as prejudiced and bigoted deny their apparent bigotry and prejudice. For a long while I thought such denials false, mere prevarications made necessary by the American commitment to fair treatment in one's dealings with others. Given the American emphasis on equity in social intercourse, I considered it unlikely that even the most prejudiced and

[12] These conditions and our investments in them are thoroughly analyzed in the following chapter.

bigoted among us would acknowledge their true beliefs and intentions. To do so would make them vulnerable to censure and likely ridicule. While this observation was probably correct in some instances, my understanding of the individual-as-central sensibility and its psychological implications now leads me to construe such denials as frequently containing more than a kernel of truth. Such people, I am now convinced, are not acting out of prejudice (as we understand the meaning of that term) when they exclude or otherwise mistreat the disinherited (the poor and the black poor in particular). They are acting out of a desperate attempt to rescue themselves from the self-derogation which comes of the sense that whatever they have accomplished is simply not enough—that given the presumed openness of American society, they should be more than they are in fact. They do not hate those they mistreat or, at the very least, neglect. They do not discriminate against the blacks because they are blacks, and they are not contemptuous of the poor because they are poor. Those acts of commission and omission against identifiable others which appear to indicate strong prejudice and unequivocal antipathy actually indicate attempts by those who author them to convince themselves of their self-worth—to convince themselves that if they have not accomplished all that they should, they have, by virtue of the quality and quantity of their own efforts, accomplished more than have others with the same opportunities. Defamation of identifiable others, understood in terms of the psychological need created by the individual-as-central sensibility, is not an end in itself (as it usually is when prejudice and bigotry are involved) but is rather a mechanism for convincing oneself, by contradistinction, of one's self-worth.

According to this view, the disinherited are necessary to those who demean them; like new automobiles, supposedly rare French wines, and liveried waiters, they are props necessary to the creation of an illusion of personal success which distracts many of us from the threat to our self-worth posed by the aspiration-achievement disparity. In the logic of bigotry, the social invisibility of the pariahs—perhaps (as in the racial insanity of German National Socialism) even their physical destruction—is the desired end; but such is not the case in the situation of the American disinherited. It is not their social invisibility, their removal from the everyday venues of American life, which is desired, but just the opposite: their sustained visibility in our midst where they personify the "failures" we might be but are not. No, it is not bigotry which moves many Americans to demean other Americans, but a desperate quest for personal salvation.

If this observation is correct, it has at least one implication of considerable significance: as long as the individual-as-central sensibility dominates our thinking about the existence of inequality in American society, it will be virtually impossible to put an end to the social stigmatization and economic exclusion of the disinherited. If it is true that the disinherited are victimized because the individual-as-central sensibility has placed the victimizers in psychological jeopardy, if it is true that, in order to deal with the threat to self posed by the aspiration-achievement disparity, the disinherited are used by many people as negative alter egos, then it should be clear that, as long as the sensibility is dominant, many Americans will find it necessary to demean and exclude other Americans. Bigots might be persuaded that their views are in error (although this persuasion is not easy to accomplish), and if they were so persuaded they might change their behavior; but when exclusion occurs out of a need to salvage the self and avoid personal despair, it is hardly likely that it will cease unless the threat to self motivating it is removed. If people persist in viewing the poor as amoral slackers because by doing so they can live with not being as successful as they believe they ought to be, then no amount of education or citation of facts is going to change their views or the behaviors these views inform. They simply have too much invested in their pejorative characterizations of the poor. Their self-respect is on the line and they will not give up what is virtually their only defense against self-derogation. If accepting the truth about the poor means exposing themselves to their own worst fears, then that truth must simply be ignored.

As long as the individual-as-central sensibility remains dominant, the threat of self-derogation will be intense. And as long as this threat is intense there will be many who, in order to save themselves from it, will employ the tenets of the sensibility to victimize other people. If this assertion is correct, there would appear to be little realistic hope for positive change in the circumstances of the disinherited within the foreseeable future. If, as I have suggested, the hegemony of the individual-as-central sensibility implies their continuing stigmatization and exclusion, then only an end to this hegemony promises an end to their unfortunate estate. Given the historic tenacity of the sensibility, there is little reason to believe that it will soon cease to be dominant. Hence, many who believe (contrary to the realities of the American opportunity structure) that they are free to achieve their most cherished aspirations and who fail to achieve them in full will continue to make hostages of the disinherited, demeaning them to feel personally successful by comparison. With no cultural revolution in sight, it would be foolishly optimistic indeed to expect significant changes for those whose seemingly unequivocal failures are necessary to the maintenance in many other Americans of even a modicum of self-esteem.[13] Until and unless the hegemony of the individual-as-central sensibility is broken, both those who are presumably "making it" and those who are not will continue to suffer, albeit differently. All (or very nearly all) of us are, one way or another, victims of those beliefs we revere—and I can see no reason to think that it will be otherwise for quite some time to come.

☆

The American culture of inequality is a tragic paradox writ large. It justifies the persistence of inequality in a society which stands firmly upon a foundation of equalitarian principle. It explains the persistence of inequality in terms consonant with equalitarian belief. It honors individual capacity, freedom, and dignity, while at the same time it is a source of profound personal discontent and, for some, of despair. It celebrates equal opportunity as a reality while it makes a fact of unequal opportunity. It troubles us, but we regard any criticism of its premises as heresy and those who engage in such criticism as eccentrics or worse. And while it is a source of contemporary social stability, the trouble which is its issue can portend, as we shall see, a de-stabilized American future.

The culture of inequality is the dialectic of our time. It contains the polarities of belief and intent which will probably shape the foreseeable future of American society—unless, of course, we are able to see it for what it is.

[13] This assertion, I think, will be amply supported by the materials presented in Chapter Three.

# 3

## Mandated Social Problems

If, as it is frequently suggested, *culture* is a collective design for living, it is nevertheless true that not all such designs are equally service-able. The values, beliefs, and normative nuances which are the essence of culture may be life-enhancing, in that they make personal fulfillment a real possibility for most of those people whose existences they define, or they may be destructive, because they make such fulfillment virtually impossible. They may be the wellsprings of creative response to a so-ciety's problems or may, conversely, so limit human imagination that collective response either has no effect or, worse still, actually maximizes the impact of these problems. Moreover, the culture or design may itself minimize the frictions in human interaction, thus reducing the potential for problems in society, or it may maximize such frictions and thus constitute a potent source of social problems. The values, beliefs, and normative nuances which constitute a culture may serve one era quite well—perhaps too well—and successive eras not at all. It is true that culture simplifies the tasks of living by providing ready answers to a myriad of questions, both simple and complex; but those answers—so powerful in their easy accessibility that they often appear to be the only possible ones—can immobilize people in the face of the new and unforeseen. Quite simply, if culture is a design for living it can also be a trap in which life is made torturous indeed.

The cultural consciousness characterized by the individual-as-central sensibility of the culture of inequality and its psychological implications is, sad to say, a trap. In the past it may have been life-enhancing; in its emphasis upon personal achievement it no doubt contributed sig-nificantly to the creativity, the burst of imaginative energy, which in the latter part of the nineteenth century and the early part of the twentieth century brought about the modernization of American society. But in the present it is a trap: its preeminence maximizes the potential for personal frustration and social friction; it is a source of much that is problematic in American life; and in its hegemony over the modern American mind it has severely restricted effective reconstructive response to that which is problematic. The values and beliefs constituting the individual-as-central sensibility have immobilized us in the face of the *trouble* which is its unfortunate product, so much so that we stand on the verge of cultural bankruptcy; and the possibility that we may be overwhelmed by our problems—unthinkable in the halcyon days of our optimistic past—presses upon us in all its awful potential.

The manner in which the sensibility maximizes the potential for personal frustration has already been chronicled in chapters One and Two above. It is sufficient to note in this context that by making a moral imperative of high personal aspiration and by making "success" or "failure" the *natural* result of the quality of an individual's effort and/or competence, the sensibility places people in a situation where the likely disparity between their aspirations and achievements must frustrate and threaten them regardless of the quality of their achievements or, indeed, the elaborate strategems they may employ to avoid the threat.

To understand the importance of the individual-as-central sensibility as a source of society's problems and an inhibitor of reconstructive responses which might render them soluble, let us consider the effects of the sensibility on some of the worst of these problems.

### Poverty, Race, Educational Failure, and Crime: The Mandated Problems

As we have seen, the threat to self-worth posed by the disparity between personal aspiration and individual achievement can only be reduced or neutralized for many people when they are able to distinguish between their moderate successes and the apparently unequivocal failures of others on the basis of their own presumed superior effort or competence. As long as many Americans are driven to make use of this strategem, apparent failure, presumed to be the just desert of those who malinger or are incompetent, will in fact be a *social necessity*. Put somewhat starkly, as long as visible failure is reassuring to the many who fear that they have not been successful *enough*, it is not beyond reason to suggest that many Americans will have a stake in insuring the

continuation of such "failure" as the lot of a significant number of
their fellow citizens. For such people, those who "fail" in American
life—the poor, the uneducated, the delinquent—are psychic hostages
against intimations of personal worthlessness. They become necessary
to the maintenance of even a tenuous sense of psychic well-being.

If indeed this description is accurate, what does it indicate about
the social problems which appear to characterize the current American
experience? It indicates, I would maintain, that some of those conditions which we facilely regard as problematic (and by implication,
those which nearly everyone would like to remedy) may nevertheless
be necessary conditions in American life. Put another way, while these
conditions may be troublesome—they certainly injure many people—
their existence is culturally mandated and they are intrinsic to the very
essence of American society.

*Poverty and Race* [1]  Is poverty a problem? Well, yes and no! It is
certainly a problem for the thirty million poor in the United States;
and we may suppose that, in the abstract, most Americans would agree
that the existence of insufficient financial wherewithal among so many
people implies difficulties for the society as a whole. But to the extent
that those who need to discredit the poor in order to buttress their own
threatened self-worth can view the poor as having, of their own volition
or incompetence, failed in this society of chances, the existence of
poverty becomes a virtual necessity in American society. All the antipoverty rhetoric notwithstanding, and irrespective of the many skirmishes entered into by poverty warriors past and present, the culturally
mandated need for visible failure in American society carries with it
a need to maintain poverty.[2]

In this light it is important to note that while Americans have
ostensibly concerned themselves with poverty remedies for years, from
the beginnings of friendly visiting and social work in the latter part of
the nineteenth century through the advent of federally supported
welfare programs during the 1930s and the War on Poverty in the
sixties, none of these remedies has had a serious impact on the existence
of widespread poverty in American life. Given the American record of
inventive and successful response to a host of challenges during this
same period (for example, the relatively successful assimilation of mil-

[1] Poverty and Race are treated jointly because, as will be seen, they are conventionally
associated in the public consciousness.
[2] See Adam Walinsky, "Keeping the Poor in Their Place: Notes on the Importance
of Being One-Up," *New Republic*, July 4, 1964, pp. 15–18.

lions of immigrants, the elaboration of successful organizational forms to meet the needs of political and economic modernization, the relative stabilization of economic process threatened by worldwide depression, the development of an awesome technology, and so on), this persistent failure to make effective inroads against poverty would appear inexplicable—unless of course the ineffectiveness of the poverty remedies is at least to some extent *intentional*, unless these remedies have been intentionally inappropriate so that even as we appear to be doing something about poverty, we are actually, out of a need to keep the poor in their place, insuring its persistence.

The accuracy of this last assertion can be demonstrated with considerable force if we take a closer look at what may be termed *institutionalized responses* to the existence of poverty, by which I mean those remedial programs and other efforts which have been and are supported by federal, state, and local governments as well as those voluntary programs and efforts which have attracted fairly widespread support.

As a general rule antipoverty programs of the institutionalized variety have been constructed and executed according to an assumption which locates the source of poverty among the poor. In a manner consistent with the individual-as-central sensibility of the culture of inequality, these efforts have generally approached poverty as a moral problem of the poor, as a problem stemming from deficiencies in competence found extensively among the poor, or in some instances as a combination of both. Locating the source of poverty among the poor as it does, the institutionalized response to poverty appears to have as net effects the insuring of the continued existence of a visible poverty population and the reinforcing of the view of the poor which holds them to be failures through their own volition or incompetence.

The most important institutionalized antipoverty program on the American scene, both in the numbers of people it has served (some, and I include myself, may question the use of the word *served*) and in its relative longevity, is the federal-state partnership which has created what we know as *welfare*, or Public Assistance. Growing out of the Social Security Act of 1935, Public Assistance programs have made use of federal and state moneys for such programs as aid to families with dependent children, aid to the aged, aid to the blind and disabled, and, recently, aid to the medically indigent. In each instance the program in question has been administered by the state (although the federal Social Security Administration has had some involvement in a regulatory capacity).

In theory, welfare, or Public Assistance, is supposed to help those indigents who literally have no other sustenance options, and it is supposed to be a right. In fact, the sustenance assistance welfare programs provide is more often than not grossly inadequate, and the right to such assistance is exercised at great social and psychological cost to those who claim it.

Assistance levels vary from state to state. In some, particularly in the south, maximum monthly payments are so low[3] that (even taking a lower cost of living in these states into account) it is difficult to avoid the conclusion that such states have Public Assistance programs in name only—that "welfare" is little more than a cruel hoax. In other states the maximums are higher, but only rarely do they exceed the federal government's estimate of the poverty threshold.[4] The net financial effect of Public Assistance is therefore to create what we may term *stabilized impoverishment*. Public Assistance literally finances poverty for the very poor. It provides them with just enough wherewithal so that they can survive in poverty. Without Public Assistance many of the very poor would simply cease to exist. They would starve, they would die of exposure, and they would succumb to disease because few physicians are committed to healing if it is not made at least minimally profitable.

[3] The sources of this information are the reports of maximums for a family of four in the AFDC programs, which are the largest of the Public Assistance programs.

[4] One study published in 1970 indicated that maximums for a family of four in the AFDC program exceeded the poverty threshold in but two of the fifty states. See Committee for Economic Development, "Improving the Public Welfare System" (New York, April 1970). Since most observers agree that the federal estimate of the poverty threshold is too low, one is safe in assuming that people on AFDC rarely live above the *actual* poverty threshold no matter what state they reside in. Another indication of the inadequacy of welfare assistance may be found in a report that a substantial majority of families receiving benefits, including social insurance, remain poor even after the receipt of these benefits. See Michael C. Barth, George J. Cargano, and John L. Palmer, *Toward an Effective Income Support System: Problems, Prospects and Choices* (Madison, Wisc.: Institute for Research on Poverty, University of Wisconsin, 1974), table 6, p. 28. In a recent treatment of AFDC, one analyst concluded that "[f]or most families the program merely makes the difference between living in more or less poverty." See Winifred Bell, "AFDC: Symptom and Potential," in *Jubilee for Our Times*, ed. Alvin L. Schorr (New York: Columbia University Press, 1977), p. 230. A recent proposal by the Carter administration would, if adopted by Congress, probably increase public assistance benefits overall, but not enough, it seems, to move those families presently on welfare over the federal government's poverty line which is too low to begin with. As best as I can tell, the primary beneficiaries of the Carter proposal would be the working poor and not those who must primarily depend upon welfare for their sustenance.

With Public Assistance the very poor can eat just well enough to avoid starvation (the food stamp supplement extends their food purchasing power somewhat beyond what it would be if they lived on their basic assistance grants alone, but food stamps are unavailable in some places); they can have access to just enough shelter to avoid life-threatening exposure; and they can purchase that minimum of medical care which, while not curing their maladies, will nevertheless keep them alive. Given the level of support which public assistance characteristically provides, given that a family living on Public Assistance will rarely have an income exceeding a realistic poverty standard,[5] there is only one conclusion to be drawn: welfare is *not* an antipoverty program but a *poverty-maintenance* program—in a very real sense it renders poverty possible for many who might not otherwise survive the life-threatening conditions which are poverty's issue.

Such a conclusion is consistent with the existence of a need for unequivocal failures spawned by the individual-as-central sensibility of the culture of inequality. By creating a system ostensibly intended to reduce poverty which actually renders protracted impoverishment possible, we have in fact insured the existence of a segment of the population who remain poor and who, given our assumption about the meaning of poverty, stand before us as visible failures.

Poverty is maintained, moreover, not simply through the inadequacy of the financial assistance offered. To a considerable degree the operating procedures of welfare agencies—ostensibly intended to improve the ability of clients to do those things which will move them out of poverty—actually insure that those who are on the rolls will remain there.

Being poor in a society proclaiming that it has the highest standard of living in the world cannot help but be demoralizing. Having so little while others apparently have so much is likely to be a source of personal depression. Given this circumstance, one should expect that a program whose apparent goal is to help people overcome the extreme disadvantages of poverty would attempt to reduce the extent and salience of such

[5] Recently some analysts have claimed that in-kind Public Assistance transfers really do lift many people out of poverty. This position is taken in the Congressional Budget Office's 1977 report, "Poverty Status of Families under Alternative Definitions of Poverty." There are in my view two problems with this claim. First, for the claim to have any accuracy at all, one must assume that the official poverty standard is not set too low, and most observers challenge this assumption. Second, statistical manipulations aside, no substantive analysis of the life circumstances of those presumably being lifted out of poverty by receipt of in-kind transfers would justify such an optimistic assertion.

demoralization. One should expect that welfare agencies would strive to enhance their clients' sense of personal esteem. In point of fact, however, the agencies operate in such a manner as to do just the opposite; their procedures are much more likely to increase client demoralization than to reduce it and are therefore likely to minimize the probability that any given client will be able to overcome the disadvantages of poverty.

All Public Assistance agencies, for example, make *suspicion* of their clients or those who wish to become their clients the first operating principle in their efforts. Those who find themselves in need of welfare assistance must be prepared to *prove* that their needs actually exist. The clients or prospective clients, must be prepared to prove that their petitions for Public Assistance are not fraudulent, that they are not trying to take unfair advantage of taxpayer generosity. Thus, from the outset of their contact with the welfare agency, poverty-stricken people are made aware that poverty itself places them under suspicion. Having committed no crime they are nevertheless *suspect*, merely because they have attempted to exercise a right! It is difficult to imagine that such treatment can result in anything but increased demoralization.[6]

There is, moreover, an ancillary point to be made about the probable effects of such suspicion on welfare recipients. If recipients know that they are not trusted by agency personnel, it is difficult to see how the recipients will, in turn, trust the agency representatives with whom they deal on a regular basis. Mistrust must invariably beget mistrust in return. If, as a welfare recipient, I feel that I am almost constantly under suspicion, I should certainly be wary in my dealings with those who suspect me. I would be careful of what I revealed to them for fear that they might misinterpret it and cause me to lose the financial assistance I so desperately need. This circumstance has two very unfortunate effects. In the first place, it results in a kind of self-fulfilling prophecy whereby unfounded suspicions of agency personnel result in guarded secretive behaviors on the part of the welfare recipients—behaviors which appear to confirm the legitimacy of the original suspicions. But in the second place and even more importantly, because welfare recipients feel that

---

[6] Frances Fox Piven and Richard Cloward, *Regulating the Poor: The Function of Public Welfare* (New York, Pantheon Books, 1971). Also see Joel F. Handler, *Coercion in the Caseworker Relationship: A Comparative Overview* (University of Wisconsin, Madison: Institute for Research on Poverty, 1968), and Lawrence M. Friedman, *Social Welfare Legislation: An Introduction* (Madison, Wisc.: Institute for Research on Poverty, University of Wisconsin, no date), in particular, p. 55.

they must be wary of agency personnel, it is quite unlikely that they will be disposed to accept as well intended any agency efforts to better their situations. Thus it is difficult to see how agency suspicion of re-cipients and potential recipients can result in anything except minimized effectiveness in helping the very people the agency is ostensibly trying to serve.

Even when the negative implications of suspicion can be surmounted, the efforts of welfare agencies to "help" their clients are often counter-productive because they imply that the clients and the clients alone are in one way or another responsible for the problems of poverty. When welfare agencies are not suspecting those they serve of fraudulent claims to indigency (a manifestation of the *moralistic* form of the individual-as-central sensibility, equating poverty with moral infirmity), they as-sume that indigency is the product of impaired capacity (a manifestation of the *modified* form of the individual-as-central sensibility, using de-ficiency explanations to account for poverty). Financial assistance is, then, almost always coupled with some form of "therapy" which—ir-respective of its actual necessity—is assumed useful in compensating for or correcting the impaired capacity which has resulted in the client's indigency. It is highly unusual for someone on welfare to receive finan-cial assistance without at least some attempt by agency personnel to "correct" the "problems" which are assumed to be at the source of that individual's indigency. For some, a form of psychotherapy may be prescribed. For others, the attempt to correct root problems may mean required attendance at group work sessions focused on "proper parenting behavior." Others still may be pressured into joining vocational training programs. And even if the individual is not pressed to participate in a specific therapeutic activity, there is always the caseworker ever ready to make suggestions about everything from household management to sexual behavior.[7]

No doubt some people on welfare do need and benefit from these therapeutic endeavors. Given that poverty makes life harder than it must otherwise be, it is probably safe to assume that as a group welfare re-cipients have greater need of such services than the rest of us. Overall, however, such efforts are ill-conceived and counterproductive, for two reasons.

In the first place, there is the absence of selectivity in the application of therapeutic measures. Insisting on therapy for those who really do

7 See Piven and Cloward, *Regulating the Poor*, pp. 176–77, in particular.

not need it can only alienate those who are the focus of such efforts. From the point of view of welfare recipients, unnecessarily badgered by caseworkers about the "need to seek some help," the legitimacy of any and all agency efforts is undermined. The relationships between recipients and caseworkers sooner or later begin to resemble adversary relationships and the recipients either avoid the caseworkers as much as possible or develop strategies for finessing the caseworkers' expectations. The recipients' demoralization is thus bound to be increased: not only do they have very severe money problems, but in order to deal with these problems, if only minimally, they have to confront what must appear to be unwarranted impositions and tensions. It is tough enough to be without money, but even tougher to do the things you have to do to get the minimum necessary for survival.

In the second place, even when therapy is called for or justified, its implicit and often explicit connection to the existence of the recipients' impoverished state has the effect of demoralizing individuals who need it. Recipients who are led to believe that they are poor because of their inability to cope cannot help but have their self-esteem considerably reduced. When the caseworker tells Mrs. Jones that she is poor because of her inability to mobilize herself to do better, and that she needs some psychotherapy so that she will be better able to function, the poverty she suffers must seem to Mrs. Jones to be something she has brought on by herself. Regardless of her need for psychotherapy, the representation of her need as the source of her poverty can only damage Mrs. Jones's self-esteem. When Mr. White is told by his caseworker that he will in effect remain poor unless he learns how to get along with people on the job, he is being told that he is responsible for his unfortunate circumstances. Assuming that Mr. White is indeed hard to get along with, a message linking his personality to his poverty is more than likely wrong-headed and cannot help but be counterproductive. There are just too many hard-to-get-along-with people who are not poor for this characteristic to be the sole source of his impoverishment. While it may complicate his economic situation, his disposition is hardly likely to be the central cause of his poverty. To the extent that Mr. White believes his caseworker, we can only expect his self-esteem to be lowered, that his demoralization will be increased—and for no good reason.

Examples such as these multiplied manifold can only result in a population of recipients whose self-confidence has been reduced, whose abilities to confront the circumstances of poverty are minimized, and who consequently are unlikely to be able to free themselves of the disadvantages and trouble which poverty brings. If this is the help which welfare agencies offer, then their clients would be better served without such "helpfulness."

In truth, the procedures employed by welfare agencies do not help the poor overcome their poverty; on the contrary, the culture-based conventional wisdom informing these procedures only results in the minimization of any resolve among the poor to struggle against their impoverishment. In employing these procedures welfare assistance not only maintains poverty but makes it appear that the poor are unable to progress and better the conditions of their existence. Far from being an antipoverty program, welfare would appear to be a daemonic mechanism for insuring the presence of a poverty population bearing the mark of unequivocal failure.

Most people do not take the time to analyze how the welfare system actually works; they are, it is safe to say, confirmed in the assumption that welfare is in fact a benevolent (perhaps overly benevolent) social service. Few would be willing to entertain the idea that public assistance actually maintains poverty. Therefore, when poverty persists in spite of the taxes they pay to assist the poor and reduce poverty, their view of the poor as failures—as malingerers and incompetents—is reinforced. All that money and all that effort to ameliorate poverty and yet the poor remain with us. If the poor have not responded, if they remain dependent, if they remain on the dole, how can we conclude that they are anything but morally unfit or woefully incompetent? [8]

If welfare is important for its longevity and for the numbers it has presumably served, another antipoverty effort—the War on Poverty of the 1960s—is important because its proponents claimed that it would constitute an unprecedented mobilization of talent and resources to rid

---

[8] At this writing (August 1977), President Carter has, as noted above, recommended a reform of the welfare system. While it is impossible to predict the legislative fate of his proposals, the tone of the president's stated intentions does not bode well for the development of an effectual system. The president appears to be putting a balanced federal budget ahead of increases in benefits sufficient to bring recipients over a realistic poverty line, and his emphasis on the necessity of reducing fraud and waste in the present system is unfortunately consistent with the view that links impoverishment with moral infirmity. Whatever the ultimate reform of the present system, there is little reason—given the tenacity of the culture of inequality—to expect that welfare will become an effectual antipoverty program. And if I am correct, reform will only make the poor look worse than ever: it will appear that even an improvement in the system can't help them, and so they must indeed be beyond redemption!

American life of the scourge of poverty. As I write this, we, all of us, know that the War on Poverty turned out to be something less than successful; it was instead less a war on poverty than an exercise, or maneuver, informed by the modified (liberal) version of the individual-as-central sensibility, an exercise which did little more than convince many non-poor Americans that the poor could be helped but little to overcome the circumstances of their lives. When it began, however, it appeared to many a veritable crusade—an effort of undeniable sincerity and force calculated to relegate poverty to historical notice as a thing of the past. A martyred president's legacy of humane conviction inspired it, and a president who envisioned himself the heir to Franklin Roosevelt's mantle as a progressive reformer gave it life by creating an executive agency—the Office of Economic Opportunity (OEO)—to spearhead what was to be a maximum effort to improve the economic situation of the poor, their education, their health, and their status in the communities they called home. Within a short time of its inception OEO conscripted an army of antipoverty warriors the likes of which had never been seen before: planners, professors, social workers, college students, clergy, public-spirited businessmen, and even the poor themselves. Under the sponsorship of OEO, as well as HEW and the Department of Labor, federal and local programs were launched with an assertiveness which promised an early demise for the enemy.

But it was not to be, and for two good and sufficient reasons. First, although the rhetoric of the War on Poverty proclaimed that its programs would mark a new departure in the struggle against poverty, these programs were, for the most part, little distinguishable from previous efforts which had given no indication that they could make serious inroads against poverty. Essentially, the programs of the War on Poverty, like their less publicized predecessors, located the causes of poverty among the poor and attempted to defeat poverty by making the poor better able to cope with the "realities" of American society. Just as public welfare agencies (and before the advent of public welfare, the charitable agencies) operated on the assumption that the indigents needed "therapy" or exhortation to motivate them and train them to do those things which would allow them to rise out of poverty, so too did the programs of the War on Poverty operate on the assumption that the poor would have to compensate for or otherwise correct *their* inadequacies if poverty was to be relegated to historical reminiscence.

The thrust of the poverty war's "new" programs—such as Job Corps, the Neighborhood Youth Corps, Project Head Start, Upward Bound,

Vista, and Community Action—was to tutor the untutored poor and to alter their attitudes so that they might cease their apathetic withdrawal from society.[9] Except for some legal assistance programs and some community action programs which got themselves involved in local politics,[10] none of the major programs in the poverty war's arsenal operated on the assumption that the causes of protracted poverty could and should be located beyond the life routines of the poor themselves. None of the programs assumed that the poor were poor because of their *exclusion* from opportunity in American society or saw the problem of poverty as endemic to the American social system, and consequently none of the programs undertook any basic reform of that system.

The issue is not whether a view holding American society as a whole responsible for poverty is accurate or whether antipoverty programs informed by such a view would have been more successful than those informed by the individual-as-central sensibility; the issue is rather the refusal of those who planned and executed the War on Poverty to give serious consideration to such a view and their consequent inability to devise reform (as opposed to therapeutic) strategies for the alleviation of poverty. As a result of this refusal or inability, the promised new departure was not new at all; for the most part what was tried had been tried previously and found wanting. No amount of ballyhoo would turn an ineffective strategy against poverty into an effective one. No public-relations hyperbole would transform past failure into current success. Because this response to poverty really differed but little from previous responses, the War on Poverty did little to reduce poverty in American life.

But even if the programs generated by all the antipoverty enthusiasts had been new and imaginative, even if they were not redolent of past failure, the War on Poverty would not have succeeded for another good and sufficient reason. For all the grandiose claims and heroic rhetoric which made it appear as though men and women of goodwill were joining together to launch the final and decisive campaign against poverty, the War on Poverty was really quite limited in scope and scale.

[9] See Ben B. Seligman, "Poverty and Power," in *Aspects of Poverty*, ed. B. Seligman (New York: Thomas Y. Crowell Co., 1968), pp. 288–323.
[10] Such efforts drew the enmity of local political "establishments" and resulted in the passage of the Green Amendment to the Economic Opportunity Act (1967). This legislation in effect placed all community action programs under the control of local governments whenever these units wished to exercise control. This provision gave local political "establishments" veto power over community action efforts and effectively ended whatever independent political activity they had generated.

Hyperbolic claims to the contrary notwithstanding, the programs it generated never served more than an estimated 15 percent of the poverty population.[11] Even if these programs had been maximally effective, fully 85 percent of the poor would have received no benefits from them. At best poverty would have been eliminated for a minority of the poor, while the vast majority would have continued to live amidst considerable hardship. After the "decisive campaign," poverty and the poor would have remained with us on a scale reduced but little.

The War on Poverty, like Public Assistance, was an antipoverty program which in its conception and scope offered little hope of obliterating or even significantly reducing the extent of poverty in the United States. At best, like Public Assistance, it made poverty a bit more bearable for some of the poor, and in isolated instances it may have even made some social mobility possible, but overall it did not have and *could not* have had much impact on the extent of poverty in the United States. The major outcome of the poverty war, it would seem, was the continuation of extensive poverty amidst the plenty which marks the American experience.

The War on Poverty should not, however, be written off as a mere failure, an attempt to do good which unfortunately did not do enough good. To dismiss it in this way would be to miss something very important about this episode in the saga of our antipoverty efforts. If the War on Poverty did not reduce poverty in American life, it *did* make poverty and the poor more visible than ever before; and in its emphasis, the character of its programs, and its very lack of success, it rendered the poor ever more visible as unequivocal failures, as those people whose inadequacies make commonplace adequacy among the non-poor praiseworthy.

The war began by pointing to the extensive poverty which persisted in the United States. It continued with a call to arms; in the name of American idealism it rallied thousands who would make an all-out effort to end poverty in our time. The problem was a big one, but something would be done; it would be surmounted just as so many other problems had been surmounted, through American determination and ingenuity. And then, with all the publicity that could be mustered, something was being done; something new and big, as we were told over and over again, was being launched. Acronym followed upon acronym, holding our attention and communicating a sense that a massive new effort to do the

[11] Seligman, "Poverty and Power," p. 291.

best we could for the poor was indeed under way. We were helping the poor to change their attitudes and to improve their marketable skills, their diets, their health, their family life; we were making an all-out effort to salvage their children from the depredations of the street; we were in sum doing all the things that would give them *another chance* to make their way in what was after all still a society of chances—or so it appeared. We would probably have kept on doing "all that we could" to give the poor *another* chance for quite some time; but we were fighting another war in Vietnam, and that awful struggle drained resources from our poverty war. By the end of the decade a conservative Republican had succeeded to the presidency, and with little public protest he proceeded to put an end to the already weakened and retrenched crusade against poverty.

The War on Poverty was over before it really began, and the weapons it used, as we have seen, were hardly likely to have been very effective. But with all the ballyhoo that surrounded each and every move of the poverty warriors, it was very easy for most of the non-poor to conclude that an imaginative new attempt had been made to end poverty. And if poverty persisted, the non-poor could conclude that the poor refused, through either lack of ambition or incompetence, to be helped; they could conclude that the poor, given *another chance*, did not take it! If anyone had any doubts about the moral infirmity and basic incompetence of the poor, the very failure of that grand effort to defeat poverty—our War on Poverty—should have removed them.[12]

What we had done was to create, with as much public attention as possible, a program which although it was supposed to help the poor could not, for reasons of inadequate conception and insufficient scale, really do so. But who looks closely enough to come to such a conclusion? To most it must have appeared that a sincere effort was made, but that the poor in their recalcitrance and their incompetence had proved unworthy of it.

Like welfare the War on Poverty was an antipoverty effort which turned out not to be an antipoverty effort at all. Like welfare it brought poverty to the public's attention, it gave the appearance of doing something about poverty even as it persisted in activities which did not accomplish much, and its net impact was to sustain the poor in their

[12] This conclusion was in fact helped along by such commentators as Edward Banfield and Daniel Patrick Moynihan. See Banfield, *The Unheavenly City* (Boston: Little, Brown and Co., 1970), and Moynihan, *Maximum Feasible Misunderstanding* (New York: Macmillan, Free Press, 1969).

impoverished state even as it confirmed their unworthiness and incompetence in the eyes of the non-poor.

I have suggested that our failure to reduce poverty effectively is intentional, that given the need of many Americans to keep the poor in their place and make of them hostages to the need for personal reassurance, our efforts to reduce poverty have been designed to confound the purposes they ostensibly serve. It is difficult, I think, to avoid such a conclusion in light of what can be and has been demonstrated about welfare and the War on Poverty—the two most important "antipoverty" efforts in the last forty years. Our failure has not been intentional, however, in the sense of representing a conscious conspiracy to construct and administer inadequate antipoverty programs. Indeed, a conscious conspiracy would make it impossible for us to convince ourselves that the poor are poor because of their own inadequacies and failures. A conscious conspiracy would inevitably lead us to view the poor as victims. But our unsuccessful efforts have been intentional in the sense that, given the need of many Americans for unequivocal failures from whom they can distinguish themselves, we have been inspired by the individual-as-central sensibility to construct and administer antipoverty efforts whose inadequacies we have been compelled (again by virtue of the cultural hegemony of the individual-as-central sensibility) to ignore; our failure has been intentional in that the effect of this culturally inspired need of many Americans—to reassure themselves by seeing their commonplace successes as extraordinary in contradistinction to the presumed failures of others—has been the suspension of critical disbelief even when the inadequacy of our antipoverty efforts stares us right in the face. There would appear to be no gainsaying that the individual-as-central sensibility of the culture of inequality has, with wonderous circularity, created a need for the maintenance of poverty in American life and a system of belief which renders its maintenance probable. Viewed in this manner, poverty may be a major social problem, but it is also a problem that many Americans would be hard pressed to do without.

Does race pose problems in American life? Certainly for those who are the objects of discrimination in jobs, housing, and educational opportunities it poses a very significant set of problems. And to the extent that those who have been discriminated against actively protest their condition or otherwise react with intense (if often inchoate) anger, the products of discrimination based upon race become problematic for many others.[13] But the social meanings attached to racial difference in American life take on a special significance in light of the need of many Americans to use the ostensible failures of others to protect their own threatened self-esteem—a significance which renders the problems posed by race socially necessary or intrinsic to society as we know it.

Non-whites, and blacks in particular, because of the historically sustained pattern of discrimination and exclusion which has victimized them, are overrepresented among the poor in American society. Constituting approximately 11 percent of the population of the United States, they constitute approximately 30 percent of the poverty population. Because of their visibility and their very real difficulties in American society, it has become all too easy in the popular mind to associate poverty and racial minority status. This association, which has some basis in fact, does not in itself mean very much. It does take on considerable importance, however, when it is viewed in light of the meanings which are characteristically ascribed to poverty. As we have seen, the preeminence of the individual-as-central sensibility in American culture, together with the need for visible failure which it spawns, virtually insures that for a great many Americans poverty will invariably be taken to signify the absence of sufficient effort or competence to escape it. If racial minority status is associated with poverty in the popular mind, such status in and of itself is likely to signify failure based upon moral infirmity or personal incompetence. Because the individual-as-central sensibility makes it so easy to overlook the structure of exclusion which has persistently confronted non-whites (even if it permits awareness of the past existence of a structure of exclusion, the sensibility makes it easy to deny the structure's importance in the present), non-whites become, through their high visibility and the visibility of their *poverty cum failure*, psychic hostages par excellence. The benighted blacks (and the Spanish speaking, the Indians, and so on) symbolize the worst aspects of the human condition; they become the representations of all that men and women might be if they did not possess the strength of character and competence to overcome their worst proclivities. In the last analysis, many white Americans, in dread of the self-derogation which they themselves harbor, "know" they are people of value simply because they are not black!

The association of racial minority status with poverty, and thus with

[13] See Lewis Killian, *The Impossible Revolution: Phase 2* (New York: Random House, 1975).

failure based upon characterological infirmity or personal incompetence, implies a subtlety often overlooked when we consider race in American society. It is not racial minority status itself but rather the association of such status with poverty and failure which frequently injures those who are so identified. When majority whites express antipathy toward minority blacks, some no doubt do so because they are committed to racist belief, to dogma which holds blacks to be inherently inferior; but most, I would venture, express such antipathy for a contrary reason. When whites exclude blacks from neighborhoods, from schools, and from economic opportunity, most do so not because they view blacks as naturally inferior, as people whose racial identity is taken to mean that they *cannot* make their way, but rather because they view them as volitionally inferior, as people who because of personal sloth or incompetence *will not* make their way. In a curious sense blacks and other racial minorities are regarded by most of their white antagonists not as inherently different (the typically *racist* orientation) but as people who possess the same potential for personal success as the whites—potential which, to their everlasting shame, it is presumed they seldom realize. In the eyes of many whites there is nothing about being born black which foreordains personal failure and consequent low status; it is simply that too many black people do not of their own volition develop the character or competence necessary for personal success.

Given the hegemony of the individual-as-central sensibility and its psychological implications, the above construction of the racial antipathy of many whites is far more reasonable than any construction premised on the existence of racist or natural inferiority dogma. In order to salvage your sense of self-worth by juxtaposing your modest successes against the apparently unequivocal failures of others, you have to assume these others have had the same chance to succeed that you have had. If you believe that blacks and other racial minorities are naturally inferior just because of their racial identity, if you perceive them as being inherently incapable of the success which you have achieved, you can take no real comfort in the juxtaposition of your success and their failure. If you assume their inherent inferiority, then the fact that you have achieved greater success does not prove your personal worth, just as winning a footrace against lame opponents could prove nothing about your speed. In order for the juxtaposition to be psychologically effective, you have to assume that there are no inherent differences between you and those who have done less well than you. In order to take pride in your successes in comparison to the apparent failures of others you must be able to assume that the only significant differences are those of will and competence. To be confirmed in your sense of self-worth you must see the juxtaposition as indicating volitional superiority—as indicating your characterological strength against the characterological weakness of the others, your competence against their incompetence. If the hegemony of the individual-as-central sensibility is as I have described it, if it creates the necessity of perceiving failure in others so that one's commonplace achievements, by contradistinction, will appear praiseworthy, racism is hardly likely to provide the major premise for racial antipathy and stigmatization in American society.

I do not mean to argue, however, that racial minority status is unimportant. On the contrary it is very important, but only because it is a convenient indicator of presumed volitional incapacity born of characterological infirmity or incompetence. The vast majority of poor people in American society are white, but it is safe to say that many Americans conceive of the poor as being overwhelmingly non-white. When Americans think of poverty they think of the teeming racial ghettos of the cities or the dirt farms of the rural south's black belt before they think of anything else. In concept, if not in reality, the face of poverty is black, and as a result the meaning characteristically attributed to poverty— that it is the just desert of immorality and incompetence—is projected upon black Americans by many of their white compatriots. Blacks and other non-whites are in effect *targets of opportunity*, a convenient negative reference group, for those whites who because they have fallen victim to the individual-as-central sensibility need to reassure themselves of their self-worth.

For this reason, I would argue, the most significant problems of race are ultimately one and the same with the problems of poverty, and all that has been said about the problems of poverty and their maintenance through inadequate response applies equally to the problems of race. In American society it has become possible, after considerable struggle and unconscionable delay, to be sure, for blacks and other non-whites to achieve a measure of legal equality (the doctrine of separate but equal has been invalidated and the law no longer sanctions overt discrimination), but non-whites have found it much more difficult to escape forced impoverishment. Obvious manifestations of racism, it seems, can be overcome, but the need for the poor made visible remains potent, and therefore poor blacks—the most visible of all the poor—are maintained in their place by the very programs which are ostensibly intended to have the opposite effect.

Race poses many problems indeed, but it also provides many of us with easy criteria for the "identification" of the malingerers and incompetents whose presence is in considerable demand. Consequently, as long as there is a culturally determined need for such negatively defined *significant others*, racial differentiation and the trouble it engenders will continue to be important components of the American experience.

☆

*Educational Failure*   American public schools annually graduate thousands of students who are in fact functionally illiterate. Thousands more drop out of school each year without having mastered the rudiments of reading and writing. In total there are literally millions of people in the United States who are educational failures.

Few would deny that the extent of this condition establishes it as a social problem in American life. Commentators are quick to point out that basic literacy is a requisite skill for independent functioning in this complex society. In spite of the important role played by the aural and pictorial media, most information necessary for an informed social existence is communicated in print. If Americans are not the "children of the book" they are nevertheless the children of the memo, the contract, the political pamphlet, the tabloid, and even the do-it-yourself instruction sheet.

Extensive educational failure must therefore be reckoned a problem of some magnitude in this society. But in spite of the fact that it is a problem whose existence is recognized and regularly bemoaned; in spite of the profusion of books, articles, and reports calling our attention to the need to do something about educational failure; in spite of the many strategies promulgated—Head Start, Right to Read, Higher Horizons, parent participation, behavior modification, the open classroom, joy in the classroom, and so on—such failure appears to persist and may indeed by accelerating.

Again one must ask why? Why is it that educational failure persists in spite of our awareness and apparent abhorrence of it? Why is it that a society with such an exemplary problem-solving record seems unable, the many attempts notwithstanding, to make its educational system work as it should? Why are so many Americans rendered unable to deal intelligently with the exigencies of contemporary social life?

In answer, some may point to the technical inadequacies of the proposals and programs characterizing the educator's response to the problem of educational failure—they do not, it seems, know how to teach some youngsters—but such an answer really begs the question. Why don't they know how to teach them? Why is it that the American genius can conquer space, but cannot come up with suitable methods to ensure that all those who can be educated are indeed educated? Surely such methods should not be so difficult to discover! Some may argue that the difficulty is not so much technical as organizational and financial, that the methods exist but, given ingrained bureaucratic resistance to change[14] and the inadequacy of the monetary resources available to the public schools,[15] it is difficult if not impossible to make effective use of the teaching methods which educational research has developed.

Few would argue with the assertions that American schools are underfinanced and that there is good reason to worry about the problem of bureaucratic rigidity in the schools, particularly when very large systems are involved, but to cite these problems as causes for the persisting educational failure of millions of Americans is once again to beg the question. If, as the conventional wisdom has it, education is so important to the well-being of this society, why is it that we nevertheless have failed to provide our schools with enough funds to do what needs to be done? If, as is so often asserted, the very future of American society depends upon how well the schools perform their tasks, why is it so difficult to raise funds sufficient to their needs? While bureaucratic unresponsiveness is to a certain extent a fact of organizational life in every modern society, and certainly in American society, the record indicates that, when priority is given to the solution of a particular problem, such unresponsiveness can be overcome. In the urgency of World War II the American military machine functioned almost in spite of the sanctity of its routines. Challenged by a strange metallic sphere launched into space by those master bureaucrats—the Russians—organizational lethargy and self-interest were overcome, so that a National Aeronautics and Space Administration could get a capitalist to the moon before

[14] So well documented by David Rogers in his study of the New York City School System, 110 Livingston Street (New York: Random House, 1968).

[15] Public education in American communities is financed primarily by the property tax. Heavily burdened taxpayers characteristically resist budget increases which they see reflected in their tax bills. There are at present movements for change in this financing system. Local school officials have been pressing for formulas to increase state and federal aid to school districts. In some states the courts have ruled the present system of local financing inherently inequitable because it favors those children who live in the wealthier communities. For a recent discussion of school financing see Michael Lewis, Urban America: Institutions and Experience (New York: John Wiley & Sons, 1973), chap. 4.

any godless communist laid claim to it. When a real priority is set, bureaucratic resistance may be a problem, but it is usually one that can be minimized. Therefore, to say that educational failure in American society continues to exist because of inadequate organization, bureaucratic inefficiency, and the like is only to say that, protestations to the contrary notwithstanding, educational failure is not the urgent problem we often presume it to be. To be sure, it is a problem, but it is one most Americans can live with; and because of the psychological need for visible failure in others generated by the individual-as-central sensibility of the culture of inequality, it may very well be a problem which many Americans would have difficulty living without.

I noted earlier that in the modified form of the individual-as-central sensibility, deficiency explanations replace moralistic explanations of personal failure, that those who subscribe to the modified form of the sensibility view failure as a matter of insufficient capacity instead of insufficient effort. Among the deficiency explanations discussed at that point was *cognitive insufficiency*, or the absence of such necessary skills as basic literacy and adequate quantitative reasoning. Considering the existence of such a deficiency explanation and the need for visible failure in society, the persistence of extensive educational failure makes sense—albeit troubling sense.

Needing apparently unequivocal failure in others to protect themselves against self-defamation, many Americans, particularly those of liberal persuasion who characteristically embrace the modified version of the individual-as-central sensibility, find their need well served by the continuing existence of widespread educational failure. To begin with, it is failure which is easily recognized in others and clearly marks them as fundamentally incompetent. Those who have not "failed" educationally can at the very least rest assured that they have mastered a set of skills which many of their fellows have been unable to claim. Cognitive competence, which might ordinarily be taken for granted, becomes, when many fail to attain it, an indicator of self-worth.

More importantly, educational failure can provide personal reassurance for those who need it by linkage with more striking manifestations of apparent failure, such as the inability to find reasonably remunerative work and the sustained impoverishment which results. It is quite true that a man or woman who lacks even minimal certification of educational attainment, usually a high school diploma, will have considerable difficulty entering those vocations which provide reasonably steady employment at income levels comfortably above the poverty line. And it

goes virtually without saying that those who lack basic literacy skills will
not be hired except for the most menial and least rewarding jobs.
Whether or not some of those who are found educationally wanting
could actually perform in jobs from which they are excluded, they are
categorically excluded on the assumption that they could not conceivably perform up to standard expectations on the job if they have failed
to do so in the schools. Thus those who are educational failures are
also among the most likely candidates for poverty. From the point of
view of those who need visible failure in others, the existence of educational failure is important not simply because it is a failure to which they
have not succumbed but also because it explains the sustained existence
of poverty in a manner which reinforces their senses of self-worth. The
poor appear to be poor because they lack the skills to escape poverty,
because they are incompetent (the deficiency explanation). If poverty is
viewed as a function of incompetence, then whatever else may be true of
people, they can believe themselves competent and therefore successful
simply because they have managed to avoid impoverishment.

Assuming this formulation accurate, it is reasonable to conclude that
because educational failure serves so potent a need it is a condition, however ostensibly problematic, that many Americans have a stake in sustaining.[16] This is not to say that there is a conscious conspiracy to insure
the existence of learning problems among a significant segment of the
population (any more than the maintenance of poverty and racial disadvantage may be understood as products of similar conspiracies). It is
to say, however, that continued support (emotional if not always financial) for ineffective educational programs is no accident; [17] that the low
priority given to educational failure among American problems is not
merely inadvertent. It is to say that the continued visibility of the prob-

[16] Such failure is probably also economically functional. It results in the existence
of what Bernard Farber calls a surplus population available and ready to take on the
most onerous tasks in the economy. In this view, failure may once again be seen as
not the problem we conceive it to be. It is certainly a problem for some Americans,
but others, perhaps the majority, actually benefit from its existence. See Bernard
Farber, Mental Retardation: Its Social Causes and Social Consequences (Boston:
Houghton Mifflin, 1968).

[17] For example, although compensatory education has proven ineffective as a
strategy for the education of the poor, its appeal remains strong. For evaluations
of the compensatory strategy see Bernard Farber and Michael Lewis, "Compensatory
Education and Social Justice," Peabody Journal of Education 49 (January 1972):
85–96, and Westinghouse Learning Corporation, "The Impact of Head Start: An
Evaluation of the Effects of Head Start on Children's Cognitive Development,"
June 1969.

lem—as *a problem*—is important to many of us, and so we do everything short of actually solving it. We publicize its existence, we launch programs which appear to address it, we train professionals whose presumed expertise holds out the promise of its solution—all efforts having the effect of focusing our attention on its persistence—but we nevertheless allow its solution to elude us.

That what appear to be our best efforts have little if any impact upon the existence of educational failure has not escaped the critical notice of some scholars and educators; but for the most part their commentary, permeated as it has been by the individual-as-central sensibility, has amounted to little more than the citation of deficiency explanations for a condition which itself serves as a deficiency explanation for the perpetuation of economic failure and consequent impoverishment. Educational failure persists, we are told by some, because problematic family backgrounds undo the good work being done in the schools; [18] others tell us that it persists because those who "fail" are imbued with a view of the world which devalues educational competence; [19] and others still claim that such failure persists because those who have learning problems are genetically (or congenitally) predisposed to have them.[20]

These postulates of deficiency are important not so much for what they explain about the persistence of extensive educational failure but once again for what they say to those of us whose sense of self-worth is threatened by the aspiration-achievement disparity. If, as suggested by some commentators, the failure to learn stems from the interference of family problems with pedagogical efforts, those who can learn adequately and those, in particular, with children apparently progressing well in school can take comfort and perhaps some pride in the notion that their family life has been successful, that they and their parents have been able to meet the complex set of demands characteristic of life in this society. In other words, if educational failure implies domestic incompetence, then the absence of such failure can be taken to signify the achievement of domestic competence. And given the public reverence for

[18] See, for example, Albert Shanker, "Where We Stand," a column printed weekly for the past several years as a paid advertisement in the *New York Times.*

[19] See Banfield, *The Unheavenly City,* and also Frank Riessman, *The Culturally Deprived Child* (New York: Harper and Row, 1962).

[20] Most "respectable commentators" eschew this view presumably because its espousal has been linked to the existence of genetic racial differences. For the most respectable, although severely criticized, statement in support of the genetic position, see Arthur R. Jensen, "How Much Can We Boost I.Q. and Scholastic Achievement?" *Harvard Educational Review* 39 (1969): 1–123.

the family, as well as public concern about what often appears to be an epidemic of family problems, the existence of domestic competence must appear no small achievement. If the failure to learn occurs among those who devalue the importance of education, those who possess a world view at some variance with mainstream expectations in American society, then those who have not failed to learn can, at the very least, assure themselves that they understand what is necessary for personal success in this society, that they are well informed, and that whatever they may or may not have achieved they are *in step*—they are full participants in one of the most successful social enterprises on the face of the earth. If educational failure signifies *cultural estrangement*, then the absence of such failure can be taken to imply a success born of commitment to one of the most achievement-oriented cultures in human history. And finally, if there is a genetic basis for educational failure, there must be a genetic basis for the absence of such failure. In the logic implied by the genetic postulate, a commonplace competence is transformed into a mark of unequivocal superiority. It is not the extent of learning that counts but what the presence or absence of rudimentary skill and even minimal scholastic certification is taken to mean. If the absence of such skill and certification means genetic inferiority, then the presence of such skill and certification means genetic superiority; and when all else fails to neutralize the threat of self-derogation, commonplace educational competence can become for some people, at least, a source of comfort. It may not represent the kind of success or superiority which is highly valued in American life—it is after all a matter of inheritance and not achievement—but it does imply a kind of superiority and for those who are desperate enough, it may have to suffice.[21]

There appears to be a consistency of undeniable force in all of this. Extensive educational failure provides many Americans with the hostages necessary to the maintenance of their psychological equilibrium, is a problem of considerable visibility, and as such reassures those who are able to distinguish themselves from those others who suffer from it; it is a prominent deficiency explanation for the persistence of the "failure" which results in extensive poverty, and it is generative of other defi-

---

[21] Given the existence of the aspiration-achievement disparity, inherited success or superiority should not ordinarily serve to sustain a positive sense of personal value. It is after all nothing over which the individual has any control. When an individual is sufficiently threatened, however, the distinction between achieved and inherited may, out of personal necessity, become blurred, and any presumption of superiority, even inherited superiority, may be seized upon to rescue the threatened self.

ciency explanations which themselves symbolically reassure those who are not encumbered by learning problems. So much about educational failure in the United States appears to have a *usefulness* related to the individual-as-central sensibility and the psychological predispositions it produces in many people. Perhaps this seeming usefulness is mere coincidence, and perhaps the meanings I have attributed to the phenomena described above have been misattributed; but convinced as I am of the existence and cultural hegemony of the individual-as-central sensibility (and I hope that at this point I have given at least some readers good reason to share my conviction), I find it difficult to write off what appears to be a very good fit between need and occurrence. Although extensive educational failure is a problem, it is unfortunately a problem made necessary by our cultural commitments; and it is, therefore, a problem that will escape solution as long as we remain steadfast in these commitments.

*Crime* Is there a social problem more threatening to our sense of well-being than crime? Surely law-abiding Americans, however influenced by the tenets of the culture of inequality, cannot be accused of behaving in ways which perpetuate the existence of criminal deviance. Failures are one thing, but criminals—people who threaten your property and menace your life—are quite another. Who in their right mind needs them? What kind of psycho-cultural need could they possibly serve? How could anyone suggest that the crime problem is anything except what it appears to be—a major threat to personal security and social order?

I, for one, find it necessary to suggest that there is more to the existence of criminality in American society than has been supposed. If crime is a problem of significant dimension (as indeed it is), then, like poverty, race, and educational failure, it is nevertheless a problem which appears to be a social necessity mandated by needs generated in the culture of inequality and in particular by the individual-as-central sensibility. The case for this assertion can be made in the following manner.

In a curious way the criminal is a comfort. Even while eliciting fear and loathing among law-abiding Americans, the criminal's presence reassures them of their self-worth. Even as their imaginations are terrorized by criminal deeds (or reports of them), their self-appreciation is enhanced. Through unconscionable behavior the criminal proves unworthy—an undeniable moral failure—and the law-abiding American, by juxtaposing his or her willing acceptance of conventional moral restraint against the criminal's rejection of such restraint, finds cause for self-congratulation in a conformity which would otherwise mean very little. Criminals, like educational failures and the poor, constitute for many Americans a negative reference group whose behavior makes avarice and cruelty a real option, the rejection of which can be understood as a self-enhancing moral choice.

Of all the problematic phenomena noted here, criminality is the most striking in the extent of its public notice. Our awareness of it is hardly surprising. We are regularly informed by the director of the Federal Bureau of Investigation that the crime rate has gone up, particularly the rate for violent crimes.[22] The news media find the excitement of criminal incidents irresistible and report them in graphic detail. Nothing, it seems, is hidden from us; we are given access to the criminal's nefarious intent as well as the victim's anguish.[23] Real crime, it seems, is not enough, perhaps because it can only be reported after the fact. Fictionalized accounts, showing the actual commission of heinous acts, leap to life in profusion on the small screens in our living rooms and the big screens of our "magic lantern emporiums."

Why this preoccupation with crime? Why this concern for the details of criminal motivation and the suffering of the victims? Surely it is not

[22] Among criminologists there is considerable debate on the adequacy of official crime statistics. Some point to the unevenness of even uniform reports, where some incidents are reported and others are not. Some critics have suggested that it is virtually impossible to tell if there has been an actual increase in crime because of the inadequacy of the statistics being used. For such criticism see Task Force on Assessment, the President's Commission on Law Enforcement and Administration of Justice, *Crime and Its Impact: An Assessment.* (Washington, D. C.: Government Printing Office, 1967). Whether the rate of crime has or has not actually increased, however, the general public has been led to *believe* that it has, and that belief in itself is significant.

[23] It is not merely the so-called scandal sheets and tabloids which have an affinity for gory details. So staid and respectable a newspaper as the *New York Times* is quite capable of competing with the tabloids. The *Times* regularly runs detailed (and with the *Times*, *detailed* means *detailed*) accounts of rape, assault, and other forms of mayhem. A *Times* "classic": A desperado invades a house, terrorizes the residents, and kills one of them. The others report that her last words were, "I thought you promised not to hurt us." There follows a report of the victim's funeral —her mother is overcome with grief—the police circulate amongst the mourners— the victim is characterized as an outstanding young woman always ready to help others. A suspect is apprehended and his background is reported. He is known to his neighbors as ill-tempered and dangerous. Married, he has been imprisoned for physical abuse of his children. The story runs almost daily for a period of ten days, with many of the details repeated in each edition.

because we are afraid. If we were consumed by a fear of crime, would we really be such an avid audience for accounts of what we fear? The psychology of such a state of affairs simply does not make much sense. When you are desperately afraid of something you flee its presence; you repress it or deny its reality if you are unable to flee; the one thing you do not do is to intensify your fear by voluntarily exposing yourself to its source.[24]

Preoccupation with crime is explicable in terms of the need for assurance of self-worth. The visibility of crime in the United States makes it easy for those who need to do so, to assert their moral superiority, their *successful* conformity to the right when others succumb to base impulse. The statistics charting the increase in crime may describe the proliferation of a social problem, but they also render law-abiding behavior ever more praiseworthy. The formula is really quite simple: the less the reported incidence of crime, the less exceptional is lawful conformity; the greater the reported incidence the more exceptional is such conformity. If little or no crime was publicly reported, if it appeared that virtually everyone was law-abiding, no claims to moral superiority could be made as a result of such conformity, since there would be no recognition of a group of people who failed to conform. To whom would those who are law-abiding be *superior?* The statistics purporting to show a steady increase in crime also serve public notice of the increasing exceptionality of lawfulness and, consequently, of its increasing praiseworthiness. Given the extensiveness of the culturally induced need for assurance of personal worth, interest in such statistics is not surprising, nor is the willingness of our law-enforcement agencies to titillate such interest.[25]

[24] Psychoanalysts tell us that some people may expose themselves to the things they fear in order to deny their fear (a counterphobic reaction); but the occurrence of such reactions in sufficient frequency to account for the extensive American preoccupation with crime is highly questionable.

[25] It is, I think, revealing to note that the publication of statistics indicating increases in crime runs counter to standard bureaucratic procedure. Organizations such as the local police and the FBI admit failure when they report increases in the crime rate. Organizations do not like to report ineffectiveness, and yet law-enforcement agencies appear to do so with little if any hesitation. One may conclude from this anomaly that their failure is less important than the need to highlight criminal incidence. Such a conclusion receives further support when we note that, in spite of their self-admitted inability to cope with crime, law-enforcement agencies—while often criticized for such things as abuses of civil rights and the existence of corruption within their ranks—are only infrequently criticized for their ineffectiveness. Law-enforcement agencies frequently blame the increased incidence of crime on judicial permissiveness, and that strategy may be an effective one for deflecting criticism. Nevertheless,

Statistics—no matter how striking their cumulative impact—tend nonetheless to be somewhat antiseptic in their depiction of crime. They describe *rates* of offense, but they do not dramatize the nefarious behaviors which result in these rates. The need to find moral superiority in the distinction between one's own law-abiding behavior and the criminality of others is thus likely to be served only in part by the notice of soaring crime rates. Law-abiding citizens, it is reasonable to assume, want to see beyond the rates to the morally abhorrent behavior they presumably represent. They want to know what they *are* by knowing what they *are not*; they want to know that they are good by identifying the bad in others. The soaring rate of crime indicates that there is a lot of badness around, and that the amount is growing, but it does not of itself graphically depict just how bad bad is, or by contrast just how good good is—thus the need for the description of repugnant evil, which the media serves with what appears to be considerable enthusiasm. The details of a gangland execution describe a professional cruelty which repels good people; so if you are repelled you must be good. The violence of a street mugging reported by the likes of the *New York Daily News*, the *Chicago Tribune*, or even the *New York Times* marks it as a crime most foul; and since the readers of the *Times* (or even the *News* or *Tribune*) are not muggers their goodness is attested to by the violent acts they refuse to commit. It is all there: assaults upon sweet innocence (children are abused and molested), violence against the aged and infirm (an eighty-year-old woman is raped, a blind man is robbed and beaten to death), awful transgressions against the sacred (a church's ritual relics are stolen, a synagogue is vandalized), mayhem in the streets (two youth gangs have at one another, a sniper shoots down three holiday shoppers on their way home with presents for their loved ones), and so on and on in a dramatization of the worst we *are capable of*, assuring us of our moral superiority because, whatever else we might do, we would never perpetrate such atrocities as these.

If, as the foregoing argument alleges, our interest in crime is a function of a culturally induced need to distinguish ourselves from criminal deviants so that we may claim a measure of moral superiority for ourselves, then crime, however problematic it appears, is another ironic necessity in American life. And if this interpretation is indeed correct, then

---

one would expect the number of unsolved criminal cases—about three in every four—to draw critical attention to law-enforcement incompetence, when in fact it rarely does so.

we can hardly be sanguine about the possibility that crime will be reduced to relative insignificance—not unless the need sustaining it is rendered less salient, and that change would ultimately depend on our willingness to reject the individual-as-central sensibility of the culture of inequality. At best, given the hegemony of the culture of inequality, the probability of such a rejection is minimal.

The visibility of crime in American society can be understood as having still another function when it is viewed in terms of the need to find unequivocal failure in others; once again that function suggests the necessity of the crime problem, given the preeminence of the culture of inequality. Just as poverty is conventionally associated with racial minorities in American society (and blacks in particular), so too is the incidence of crime. Whatever the actual distribution of criminal acts among Americans of every station,[26] the visible distribution is skewed in the direction of poor non-whites. Whether or not non-whites actually commit more crimes than whites, they are more likely to be arrested, charged, tried, convicted, and sentenced to prison terms. Moreover, the reported rates of serious crime (felonies—crimes against persons) are significantly higher for the slum-ghettos of American cities than for other residential sections of these cities.[27] It is difficult to think of Harlem and Bedford Stuyvesant in New York City, Roxbury and Dorchester in Boston, the South and West Sides of Chicago, Hough in Cleveland, or Watts in Los Angeles without thinking also of mugging, marauding juvenile gangs, narcotics use, and apparently purposeless street violence. Whatever the real distribution of crime, differentials in criminal visibility have resulted in a conventional apprehension which construes minority group status as criminogenic.

When we consider that for most Americans crime represents inexcusable moral failure, it should not require much effort to understand that its skewed visibility reinforces the conventional white conception of blacks and other racial minorities as morally unfit. Just as the meanings ascribed to poverty make minority racial identity symbolic of moral

[26] The actual distribution includes all acts in violation of the law, reported or not. Many crimes, such as white-collar crimes committed by advantaged people (particularly whites), do not receive official police attention and therefore do not become part of the reports. See Marvin Wolfgang and Bernard Cohen, Crime and Race: Conceptions and Misconceptions (New York: Institute of Human Relations Press, 1970).
[27] See Phillip Ennis, Criminal Victimization in the United States (Chicago: National Opinion Research Center, University of Chicago, 1967).

infirmity (as well as incompetence), so does the social meaning of crime render such identity symbolic of the failure to live up to society's expectations for acceptable intentions and behavior. The association of crime with non-whites serves therefore to make those who are presumed failures easily identifiable. To many white Americans, not only are blacks poor by their own volition and incompetence; they also fail to exercise sufficient self-control and as a result are wanton in their disregard of common decency and the law which protects it. As visible criminals they once again come to symbolize the most objectionable of human possibilities, those possibilities which good, law-abiding people have been successful in avoiding.

Criminal visibility is important, then, not only because it reassures many Americans that their law-abiding conformity is an increasingly praiseworthy achievement but also because in its skewed representation it contributes to the pejorative meaning of racial minority status, placing non-whites in an easily recognizable negative reference group. It makes it possible for those whites who need to be assured of their self-worth to consider themselves successful if only because they are white. Unfortunately, it is once again reasonable to suggest that, as long as many Americans are forced to rely upon clear, unequivocal failure in other Americans in order to quiet doubts about themselves engendered by the aspiration-achievement disparity, crime, made dramatically visible, will be a necessity—a problematic necessity but a necessity nevertheless. And as long as the culture of inequality—and in particular the individual-as-central sensibility—dominates the American imagination, those doubts will be a reality for far too many people.

Our characteristic response to the persistence of crime is quite revealing. Crime is ostensibly a major social problem in the United States. It is a problem most Americans claim to be enthusiastic about solving. And yet, for all the apparent anguish crime seems to generate, the American anti-crime response has been and continues to be grossly inadequate and, in some instances at least, actually criminogenic. Our response to crime has in fact been more consistent with the need to sustain it as a highly visible component of the American experience than with the ostensible desire to reduce its impact upon our lives. Quite simply, our response gives the lie to our protestations of fear and loathing of crime, even as it validates the assertion that, for many Americans, criminals serve as a negative reference group whose violations of common decency render such decency uncommon and praiseworthy.

For example, is the fact that our police have been and are still underpaid, and therefore frequently underqualified, an indication of our commitment to crime reduction, or is it an indication that we may not be as concerned about the "crime problem" as we would like to believe we are? [28] The relatively low salary of police officers in many communities not only serves as a barrier to the upgrading of personnel but also encourages those who do serve to give less than their best effort; often enough it may even encourage criminal malfeasance on their part. Police work requires maximal alertness and a high order of physical competence; the officer who for financial reasons must "moonlight" is likely to operate at less than peak physical and mental proficiency when he is on duty. Police work—particularly in urban settings—is arduous and frequently dangerous. Given the job's difficulties and the threat of imminent danger, low salaries (low at least in comparison to other less arduous and dangerous lines of work) cannot help but contribute to morale problems on the force. It is very easy for a police officer to conclude that the people he serves just "don't give a damn" and in doing so to conclude that sloughing off and taking it easy is justified. Such an attitude is hardly conducive to maximally effective law enforcement.

For some police personnel, the morale problems created by insufficient salaries make it easy to drift into illegal activities. Not only is graft (and the consequent protection it affords to criminal activities) common to the police in American communities, but the phenomenon of the "rogue cop" who actually perpetrates the very crimes he is sworn to oppose is quite familiar to even the most superficial reader of our daily newspapers.[29]

[28] For a depiction of the relationship between salary and police competence see Robert L. Derbyshire, "The Social Control Role of the Police in Changing Urban Communities," in Crime in the City, ed. Daniel Glaser (New York: Harper and Row, 1970), pp. 210–18.

The median entrance salary for a patrolman in all U.S. cities was reported to be $7,826 in 1972, the last year for which figures are available. The median maximum salary was $9,280. These medians indicate that fully one-half of all those in the appropriate categories were earning less than the stated figures. See United States, Department of Justice L.E.A.A., National Criminal Justice Information and Statistics Service, Sourcebook of Criminal Justice Statistics (Washington, D.C., 1974).

[29] Jerome Skolnick, The Politics of Protest, A Report Submitted to the National Commission on the Causes and Prevention of Violence (New York: Ballantine Books, 1969), chap. 7, "The Police in Protest." Also see Arthur Niederhoffer, Behind the Shield (New York, Doubleday and Co., 1967).

In sum, the relatively low salaries paid to police officers work against effective crime reduction efforts by skewing recruitment in the direction of the minimally qualified, by lowering efficiency and morale, and, in some instances at least, by contributing to circumstances which foster dereliction of duty and criminal malfeasance. One can only wonder at this state of affairs. All that clamor for a maximum effort to root out crime begins to sound hollow indeed!

Is the quality of justice in the United States such that it speaks well for our collective determination to be rid of crime, or does it once again reveal that our determination is suspect? The courts, particularly the lower level courts (municipal courts, criminal courts, juvenile courts, and so on), are probably the most important component in the criminal justice system, and as such they must be reckoned crucial to our response to crime. While the police may apprehend alleged criminals, it falls to the courts to decide guilt or innocence and to determine for the guilty a course of action which will reduce their threat to the law-abiding. The courts are the definers of criminal justice in the United States, deciding what crimes shall be punished and how severely, who among those standing in the dock must be isolated from the rest of society, and who among them can and should be rehabilitated. If the crime problem is to be solved, the courts must, no doubt, be among the prime contributors to its solution; but an examination of how the courts have been functioning leaves us with little reason to be optimistic about the resolution of this problem.

Those courts which deal with alleged criminality are understaffed and poorly organized. In many instances personnel assigned to them, from the judges down to the court attendants, have been appointed as a reward for loyalty to a local political machine. Competence, it often appears, is at best a secondary qualifier for such appointments.[30] But even if competence were not a problem in these courts it is unlikely that they could do an effective job of dispensing justice. Courts dealing with criminal violation typically have too little of everything except cases to be adjudicated. There aren't enough judges, and there are rarely enough support personnel—from file clerks to probation officers—for an effective and equitable processing of the high volume of cases on their dockets.

Understaffed and marred by incompetence, the criminal term courts

[30] See Abraham Blumberg, *Criminal Justice* (Chicago: Quadrangle Books, 1967).

dispense what often seems a perverse form of justice. The speedy trial assumed to be a right of the accused is a commitment more spoken of than honored. It is not unusual for someone charged with a crime to have to wait a year or more for his or her trial. And it should be noted that such delays can have serious criminogenic consequences. For some, particularly the indigent who cannot post bail, these delays can mean a year or so of imprisonment even if they are ultimately found innocent of the charges against them. Embittering experiences of this sort can only encourage the antisocial attitudes that foster criminality. For those who are fortunate enough to be able to post bail and gain their "freedom," the delay can have consequences nearly as serious. Stigmatized by the accusations brought against them and having no opportunity to refute the charges, those awaiting trial frequently have difficulty keeping their jobs (or finding new ones); they frequently suffer the loss of friends, and even among loyal friends and relatives they must confront the doubts of innocence which invariably surface. For the innocent, living for a protracted period under a cloud of suspicion—losing so much without any recourse—can only be embittering and may even motivate crimes otherwise unthinkable.

The crowded court calendar and insufficient staff often combine to the end that an individual—innocent or guilty—may never have his or her case adjudicated on its merits. With the connivance of the judge, who wishes to clear his calendar and save money for the taxpayers, and of the prosecuting attorney and the defense attorney, the defendant is often encouraged to "cop a plea," that is, to plead guilty to a charge less severe than the one of which he or she stands accused. This practice is of course pernicious to an equitable system of criminal justice, and, again, it is likely to be criminogenic as well. To begin with, many people who are guilty of relatively serious crimes wind up with sentences which, by law, cannot be as severe as their actions warrant. Aside from the fact that this procedure is offensive to the concept of *just deserts* which should be the moral anchor of our system of justice, it can also be viewed as criminogenic. One doesn't have to take a hard line on law and order to conclude that the practice of allowing guilty pleas to reduced charges undermines any deterrence potential in the law. Although some criminals may very well continue to violate the law even when corresponding punishment appears certain to follow upon apprehension and conviction, common knowledge that the law will *not* be applied in full measure can only encourage its violation among those who are tempted to do something illegal but who are not as yet committed to criminal careers.[31]

Pleading guilty to a lesser charge can have another potentially criminogenic effect. Many indigent defendants, poorly served by public defenders whose caseloads prevent them from giving each client the individual attention needed, are virtually forced into guilty pleas on lesser counts regardless of guilt or innocence. A man charged with grand larceny (theft of over $100), having insufficient resources to hire an attorney, finds that he will be represented by an attorney from the public defender's office. Because the public defender already has a case overload, he or she is unlikely to have either the time or the resources to follow all the leads and search out all the evidence which might provide a credible defense. The prosecutor, not wishing to expend resources in trying this case and knowing that the judge assigned to hear the case has a crowded calendar, approaches the public defender with a proposal. The prosecutor will agree to reduce the charge from grand larceny to petit larceny (theft of less than $100) if the defendant will agree to plead guilty to the lesser charge. The public defender presents the options to his client, informing him that he has a right to a trial but that if he is found guilty of grand larceny he will probably have to spend at least a year in prison. Pleading guilty to petit larceny, on the other hand, will get him a six-month term (if he has had a previous conviction) or quite possibly probation (if he is a first offender). Let us assume the accused is actually innocent: he quite naturally pleads his innocence to the attorney and inquires about his chances if he does exercise his right to trial. The public defender, having had time for only a minimal investigation of the charge, responds by noting that, while the prosecution's case has some weaknesses, anything can happen in a trial, and tells our innocent man that his chances of being acquitted are probably fifty-fifty. The risk is too great to take; the possibility of conviction is real—a year in prison is a long time to be away from your family and

[31] There are of course crimes upon which even the strictest application of the law will have but a minimal deterrent effect—for example, murder and manslaughter, which frequently occur in contexts where rational calculation of gains and losses is unlikely to precede the act—and in these cases even a clear conception of punishment is unlikely to deter perpetration. There are, however, reasons to believe that the certainty of punishment can have deterrent effects on many potential crimes. See James Q. Wilson, *Thinking about Crime* (New York: Basic Books, 1975). For a theoretical treatment of rational calculation in criminal choice, see Anthony Harris, "Imprisonment and the Expected Value of Criminal Choice," *American Sociological Review* 40, no. 1 (February 1975): 71–87.

your friends, particularly when you are innocent—and so our innocent man agrees to plead guilty to the lesser charge in the belief that he really has no other option.

This unfortunate scenario does not end, however, with the injustice of an innocent man admitting spurious guilt. He must now suffer the consequences of his plea, and these consequences can very well be productive of crime. A prison term is still a prison term, however reduced, and it cannot help but embitter an innocent man. As he spends the long days locked away from his family and friends, knowing that he has been imprisoned for no good reason, the innocent man comes to believe that "the system" has done him an injustice, that the law, far from being his protector, is in truth his enemy. He has done nothing and yet the law has deprived him of his liberty and humiliated him. If nothing else, he will never again respect the law as righteous, and upon his release his potential for violating its strictures will have been increased.

If our innocent man has managed to escape imprisonment, the liberty he has gained is likely to be more apparent than real. If he is free he is nevertheless a convict; he may be able to walk the streets, but he carries with him the stigma of criminal conviction. If he had difficulty getting a reasonably good job before his encounter with the law, his difficulties will now be multiplied manifold. He finds himself disadvantaged and humiliated by the law, all the while knowing that he has done nothing to warrant the trouble which has befallen him. With justification he begins to see himself as a victim. The law which is supposed to protect him has forsaken him. Its legitimacy is thereby undermined in his eyes, and his willingness to violate its strictures will most certainly be increased.

Much as we might wish to avoid such a conclusion, it seems clear that our criminal term courts do little to mitigate crime. Indeed, as I have indicated, these courts can very well contribute to increases in the commission of unlawful acts. Court reform is a much-discussed enterprise, but little has been done. If we were really enthusiastic about reducing crime in American society, should it not be otherwise?

If, finally, we look to American penology in the hope of finding efforts effective in reducing crime, we can only be devastated by what we discover. A major assumption informing American penology is that imprisonment should be rehabilitative, that those who are committed to penal institutions should be exposed to programs and influences which will lead them to perceive the errors of their ways and return them to society ready and able to participate as law-abiding citizens. This assumption notwithstanding, the actual experience of imprisonment appears to be just the opposite in all too many cases.[32] Critical observers indicate that prisons are overcrowded, dehumanizing institutions, staffed by men and women who are undereducated and underpaid. Rehabilitation may be an ultimate goal of correction professionals, but the day-to-day realities of American prisons make the maintenance of order their primary concern. Prisoners may get some attention from the prison psychologist but then again they may not. They may be able to take courses to upgrade their literacy or provide them with vocational training useful in the "straight world," but it is more than likely that such rehabilitative experiences will be denied. Most of the time spent in prison is dead time, time spent either in idleness or in activities with no positive carry-over on the "outside" in the straight world. Indeed, as it has frequently been suggested, if the convict learns anything during the period of imprisonment, he or she learns it as a result of association with other convicts; and consequently it is more likely than not to be predisposing to continuing criminality. Viewed in this manner, the prison is actually a school for crime.[33]

If rehabilitation is to succeed, one would assume that prisoners must be motivated to give up their antisocial behavior. In order for this change to take place, the prisoner must come to see the world of the law-abiding citizen as hospitable and desirable. In this context, it must be clear that the prison experience can in no way be rehabilitative. The "straights" have put the prisoners in a place not only where they have been deprived of their freedom but where every attempt is made to deprive them of their persons. They are identified by number; they must dress in a manner determined by others; they have no real say in the way the rules are made and are unlikely to have any control over the way they are administered. All in all, their daily existence is regimented by others. Their lives are managed by people who know little about them, about their needs, desires, strengths, and weaknesses, and who could care less about them. The straights in the prison, the guards and other officials, often appear to represent an authority which is illegitimate and,

---

[32] See Thomas O. Murton, *The Dilemma of Prison Reform* (New York: Holt, Rinehart and Winston, 1976), and also Daniel Glaser, "Some Notes on Urban Jails," in Glaser, *Crime in the City*, pp. 236–44.
[33] Arthur B. Shostak, *Modern Social Reforms: Solving Today's Social Problems* (New York: Macmillan Publishing Co., 1974), chap. 13, "Prisons and Punishment."

in some instances, corrupt. In order to avoid difficulties, they frequently look the other way when some prisoners dominate and victimize others. They are often content to let the strong prey upon the weak if it will insure the appearance of order. Some straights can even be "bought": guards are bribed to pass contraband to the prisoners, even such contraband as narcotics. From the perspective of the prisoners the straight world as it is represented to them in the prison setting must often appear hypocritical, an inherently dishonest sham. They hear a great deal about rehabilitation, about the help they can get in learning to do those things that will make life in the straight world both possible and rewarding. They hear a lot about it, but they see little of it. The straight world promises a great deal but delivers little, if anything at all.

All in all, the prison experience presents the straight world at its worst. Accordingly, there is little likelihood that prisoners will be persuaded, in their contact with prison straights, to join their fraternity. If anger and contempt have moved them to violate the straight world's strictures—the law—then that anger and contempt can only be reinforced while they are "doing time." The prison manifestation of the straight world has little or nothing to offer the incarcerated.

This picture of prison life should not surprise most people—and that absence of surprise in itself is revealing. For even though reformers have persistently drawn our attention to the inadequacies of our prisons, to those characteristics which render them counterproductive more often than not, we have done very little to change them. In spite of the proliferation of books, tracts, position papers, television documentaries, and so on calling for an overhaul of our prison system, little change has occurred. Halfway houses to ease the convict's reentry into society, work release programs, and the use of furlough programs no doubt constitute some improvement, but despite the advent of such programs the character of American prisons has remained basically the same, even though we know of their inadequacies, even though we know that they do not reduce crime but on the contrary probably contribute to its persistence. If we are as enthusiastic about reducing crime as we proclaim, we once again must ask, should it not be otherwise?

Indeed, if we are as enthusiastic about reducing crime as we claim, should not the things we do and do not do about all facets of the criminal justice system—the police, the courts, and the prisons—be different? Why have we not rectified their failures? Why, if crime reduction has as high a priority as is presumed, have we not been able to conquer the financial and organizational obstacles to reform which are often held up to us as reasons for our failure to make real progress against so "troubling" a problem as crime?

Once again, our behavior—our support, overt or tacit, of practices which are counterproductive to the reduction of criminal incidence—is suggestive of a need for crime, of a need for visible criminal malfeasance to render ordinary law-abiding behavior extraordinary in the eyes of those many who, driven by the individual-as-central sensibility of the culture of inequality, can be assured of their self-worth only so long as they can distinguish themselves from those we have made to stand before us as unequivocal failures. Criminals are moral failures par excellence, and as long as the individual-as-central sensibility is allowed to maintain its hegemony over our psyches we will have need of them. As long as this need persists among so many of us, we shall—without being conscious of it—continue to sustain a criminal justice system which is in fact *criminogenic*.

☆

Poverty, race, educational failure, and crime are obviously not the only social problems characteristic of the present American experience. No one, however, would deny their significance for that experience. Find someone who doesn't have an opinion on the causes of poverty, on the character of racial justice or injustice, on the sources of educational failure and what to do about it, on the threat posed by crime and the "criminal element" in our midst, and you will have discovered a man or woman so atypical as to appear almost un-American. If you find such a person, you want to shake him or her out of an apparent torpor; you want to roar, "Good God! wake up—don't you know what's going on around you?—don't you realize what's going on in this society?—how much difficulty we're all in?" Life in America may encompass many things, but the problems of poverty, race, education, and crime are sure to be among them.

The synchronic appearance of these problems in our midst is, it would seem, no mere happenstance. Their appearance and their character are to a very considerable degree the functions of a collective psychology engendered by the culture of inequality (and in particular by its major theme—the individual-as-central sensibility). Nor are they discrete implications of the culture of inequality. The problems of poverty and race are intertwined, as are the problems of poverty and educational failure and, to a certain extent, those of crime, race, and poverty. In effect, each of the problems is really linked directly or indirectly to all of the others; it is difficult if not impossible to comprehend fully the character of each of them without recognizing its functional connection to the others. In light of the argument made throughout this book, what at first surmise appear to be four major social problems, whose existence is a source of considerable chagrin and whose remediation is to be devoutly wished, turn out on more careful consideration to be four *necessary* manifestations of what might be termed a master problem—the need for unequivocal failure in others to render our otherwise ordinary behavior meritorious.

The problems of poverty, race, educational failure, and crime—real as they are in their tragic consequences—are but the epiphenomena of a problem few dare talk about: the desperate search for personal reassurance which marks in so many Americans the overwhelming threat posed by the aspiration-achievement disparity. As long as there is a threat to self-esteem posed by the disparity between what we expect of ourselves and what we are in fact capable of, poverty, the racial dichotomy, educational failure, and crime will cast their long shadows. They will remain our necessary problems; notwithstanding high-minded protestations to the contrary, we will not really wish to remedy them. And there can be but little question that the threat posed by that disparity will remain in force as long as our individualized culture of inequality (our individualized culture of success and failure) maintains its hegemony. In the last analysis, then, where the issues associated with the existence of poverty, racial injustice, educational failure, and crime are concerned, we have but one problem—the culture of inequality itself.

### A Short Reprise

Before we proceed to Part Two of this volume, a brief summary of what we have thus far encountered would, I believe, be helpful.

Because of its peculiar history American society has given rise to an interpretation and explanation of inequality—a culture of inequality—which emphasizes the individual's central role in determining his or her social and economic circumstances and the degree of conventionally defined success or failure. Inequality in American life has come to be understood in light of what I have called the *individual-as-central* sensibility, according to which one's status and perquisites are perceived as functions of personal attributes, personal morality or immorality on the one hand and personal competence or incompetence on the other. The individual-as-central sensibility, in its hegemony over the American imagination, may free many people from social restrictions of arbitrary ascription, but in doing so it engenders widespread anxiety about the extent of one's personal achievements compared to one's aspirations. The threat to self posed by this *aspiration-achievement* disparity is a significantly troubling preoccupation in American society. Ultimately, it makes necessary pariahs of the disinherited—the poor, the non-white, the criminal. In the attempt to manage out of existence the threat posed by the aspiration-achievement disparity, many Americans come to view their worthiness in contradistinction to the presumed unworthiness of the disinherited. Invoking the individual-as-central sensibility—the very same sensibility that has engendered the threat to the self—many Americans make of their commonplace successes praiseworthy achievements by viewing disadvantage as the just desert for insufficient effort born of moral infirmity or incompetence. In doing so they invest in the maintenance of inequality in American society and particularly in the perpetuation of an under-class of objectionables. In doing so they help to maintain those social problems associated with the existence of this under-class. Protestations to the contrary notwithstanding, for the many who are threatened by the aspiration-achievement disparity these problems are themselves a comfort—an indication of the insufficiencies of others to which they might also have fallen prey, but which they have, through their own praiseworthy efforts, avoided. Ultimately, the culture of inequality in American life is a closed and self-fulfilling system. It creates psychological need which only the invocation of its basic premise —the individualization of success and failure—can serve. It is sustained by the very trouble it creates.

The cost of all this circularity is, however, considerable. By virtue of its self-maintaining hegemony, the culture of inequality has rendered the American experience far more difficult than it needs to be. By virtue of its self-maintaining hegemony, the culture of inequality has minimized the human serviceability of American society.

# PART TWO

# THE CULTURE OF INEQUALITY
# IN VIVO

# A Short Preface

Having argued the existence of an individualistic culture of inequality in American society and having explored its implications for the way we live our lives, I should like to illustrate its existence by asking the reader to enter with me into the recent life of an American community. While what follows does not constitute a proof of the argument developed thus far—there are no systematic tests of hypotheses, no formal method of verification is employed, and the community in question does not constitute a sample from which it would be prudent to generalize— it does constitute a showing of the culture of inequality in a real-life context. As such, it will hopefully deepen the reader's appreciation of the culture's domination of us in ways counterproductive to our happiness and to our collective ability to solve those social problems which render the American experience more troubling than it should be.

The major source of this illustration is a community study I undertook several years ago with the sponsorship of the United States Office of Education. The study, which had a three-year field period, was an intensive inquiry into a middle-sized community's response to pressures for change in the character of its race relations and, more generally, the character of its existing relationships between the poor and the non-poor. During the field period, the community was in the throes of a struggle over de facto segregation in its elementary schools; there was considerable conflict over local antipoverty efforts; and there were frequent skirmishes over such things as the character of public housing, the procedures of the local welfare office, the availability of recreational facilities for the poor, the quality of local health care, the treatment of the poor (and the non-white poor in particular) in the community's criminal justice system, and more generally the character of public services presumably available to every citizen.

The intent of the study was not to search out evidence of the culture of inequality and its impact on the life of the community in question (at the time of the study's execution I had not even given much thought to the existence of such a culture); the intent was simply to analyze the source of and resistance to changes in the areas of race and poverty within the community. It was hoped—perhaps vainly—that such an analysis would improve future efforts to intervene in similar communities on behalf of increased equity.

Nevertheless, assuming the existence of a culture of inequality, such an inquiry would almost surely uncover signs of it. The issues that troubled the community during the period of our study were precisely those issues which would highlight the existence of the culture if it were there. Whatever your position, you cannot be concerned with segregation, poverty, the fairness of the criminal justice system, welfare, and so on without dealing with and interpreting the character of inequality in your community. It is just these issues which call forth culturally based beliefs about the existence of inequality and what, if anything, should be done about it. When such issues are raised, one is virtually forced to take sides, and in doing so one has to decide whether and to what extent the contested inequalities implied in these issues are justified or unjustified. Such a decision in turn must invariably depend upon the interpretation given to the existence of inequality. Therefore, such issues as those confronting the community we studied are likely to call forth basic beliefs about inequality, and if a culture of inequality underlying these beliefs does in fact exist, the raising of such issues should render its parameters observable.

For three years the study staff monitored the life of the community I shall call Middle City. During that period we entered virtually its every precinct. We collected interviews on the issues with community influentials, public officials, "average citizens," the wealthy, those in what might be termed the middle-income brackets, and the poor, with blacks as well as whites, liberals as well as conservatives. For three years we attended public meetings of the community's city council, of the antipoverty agency, of the school board, board of health and park board —making note of the positions being taken as the issues were debated and decided. We studied the operations of the courts, observing them and interviewing judges and attorneys. We were present in and studied the operation of the local welfare office, the schools, the department of health, and the public housing authority. We analyzed editorials, letters to the editor, and local news reports in the community's newspapers. We attended the community's churches and monitored the sermons which were their regular fare. We were not in all of this looking for evidence of a culture of inequality; but, for the reasons stated above, the voluminous data we collected are likely to provide evidence of its existence—*assuming* its existence—and therefore I have returned to that data as a major source for what I have called an illustration of the culture of inequality.

For two years before the inception of the study I had been a resident of Middle City. Except for the time I had spent in graduate school at a university in a small town and two childhood years in a Pennsylvania town, my life before coming to Middle City had been lived in big cities, for the most part in the biggest American city of them all, New York. Living in Middle City, with its moderate population of one hundred thousand, was thus a new experience for me. Not only was I from another part of the country—I possessed all of the easterner's biases toward its midwest location—but Middle City was a community much smaller than those to which I had been accustomed. During the first two years of my stay I was, in fact, a "greenhorn," someone who could not take the community for granted, someone who had to learn how to make his way in the community.

When you are a "greenhorn" you are sensitive to many things in your environment you might otherwise miss. As one trying to become familiar with an unfamiliar social setting, the newcomer has to be a learner, and as such is more likely than anyone else to be a conscious assimilator of local styles, practices, and beliefs. What may be taken for granted and relegated to the unconscious later on is, at the outset, consciously and carefully assimilated in order to find out what's going on and cope with it.

As a "greenhorn," I assimilated a great deal about the way of life in Middle City even before I undertook the direction of the community study. During the course of that study what I had learned as a newcomer proved useful, and I have decided to use my personal observations from that period as well as those from the remaining three years of my stay in Middle City as sources in constructing my illustration of the culture of inequality.

Some, no doubt, will have serious reservations about such a course. After all, how will it be possible to assess the reliability and the validity of information collected unsystematically in the course of daily life and recollected several years later? The answer is that it will *not* be possible to do so in any formal sense. If I were trying to prove the existence of the culture of inequality by recourse to these materials, the impossibility of a formal assessment of their quality would be troubling indeed.[1] However, since the object of their use is not proof but illustration, since I am not endeavoring by the use of these materials to prove that the culture does in fact exist, the impossibility of formal assessment of their quality would not appear unduly problematic.

The object of this book, and I include the following illustrative section, is interpretation. In it I am trying to make some sociological sense of experiences most of us have but few of us fully understand. To make sociological sense of these experiences, to interpret them, is not, however, to claim the mantle of inviolable truth for the sense or interpretation I have made. What I am attempting to do is to make a prima facie case; I am not rendering a final verdict. I am saying to my readers: "This is what I see when I look at the way we live; there it is for you to think about, to test against your own experience. Ultimately, you must judge the clarity of my vision, the sense I have made of our common experience. Ultimately, on the basis of what you know and what you have experienced you must render a verdict about the illumining power residing in the arguments I have made." I claim nothing more for what appears in this book than the *likelihood* of its truth, because, for the reasons I try to make explicit in these pages, it appears true to me.

The illustration of the culture of inequality which follows here is thus nothing more than an attempt to enrich and extend the interpretation manifest in the whole of this book. Therefore, it matters little if some of the materials used to develop it are unsystematic in origin and are as a consequence incapable of formal assessment with regard to reliability and validity. *It is the interpretation itself which requires assessment,* and readers making such an assessment will render a concomitant judgment about the adequacy or inadequacy of all the materials, systematic as well as unsystematic, used in its formulation. What follows, as well as what has already been presented, either will ring true or will not. Having made such an assessment, my readers will have made the crucial judgment, and any question about the validity and reliability of the data used to construct the illustration will have received its answer.

[1] The circumstances of most community studies, whatever their claims to systematic data collection, actually render such assessment a methodological ideal honored in the breach. It is highly unlikely that any community study can be effectively replicated.

## 4

### "A good community for those who are willing to work hard and make good use of their God-given talents"

Before we immerse ourselves in the social and cultural milieu of Middle City it would be good to become familiar with some of the community's basic characteristics.

Middle City is located in the central region of one of America's major agricultural states. As one might therefore expect, its economic destiny is closely bound to the farm economy. The banks in the community specialize in agricultural loans; some even employ specialists in financial management to deal with large-scale agricultural holdings. The city houses a number of seed companies, farm equipment outlets, and crop-leasing firms; and because it has both an east-west and a north-south rail link, Middle City has for many years been a shipping depot for agricultural production.

The city's economy is, however, not solely dependent on agriculture. There are several good-sized manufacturing operations within its environs (companies such as Alcoa, Kraft, and General Electric have located in Middle City), and the community is the site of a university. Thus, although Middle City's income-producing sector (or, as the urban economists like to call it, the export sector) is dominated by agricultural pursuits, the sector is fairly well diversified and consequently has been less subject to those boom and bust cycles which often result in periods of extensive economic hardship than is the case in a single-industry community.

Although the quality of public services provided in the community has been the focus of considerable controversy in recent years, Middle City appears at least superficially to provide its hundred thousand citizens (approximately 10 percent of whom are non-white) with an adequate range of such services. Its schools have, for a number of years, provided programs for the intellectually gifted as well as the intellectually handicapped, while offering the standard range of college preparatory and pre-vocational programs for average students. The people of Middle City have access to three hospitals, and the public health department administers a well-baby clinic and a visiting nurse service. There is also a state-supported mental health center in the community. As far as social welfare is concerned, Middle City houses a department of welfare, a township supervisor's emergency relief fund, a children and family services agency, a vocational rehabilitation center, and a juvenile authority, as well as several small-scale and often sectarian helping agencies such as the Salvation Army and the Catholic Charities. Middle City appears to have no lack of recreational facilities. Its elected park board administers six parks and one community center. The local YMCA runs programs theoretically open to all (although not long ago blacks were prohibited from using YMCA facilities), and the university makes some of its facilities available to the community on a regular if somewhat limited basis. Although one does not encounter massive high-rise public housing developments in Middle City (as one characteristically does in large cities), the housing authority rents more than a few low-income units within the city limits.

Government and politics in Middle City have traditionally been dominated by the Republican party. Although the city elects its officials on a theoretically nonpartisan basis (where party labels are supposed to be meaningless), those elected have, in the vast majority of cases, been relatively conservative Republicans. This has been particularly true of the city council, where the slate endorsed—unofficially, of course—by the conservative Chamber of Commerce has usually been able to muster enough votes to dominate.

In recent years, however, the growth of the university within its midst has resulted in increased Democratic strength within the city. The university is an importer of people. It brings into the community outsiders who tend to be rather liberal in their political orientation. During the recent period of academic expansion in the United States (late fifties to about 1968), the university in Middle City attracted people from throughout the country in considerable numbers. Many who came as new faculty became more or less permanent residents in the community; and while they lacked sufficient numbers to tip the local balance in favor of the Democrats, their propensity for involving themselves in a visible and highly articulate manner on behalf of liberal causes gave the Democrats in Middle City a significant increase in political presence. When the eighteen-year-olds got the vote and when federal court rulings made it possible for college students to vote in the communities where their schools were located, Democratic strength in Middle City received an additional boost. Therefore, while the Republicans still dominate the politics of Middle City, the Democrats in recent years have increased their local influence; and as a consequence local conservatism has to a degree been moderated.

Like many middle-sized cities in the United States, Middle City has for a number of years had a council-manager form of municipal government. The council-manager form—a favorite of middle-class proponents of "good government"—is based upon the assumption that there can and should be a clear distinction between municipal policy-making and municipal administration. Policy-making is of course assumed to be the province of representatives elected by the citizens of a community. It is believed to be inherently and justifiably political in character. Administration, the management of municipal government and the many services it provides, is believed to be best accomplished when removed from politics and made the responsibility of a professionally trained city manager. The city manager, serving at the pleasure of the council, is presumed to have a special expertise which when applied to the operations of municipal government enhances their quality. Instead of the waste caused by the machinations of politicians easily persuaded to act in behalf of narrow interests, rationalized functional efficiency in the service of the community as a whole is presumed characteristic of government operations given over to the ministerings of a professional manager who is assumed to have no political axe to grind. Whether municipal government is actually improved by the adoption of the council-manager scheme is a matter of some debate,[1] but the assumption that depoliticization will in fact bring about such improvement has proved very attractive in many communities, particularly middle-sized communities, and the people of Middle City for the most part share that assumption.

The people of Middle City take pride in what they see as the many opportunities for citizen participation in local government. One of the things frequently brought to my attention by politically active people in the community was the view that no one group or small clique could

[1] Edward C. Banfield and James Q. Wilson, City Politics (New York: Random House, Vintage Books, 1963).

monopolize public decision-making in Middle City—a function, they argued, of the dispersal of decision-making authority, its decentralization in a functionally specific manner.

Many in Middle City would dispute the asserted impossibility of decision-making monopolization. Many of those who sought to work out an effective desegregation strategy or to maximize antipoverty efforts did, in fact, refer frequently during the course of our study to the "power structure" or the "establishment," as though a clique in the community had the power to advance or more likely to impede their cause or, for that matter, any other cause.

Nevertheless, as far as formal governmental decision-making is concerned, Middle City was and still is characterized by considerable decentralization. Whereas in some communities members of the school board are appointed by the mayor, in Middle City the members of the school board are elected and the board as a body has considerable autonomy. The park board is likewise elected, and it too has considerable autonomy: it can, for example, decide when a new recreation facility should be built, what type of facility it should be, and where it should be located. Then there are various commissions—civil service, public safety, planning, human relations, and so on—which, although they do not possess the autonomy of the school board and the park board, do have mandated authority in specific functional areas. Whether this dispersal of decision-making powers in Middle City prevents the monopolization of decision-making is, as I have noted, debatable,[2] but clearly

[2] During the course of the United States Office of Education community study, we attempted to analyze the actual as opposed to the formal distribution of community power in Middle City. The analysis was inconclusive. We did find an economically powerful group, similar to Hunter's business influentials (see Floyd Hunter, *Community Power: A Study of Decision Makers* [Chapel Hill, University of North Carolina Press, 1953]), who while remaining behind the scenes were in a position to exert considerable pressure on the public decision-makers. When interviewed, members of this group displayed considerable similarity in their views of life in Middle City and of what should be done to make Middle City—"a good community"—even better. Nevertheless, although these economic elites were in a position to exert pressure to implement their views, we were unable to discover any evidence that they were doing so in an organized or concerted manner. No doubt they did act when they felt their interests were directly affected by a particular issue, but we were unable to unearth any evidence to indicate that they "passed the word along" with any regularity. It may be that the exercise of their potential power was unnecessary in Middle City, for as our interviews indicate their views of the good life in the community were shared by many of the non-elites. Such a consensus might very well make the exercise of elite power unnecessary.

the functional decentralization of authority in the community does encourage the assumption—not necessarily borne out by fact—that if an individual wishes to pitch in and work for the good of the community he or she will be able to do so in a manner consonant with his or her interests and talents.

Consistent with this participatory ethos, the practice of politics in Middle City is rarely if ever a vocation. It is safe to say that, during the period I was observing in the community, no one save perhaps the city manager (and he would deny it) practiced the political arts in the style of the professional, full-time politicians one finds in large cities. The livelihood of each public figure (other than the city manager), of each office-holder and party functionary, was not primarily derived from his or her role in Middle City's political life. During the period of our study the mayor, for example, was the president of a local construction company, and the council members earned their livelihoods by such varied occupations as veterinarian, owner of a sporting goods store, insurance agent, real estate broker, housing officer for the university, owner of a shoe store, and professor of accounting. Politics was seemingly a side interest, an avocation, for those who engaged in it.

A few other characteristics of Middle City require mention. In order not to delay I shall simply note them without extended comment.

There are some ten thousand blacks in Middle City, the vast majority of whom live in a run-down ghetto area called the North Quarter. The blacks as a group are very poor. While they constitute but 10 percent of the community's population they make up 65 percent of the community's welfare cases; while unemployment among whites in Middle City rarely goes above 4 percent, among the blacks it often goes as high as 20 percent. Because so many of Middle City's black people are members of a real under-class, anger—often inchoate in its expression—runs high among them.

The blacks, however, are not the only people in Middle City who are desperately poor. There are poor whites—known locally as hillbillies —who live semi-rural lives in little communities at the outskirts of the city. Unlike the blacks, who, no matter how difficult their situation, seem to be a part of Middle City, these poverty-stricken whites appear to exist in near isolation from the community as a whole. Their children attend the public schools and they make use of the welfare services provided by the community, but for the most part they remain on the periphery (physically and socially) and display little interest in becoming part of Middle City's social ambience. Most people in Middle City view them with disdain; they are the ne'er-do-wells who would rather spend their time getting "whiskied up" than doing an honest day's work.

Most of the people in Middle City are white Protestants who regard themselves as part of the American middle class.[3] Some would, according to usual sociological usage, be located among the working class or even the upper class, but most nevertheless think of themselves as solid middle class. People in Middle City typically regard themselves as hardworking and God-fearing, as committed to their families, and as seekers of success earned honestly, the fruit of their own efforts. Most live in houses which they own; there are very few apartment buildings in the city, and these usually cater to students and younger faculty at the university. They attend church on a fairly regular basis. They join such organizations as the Rotary, the Lions, the Elks, the Exchange Club, and so on, although the more well-to-do among them show a special fondness for the society of the Middle City Country Club. Among the people of Middle City, "respectability" and "decency" are reified. The conclusion that Middle City has a puritanical cast probably overstates the case somewhat, but it is nevertheless true that there is little tolerance in the community for those whose life-styles deviate in any recognizable manner from middle American conventionality.

Middle City is not necessarily typical of urban communities in American society, but then neither is New York or Chicago. It is, however, an American community; there is nothing about Middle City to mark it as curious or deviant in light of what we know of the American experience. Thus, if that experience harbors what I have been calling the culture of inequality, we should expect to find that culture made manifest in the beliefs and behaviors of those who live their lives within its environs; we should expect to find it in the ordinary as well as the extraordinary characteristics of the Middle City experience.

[3] Perhaps because of its location, Middle City does not have many people who have maintained distinct southern or eastern European ethnic identities. As a consequence, the illustrative materials presented here do not reflect the experiences of such groups in American society. I realize that the views of these groups on inequality—on success and failure—are important and may vary somewhat from those articulated here, and I regret that they cannot be included. The absence of such views should of course be considered as the reader assesses the instructiveness of the Middle City materials.

### Encountering Beliefs about Success and Failure:
### Some Middle City Profiles

Dr. Norvell Grooms [4] is an important man in Middle City. He is a physician, one of the senior internists at the Bard Clinic (a combined medical group and hospital facility), and for all of twenty years he has been a member of the Middle City Board of Education, serving several terms as its president. Close to sixty years old, Dr. Grooms is pink-faced and rather cherubic looking, but his mild appearance is more than just a little misleading. People around Middle City will tell you that Norvell Grooms is a good friend to have but you had better not make an enemy of him. The best way to deal with Grooms, they'll tell you, is to let him believe that you think he knows all the answers—because he certainly believes that he does, particularly when it comes to medicine and education. Let him think that you're questioning his judgment and you're in trouble. It's not that Dr. Grooms is a vindictive man, they say; it's just that he has such supreme confidence in his own views and capabilities that he regards anyone who questions them as obviously incompetent and any proposals from such a person as likewise incompetent and unworthy of serious consideration.

Dr. Grooms believes that credit ought to be given where credit is due, and when it comes to the quality of education in Middle City he believes a lot of credit is due his own efforts. In an interview he consented to give—because, as he put it, "Sociologists are ignoramuses, they don't know what to look for, and if you're going to study anything about education around here I guess I'd better set you straight before you write something foolish"—Dr. Grooms let us know what he had done about Middle City education.[5]

When I got on the school board the schools were in a pretty bad way. I was shocked. I thought when I came to this town the schools would be no problem. After all, there was a university here and you just kind of expect that any town that has a university is also going to have good schools. But, as I said, I was shocked. Buildings were run-down because the business-minded people who had been on the board didn't want to repair them—and the school administration was full of incompetents or worse. One high school principal had to resign because he was using

---

[4] In chapters four, five, and six, names have been changed to protect the anonymity of individuals.

[5] In this and other statements here and in the ensuing chapters, questions eliciting the speakers' remarks have been edited out for dramatic effect.

school money for his own personal reasons. . . . When I got on the board I got them to see that things couldn't go on this way. And once I did that, things were on their way to getting better. Better people who had a real interest got elected to the board, people like myself who understood that you had to work together to get things improved. I got them to see that we had to get more professionals into the school administration and we did just that. You know, we have some of the best administrators in the state here because we go out and look for bright people and we offer them an opportunity to come in here and earn a good salary while they get an Ed.D. over at the university. They see it as a real opportunity to get ahead because they get experience and a degree and then they can go on to an even better job somewhere else. . . . So as a result of my efforts and the work of other people who joined me on the board things really got going around here. We got better management in the schools—new programs—and over the years our schools have just about become the best schools in the state. . . . I don't mind saying that I had a lot to do with it because I did.

Norvell Grooms spent a lot of time trying to prevent us from writing "something foolish" about education in Middle City, and in doing so he went to great pains to insure that we would understand the relationship between success or failure and the role of education, largely, I think, because he and his colleagues were under some pressure to improve the services provided to the poor and the black poor in particular.

You know, you can do a lot of wonderful things if you've got an education. But you've got to want to get it, you've got to have some commitment to it, you've got to understand what you can do with it, and you've got to want to do it. . . . I know, because that's the way it's been in my own life. I was a poor boy in Kansas—I know that sounds corny but it's true—a very poor boy, let me tell you, but I can't remember when my folks weren't telling me how important education was and I can't remember when I didn't go to school thinking that I wanted to be a doctor, that I would be a doctor, and that school was necessary to be what I wanted to be. As I say, I was a poor Kansas boy but I had instilled in me the idea that I could grow up and make something of myself if I attended to my studies. And I did . . . and well, it's true— I got myself an M.D. and then I even went on and got a Ph.D. in neurology. . . . I remember what I learned from my parents and I've taught the same lesson to my children. They had it easier than I did. They weren't poor but that doesn't mean anything. You won't amount to much if you don't apply yourself and take advantage of the schools.

So they had to learn the same lesson I had to learn and they learned it. I've got two daughters in college—one is going to go to medical school and the other is going to be a remedial reading teacher. I've also got a boy who is a junior in high school and he's doing just fine. So I think they've learned the same lesson I learned way back when I was a boy in Kansas.

Now these people—you know the c.e.c. [Citizens Education Coalition, a local group of blacks and white liberals] and their friends—well, they just don't know what they're talking about. They want to do something fast that'll change things. They've got these gimmicks, you know—more poor people controlling the schools, more Negroes teaching in the schools. . . . Lord knows, I'd be happy to have more qualified Negro teachers here, but where are we going to find them? . . . You know, they have these gimmicks, but that's not going to change things. I've been thinking about this for twenty years and the only responsible way to change the way these people live is to get them really involved in education. Get the kiddies when they're young and you can break the cycle. If you can get the mothers of these children to have a yen for education the way they once had it and if you can get those kiddies into the schools before they're five years old you can teach them the lesson I learned from my parents, the lesson I've taught my children. You do that and you can break the cycle; break the cycle of hopelessness—lack of identification, lack of manliness, self-esteem, and all the rest. You do that and there'll be a lot less failure and a lot more success among these people. It won't happen overnight—no matter what the c.e.c. says—but it can't help but happen. . . . I'm willing to change some of our school programs—maybe we need to do some of that—but I won't go for these gimmicks just because some people who really don't represent anybody except themselves start to make a lot of noise. This is a good community —it's good for everybody, for the poor people and the Negroes too— and if they get that yen for education, if they really want it, they'll get a chance to do things here; they'll get a chance to show what they can do with their God-given talents because nobody I know wants to stop them. But I won't go for these gimmicks. They won't change a thing and if I did approve of them I'd be irresponsible. . . .

Dr. Norvell Grooms is an important man. His views carry a lot of weight. He is a good friend to have, particularly if you want to get something done in the schools.

☆

Harold "Bud" Branson is a booster. He is "bullish" on Middle City. He was born there forty-two years ago, grew up there, went to the university there, and married into one of the city's more prestigious families. He is a successful realtor and serves as chairman of the Middle City Board of Realtors. He has been a director of the Chamber of Commerce and has for a number of years been chairman of the Middle City Park Board. Bud Branson has a quick smile and he is eager to tell anyone who will listen what he thinks—particularly when it comes to Middle City and its future:

I'm 100 percent for Middle City. Anything that's good for this town, I figure is going to be good for me, so I support it all the way. That's the whole game, my whole theory—so whatever I can do to make Middle City even better than it is right now, I want to do it. . . . But I don't want to do it with that fat federal bureaucracy looking over my shoulder and telling me how to run my business. I'm really an old-fashioned liberal, the kind people call conservative nowadays. I don't want any bureaucratic security, I want to make it myself, and when you leave me alone to make it myself you'll get my best effort and Middle City will get my best effort and I'll do what I can just like I've been doing to make this town a good town.

I've been a member of some organizations—but I don't waste my time joining groups that don't do any good for this community. Now you take the board of realtors. . . . First of all it insures honest practices in the industry and second of all it serves the individual broker by keeping him up to date. You see, by serving individuals trying to make an honest living it serves everybody in Middle City. . . . As far as the chamber is concerned I think it speaks for itself. I guess you'd say it encourages a good climate for business around here so that a guy who has a good idea will be willing to try it out here. That's good for the guy who has the idea and good for Middle City and that means it's good for me. . . . So you see I'll do my best as an individual to make sure that anybody who wants to do some good will get a chance around here. . . . But I'll tell you one thing—sometimes I get awfully tired because in this town like any other town, I guess, you can run into a lot of resistance.

Now you take this whole Negro thing. I'm an integrationist. I mean, and I know this is going to sound bad, but I'm an integrationist because I think that's the only way they're going to get a different view of things —that's the only way they're going to meet people on . . . on . . . well, you know, on a higher level, people who've got something because they know they can't expect handouts and they have to work for what they get. Well, anyhow, I'm an integrationist . . . but sometimes I think I'm going to go all the way over to being a racist. The resistance you get from those people! I've tried to work with 'em on the park board but it's really no use. They tell you they want one thing one time and then when you give it to 'em another group comes in and says, "We don't want what you gave us." It's almost like they really don't want to join in, in this community—like they think they'll succeed by standing off by themselves on the sidelines and yelling, "You white guys don't know what you're doing—you don't know what we need." Well, if that's their theory they never will succeed. You can't succeed if you don't really try —you can't do anything around here if you just stand around and make life miserable for those folks who are trying to help you. . . . When they started to give me the business at the last park board meeting, I just said, "Listen, you need me more than I need you," and then I just got up and left. You know, people have got to learn that they won't make it on handouts, that you can only get if you give. . . .

I think a lot of the future of this community depends on how this race thing comes out. Like I say, I'm an integrationist because I think these people have just got to learn that there's no "free lunch," that they've got to get a better education—and I think they won't learn this until they associate with people who are on a higher level because they already know this. . . . I'm an integrationist but from what I see it may not work. They may go in the other direction, they may become lost because they can't compete. I don't know the answer to that. If they get lost then we've hurt 'em more than we've helped 'em. . . .

Jasper's sporting goods store is a kind of landmark in downtown Middle City. It's not that it's a very big store—it's about average size—but it has been there since 1930 and just about everyone knows where it is. Just about everyone also knows that it is owned and operated by Sam Jasper, who, if nothing else, is one of the most visible men in Middle City. Sam Jasper has worked quite hard at making himself visible; some in Middle City would say, with more than just a hint of sardonic condescension, that he has devoted his life to it. At seventy-five, still a member of the city council (an office he was first elected to at the age of sixty-nine), he looks back at his life and proclaims it a life of good works and service to the people of Middle City.

As Sam Jasper himself told us: "My kids say that if anyone will listen

I'll talk their ears off about my life. I guess that's true but I don't think people mind too much because it's been a real interesting life—what with all the things I've done and all the famous people I've met—like Bob Hope and all the governors."

Whether people mind or not, there is something disconcerting about Sam Jasper's talk. You don't have to listen long before you realize that Sam appears to have forgotten you are there. It is as though your presence has been taken as a signal for the start of a soliloquy that takes little or no account of the listener once it has begun. You get the distinct impression that Sam Jasper is talking for his own benefit. It's curious, and the man's solipsistic volubility makes you wonder if he isn't trying to allay some potent doubts of his own about himself:

There's been a lot of things I've done. Formed the first kid baseball league in the state—now they call it Little League—and I've been president of the county semi-pro league. Lots of things in sports that I have had an interest in. I was one of the first members of the Front Line Club, which is a group of men that's really interested in supporting the football team at the university. We raise funds for athletic scholarships and stuff like that and we get together with the coaches and they tell us what really happened and stuff like that. Red Grange—he used to come right into this store. Not when he was playin'—because I hadn't opened up here yet—but later when he used to come down to visit, and we got him elected a trustee out there at the university kind of to look out after the athletic programs which do so much for the university. And that minister that was a pole-vaulting champion—held the world record—he worked for me right in this store. Lots of 'em have been right in this store. And back in the thirties I had the best independent basketball team in the state—played all over the state—the Jasper Jumpers—had lots of boys who played right on the university team and the high school varsity. . . . Yeah, I have had lots of interest in sports. I organized a baseball league over in Post County and I even organized a Lassie Softball League over here—the first league for girls.

But sports is only a part of my life. I keep active in my fraternity. I'm a Deke. A couple of years ago we had the national convention right here in town. People came from all over—lots of distinguished gentlemen. I was chairman of the arrangements committee. I'm proud I'm still a member because that's as fine a bunch of men as you'll find anywhere and we do lots of good things, we give lots of scholarships. And I was a charter member of the Exchange Club over here. I was the first secretary and I'm still a member—one of the two original members—me and Professor Phillips, we're the only ones still there—and I was secretary for the State Exchange.

Been involved, too, in lots of things to benefit this community. Lots of fund drives like cerebral palsy and cancer, which I'm very proud of because a lot of money was raised and nobody turns you down for those things. They just reach into their pockets and give you what they got. And I was president of the municipal cemetery association, which I guess some people wouldn't want to be—but I enjoyed it. I got letters from all over the country from people thanking me for looking after things like making sure that their parents' graves was being taken care of the way they wanted.

And I'm a board member of the county fair association—which is great, just great. We have these special days where certain people can get in free and I'm in charge of two of 'em—Senior Citizens Day and the Armed Forces Day. We bring them in—send out busses to get 'em and we show 'em a real good time. I arrange it so as that they get in free to the exhibits and they get a free meal. It's a lot of coordination and you got to have a lot of respect to get it done. The general over at the base came over and we had a special ceremony and a dinner and he told me how great he thought it was that we could get these different kinds of people together to get to know each other better. . . . And another thing about the county fair is you meet some real important and real fine people. I guess my favorite—and he's become a real fine friend —is Bob Hope. He's a real fine American. And I had the Lombardo boys over for dinner in my house and Wayne King and the governors and senators who come every year when we have Republican and Democrat days. And it was a real honor to meet Mr. Nixon a few years ago—that's before he was president. Fine people like that who come out here to meet the people. Real positive people who have made something of themselves and they appreciate the job we do out there at the fair. Just before he left Mr. Nixon took me aside and he said, "Sam, I want you to know what a good job you and your people have been doing." He said it and I guess he really must have meant it because he goes to a lot of places like this and so he can compare the way we do things. . . .

I'm a member of the Chamber of Commerce and I'm real proud of my association with the fine men there and all they do for free enterprise, which is my philosophy of life. I go on the basis of every man for himself and you have to really take care of your own ups and downs— the Chamber of Commerce doesn't take care of me, it's not an organization that's trying to guarantee me that I can open these doors day after day. I have to take care of myself and I do, and the other men at the chamber, they take care of themselves too. We all understand that and we support that philosophy so that we keep this town good for business —good for people who can take care of their own business. . . . That's what I try to do on the city council, which is a great experience, too. I wish that everybody who has the ability to do it would have the experience of being on the city council. That's the only way you really learn the ins and outs of city government. . . . Anyway, I just try to keep this town good for business, not good for any particular business, but good for business. Then it's up to you to keep your doors open just like it's been up to me to keep these doors open for going on forty-one years. . . .

There's been other groups that I have been associated with, too. There's the Elks, which I been in for over forty years, and there's the Moose, which I guess I been associated with them for a shorter time, must be somethin' like thirty-five years—and there's the country club which my daddy gave me a membership in and I'm real proud of that. And I'm on the board of directors for the Goodwill—that's for the whole state—which is a real fine organization. What the Goodwill does is put handicapped people to work remaking things and clothes and that's good because those people don't want pity and I'm glad I'm involved in that because that's my free enterprise philosophy—give 'em a chance to work and if they do, fine. . . .

I guess that about covers it. Let's see, I guess there's a few other things. I'm in the American Legion—won the Man of the Year Award back in 1955—and the Jaycees and the Optimists. I guess that's about it except for my philosophy, which as I say is free enterprise. People shouldn't expect handouts. I don't go for that at all. But there's people that do. In most cases people try to uplift themselves but there is definitely a certain amount that does expect a handout and I don't believe in any way, shape, or form in a guaranteed income because I believe in free enterprise. There's people who do need handouts—the elderly and the people that's sick. If a farmer, a professor, a business man all of a sudden had sickness in the family and needed help, then there's a place for that. And that's where I would want to help, but the ones that are physically able to work and don't do it, I don't want to subsidize them. There's little you can do for anyone and you shouldn't do it unless there's a real need. Every man has to take care of himself and every man has a right to have his property which he has earned and which nobody should tell him what he has to do with it. . . .

☆

The Bennett house is a knockout. It's a low, long building that seems to sprawl all over its lot, but the sprawl is not at all unpleasant. It is, on the contrary, very interesting, and an architectural writer could probably fill several pages with a description and analysis of just how the interesting Bennett house makes interesting use of the interesting Bennett lot. The house is built around an inner courtyard, a description of which tells something about the Bennetts themselves and particularly about Mrs. Rita Bennett, who designed it.

The first thing you notice in the Bennett courtyard is the waterfall cascading into the swimming pool from the top of what seems to be a concrete bathhouse. As it turns out, this structure, which is about eight feet tall, is something else—the entrance to the Bennett family's bomb shelter. "Since we had this shelter anyway," says Mrs. Bennett, "I decided to make it aesthetically pleasing, so we just put some pipes up on the side which you don't generally see and the water just flows out over the top and into the pool." As pleasing as it may appear during the day, at night, the Bennetts believe, it is spectacular. With the flick of a few switches they can turn on multicolored lights attached to the wall of the shelter behind the cascade, and the water flows in hues reminiscent of a Jackson Pollack action painting. Then, of course, there is the pool itself, which is bigger than most. (When she was younger, Rita Bennett was a competitive swimmer, and she wanted a pool which would allow her to do the backstroke without having to change directions constantly.) The pool is long and narrow with a curve at one end leading into the diving area. Next to the pool there is what can best be described as an ersatz Japanese rock garden and to one side of the rock garden a sitting area outfitted with a canopied table, the mandatory chaise lounge, and several comfortable chairs. On the other side of the pool there is a children's play area complete with the latest outdoor apparatus from Creative Playthings. When newcomers enter the Bennett courtyard for the first time, there are the expected "oohs" and "ahs," the "how beautifuls," the admiring "you designed this all yourself my but isn't that wonderful's"—to which the gracious Mrs. Bennett replies with a bit of recreational philosophy:

When it comes to recreation I believe facilities have to be functional. That's what's wrong with the parks we have in this community. Of the six parks we have only one—only one has things for people to do in it. The rest are just pretty and the only thing that people can do in them is have a picnic. That's why we built this little park back in here, I guess—so that we could have some recreational facilities which the city doesn't provide. . . . It's not so much of a problem for people like us; we can afford to do it on our own; but there are people in this town— for example, over near the housing projects or near the special housing for the elderly—who couldn't possibly afford their own recreational facilities and all they have are these empty parks where there aren't even benches for people to sit on. I've tried through my membership in the League of Women Voters to get the city to do something about this but I haven't succeeded and I probably won't succeed as long as Mr. Waters is the park manager in this city. He's all for beautiful parks but he has no sense of the fact that it doesn't matter how beautiful the parks are if people can't really use them. . . . I really think Mr. Waters is in the wrong job. He ought to be a cemetery manager. I'm sure his cemeteries would be very beautiful and he wouldn't have to worry about providing things for people to do.

I shouldn't get so upset about it but I guess my background just makes me very sensitive on this issue. You see, I grew up in the Pacific northwest, which is a natural playground for people. Out there, there are always things for people to do and you really don't have to worry too much about it. But in this part of the country you really don't have natural recreational resources which are easily accessible—no lakes right nearby to swim in and, my goodness, not even a little hill to climb— so you really should be giving it much more thought than we seem to be giving it—especially where the disadvantaged are concerned.

I went to a graduate school in Philadelphia. I got my doctor's degree at the University of Pennsylvania, you know. I teach now and then at the university but not on a regular basis. Big cities have this problem too, of not having natural recreational facilities, and the disadvantaged suffer most of all from that; but the big cities like Philadelphia or New York have these parks or playgrounds—they can't take up more than a half acre, but they are really very good parks; they have lots of swings, basketball hoops, shuffleboard, wading pools, and benches where people can just sit around and have a conversation if they want to. They have these good parks because people have given some thought to what the people and particularly the disadvantaged people need. They're not beautiful parks and they don't take up a lot of space like ours do, but they're better parks because people can do things in them that they can't do anywhere else. . . . I don't see why with all the superior people we have in this city—and I don't just mean the people at the university; the local people are really quite superior—they're the descendants of a superior group who came out here and made this into the most fertile farmland in the world—I don't see why with all these people, with their abilities, why we haven't come up with parks that are really functional —parks which serve the needs of the people who can't do what my husband and I have done back here. . . .

I guess I sound pretty critical, pretty negative, but I really don't mean to be. There are a lot of very good things about this community. For example, there are a lot of very successful people here—a lot of very open people who are willing to try and help those who are unfortunately disadvantaged. And I'm not just talking about liberals like my husband or myself—I'm talking about people who are probably pretty conservative on most things, people who are my neighbors, people I meet at the country club. They may not come right out and say—the way I would— that something has to be done about poverty, about breaking the cycle of poverty and failure which the disadvantaged are caught up in, but they're non-resistant. They don't oppose programs for the disadvantaged even if they're not convinced that programs like Head Start and job training are going to do much good; and they don't go around the way some people do and call you a communist or a "nigger-lover" if you're trying to help. Given half a chance I even think that some of them would pitch in to help also. Some already have with the o.i.c. [Opportunities Industrial Center, a primarily black program of self-help and vocational training founded by the Reverend Leon Sullivan in Philadelphia; it is very popular with white moderates in general and certainly was so when we were observing in Middle City], and that's why it's a shame that the disadvantaged are so disorganized, because I really think these people who have a lot of talent and who have shown that they can achieve things in their walks of life can be convinced to extend some help. . . . This is a community that doesn't have the problems of the big cities which, let's face it, are almost impossible to cope with. This is a community in which the cycle could be broken because the problems aren't that big and you don't have that resistance which you have in the big cities. You don't have to be a failure here just because your father was one. Things can change and I'm optimistic about it. . . .

I guess I've sort of wandered a bit, but about this little park I guess you might call it in here. . . . It's a retreat for us, although I know that some people might question our motives for having it—and I hope to

see the day when everyone in Middle City, no matter what their position in the community is, will be able to enjoy the kinds of things we
have here because they will be part of our public facilities. . . .

☆

. . . This fair housing ordinance just isn't fair at all and I can tell you
that if you pass it you will be doing great harm to the people of this
community: the real estate broker who will be put in such a bind that
he'll be afraid to stay in business; the homeowner who may be unjustly
accused of bigotry, whose reputation will be ruined, whose money will be
wasted in a needless defense; and even the Negro buyer who, after
pressing his case under this law, will find that it is after all unenforce-
able. . . . Yes, gentlemen, there is discrimination in this community and
no one regrets this discrimination more than I do, no one is more
sympathetic to the rights of the individual—any individual—to the pursuit of his personal happiness; but this ordinance, this so-called fair
housing law which these "spokesmen"—and I use that word advisedly
. . . spokesmen for whom?—want you to pass, won't end discrimination;
it won't accomplish anything at all except to deprive individuals of their
rights—yes, even their right to be misguided and to discriminate—it
won't accomplish anything at all that's positive but it will, I assure you,
harm a lot of innocent people. Thank you.

Having thus expressed himself amidst both cheers and catcalls in the
city council chamber, Leon Neighbors, attorney for the Association of
Real Property Owners (ARPO), sits down and listens to the remaining
statements by citizens interested in going on record as opposed to or in
favor of the fair housing ordinance which the council is considering.
Leon Neighbors listens intently, and while others are moved to heckle
the opposition or cheer their side, Leon Neighbors just takes notes; and
no matter what is said, no matter how he is excoriated for the sentiments he has just expressed, he remains, to anyone observing, visibly
cool and under control.

Leon Neighbors, age thirty-six, is an attorney who is rarely in the
public eye. For the most part his practice consists of civil liability and
divorce cases. He is not part of the legal establishment in Middle City;
he is just a fairly young lawyer who was asked by one of his neighbors—
the secretary of the newly organized ARPO—to represent the "decent
little people" in this fair housing business:

There never was any objection by the members of ARPO to a fair housing ordinance as long as it was really fair. They never said to me, "Let's

beat this thing in the core like they did in Chicago!" They never did that. I was retained to examine the proposed ordinance and to give my opinion as to whether it was a good one, whether it was actually legal, whether it was fair to innocent people who simply wanted to protect their individual rights—their rights to the property which most of them had to work very hard to get. And when I read the ordinance, when I looked into it, I just had to conclude that while it might be legal—and I would like to emphasize might—it certainly wasn't fair. I just saw too many ways in which the local government would be interfering with the rights of individuals and I saw too many ways in which the little guy— the guy who has put everything into his little house with a picket fence —could get hurt. . . . I don't think the city has the right to tell the individual how he must sell his house or to impose restrictions on him. I don't think that the city can put a man in a position where anyone, just because he thinks he might be the victim of discrimination—and again I would like to emphasize might—can complain and cause that man to be damaged even though he is actually innocent of the complaint and even though he is eventually exonerated.

Just take yourself for instance. Suppose you were leaving Middle City —suppose you got a chance to better yourself in some other job in another community. You put your house on the market. Somebody calls you and says, "Will you sell to a Negro?" and you say yes and a Negro comes to look at your house—but by that time you have a buyer who happens to be white. So when the Negro comes you tell him the house is being sold and you're sorry. So he goes away and someone tells him, "Look, that guy's discriminating against you so why don't you file a complaint." And he does and you're stuck. You can't go through with your sale for several months until the case has been decided. And by that time you may have lost your buyer and because you have been tied up in litigation you may even have lost your chance for that better job. You're innocent, you didn't do anything wrong, and the fair housing board finds that you are innocent. But who is going to compensate you for your trouble? Who is going to pay your lawyer's fees? Who is going to give you back the job which you earned? Who is going to compensate you for the money—your money—which you lost just because someone thought that you were discriminating? That's why I think the fair housing ordinance is really very unfair and that's why in behalf of ARPO I spoke out against it at the city council meeting.

But I think it's the temper of the times. There are just too many people who think that by the magic of the law you can make everyone equal. And when you try to do that you disregard the rights of the individual, you fail to protect his investments and his achievements. I don't expect us to ignore real injustice, I don't expect us to condone real discrimination which blocks any person's right to advancement, and I don't expect people like the Negroes to say thank you to us when we give them the rights they should have had in the first place, but I wish we were more positive about all this and I wish those people who want to do good would realize that you can't do it by interfering with individual rights and that there is always going to be some inequality between people because people don't earn the same things. I think we should do all that we can as individuals to give people a chance to advance themselves. I don't think you can hide behind groups in this business. I think we should try to make sure that all people have the opportunity to get the skills which if they have them and use them will get them the good things that you and I have. That's why I support the o.i.c.—it's a tremendous idea and I hope they raise a hundred thousand dollars this year—but what will happen if it fails? If people lose interest in it next year, will we say that these people should have these things anyway?

I see this whole thing in my own profession. We have this legal aid situation which in principle is very good. In fact, a few years ago I ran the legal aid for the bar association for one year. But now we have this situation which is becoming a real problem. There are poor people who think it should be their right to have not just an attorney but the attorney of their own choice free of charge. They think it's their right to have what they regard as the best, free of charge, and I think that's just incredible. I think in Middle City anybody charged with a felony has a right to a good lawyer no matter how much money he has or doesn't have. That's why we've consistently had good public defenders. But to say that you want the best and that it's your right to have the best even when you can't pay for it, that's incredible. When I get the flu I don't say send me up to the Mayo Clinic, I don't want the doctors around here because they're not as good as the ones at the Mayo Clinic. I don't think it's my right to go up to the Mayo Clinic every time I get sick and say it should be free of charge because I can't afford to pay for it. But that's what these people are saying about legal services. I don't think you or I have the right to say, "I want this so you give it to me because I'm not rich or because I'm poor." I don't think this is how our society should be and I think it could lead to some problems. . . . A poor person should never be deprived of his rights but I don't know of any place in our constitution or in the laws which govern this state where it says that a poor person has a right to have what a rich person has. A poor person has the right to try and earn what the rich person has but he doesn't have the right to have it just because he wants it. But that's how some people are thinking these days and you can just imagine what kind of society will result from this. You don't have to earn anything, you just have to want it. It's incredible. . . .

If Leon Neighbors is not an attorney of any particular distinction he is nevertheless an articulate one. He says very well what others in Middle City only think. It would seem that the Association of Real Property Owners chose very well when it retained him.

Paul Dahlberg doesn't get involved. He doesn't champion any causes. About the only time he has been moved to protest anything was when a supermarket chain attempted to get a zoning change which would have allowed it to build a market nearly at the Dahlberg doorstep. Together with his neighbors, Paul Dahlberg waged an apparently successful fight against the zoning change, for while the planning board did not decide against the petition for change, it simply made no decision, postponing the decision indefinitely and causing the supermarket chain to look for some other location. Other than this one foray into the world of public affairs, Paul Dahlberg has kept his own counsel, remaining very much the private man in pursuit of middle American normalcy.

Paul Dahlberg is married; he has a teenage son and a pre-teen daughter; he owns two modest houses, living in one and renting the other. He and his family attend the Lutheran Church—Missouri Synod—with some regularity. With a degree in agricultural economics from the University of Iowa, he makes a reasonably good living as a crop-leasing agent for the National Grains, Inc. Except among his circle of friends and business acquaintances, Paul Dahlberg has little visibility in Middle City. He is a member of the "silent majority"—the average man personified.

I don't begrudge anybody anything they have earned and I don't care who they are. A lot of people, I guess, would call me naïve about the world, but I really think that people should have the right to have the best they can get. If a Negro could afford to rent the house that I rent out, I wouldn't hesitate to rent it to him. If one of these hillbillies in the Addition wanted to rent my house and if he was respectable he could rent it. I don't think you can restrict people. I don't think you can tell a man who is trying to better himself and his family that he can't do it because you don't think he is going to fit in. But by the same token I don't think you should be giving people things that they don't deserve. I don't think that anybody can say, "Look, I deserve this or that because I've had it rough or because I've been kept down." I mean, of course they can say that, but I don't think we have to take it seriously. If a man were to say that to me I guess I would sympathize with him but I would tell him that whatever has happened has happened and now he has got to go out and do the best he can for himself and his family. I'd tell him that I never did anything against him and so I don't think I have to give him anything to make amends. . . .

A lot of people I think have lost faith in themselves and what they can do by themselves, particularly people who lived their whole lives in a city. Sometimes I think that a city is the worst place to grow up in because you learn to expect other people to do things for you and you don't have any faith in what you can do yourself. In the city, the garbage man picks up your garbage for you, but when you're on a farm you take care of that yourself. When you grow up on a farm the way I did, if something breaks down—unless it's something very complicated or technical—you learn to fix it yourself. That's a good experience because it carries over into other things. You learn to do things for yourself, you learn that you can have confidence in yourself, you learn that you don't have to depend too much on what other people say or do, and you learn not to blame your situation on other people. . . . That's why my wife and I work with the 4H Club even though we live in the city now. And that's why our kids are members even though the only time they're on a farm is when they visit their grandparents. But in the city you learn to be dependent on others—and I guess that's the way it has to be—but when you learn that, there's always the danger that you are going to lose faith in yourself and once that happens it's very easy just to stop trying to better yourself. . . . That's really kind of sad because there's really a lot that some of these people could do to make their lives better than they are. But they get demoralized. Sometimes I think if this wasn't a democracy you could solve a lot of the problems we have just by shipping a lot of these poor city kids out to the farms for two or three years. That would restore their confidence and some of them anyhow would be ready to better themselves. . . .

Also you've got to learn to be patient. Nobody has everything they want. I don't have everything that I want, but maybe my children will have those things. That's another thing about growing up in a city, you

always see other people who have more than you have. It's all around
you. And you say, well, if they have all those things why shouldn't I
have them too. What you should be learning is that it's okay to want
these things but you may not get them all because you may not be
able to earn them. You don't learn patience about these things. There's
lots of things that I want—like I said—that I don't have but I don't go
around saying it's unfair. I'm just willing to keep working and to be
patient because the more I work the better the chance that my kids will
get these things. As I said at the beginning maybe I'm naïve but I think
you should rely on yourself to better yourself and when you do that I
won't stand in your way. . . .

In the fifteen years Freeman Willett has lived in Middle City he has
seen things get better for black people, which is not to say that Willett
thinks they are as good as they should be. Nevertheless, according to
Freeman Willett, father of two teenage boys, purchasing agent at the
university, and one of the two black members of the Middle City Democratic Committee, things have been getting better for black people
and the main difficulty is that blacks haven't changed with the times.
According to Willett, too many of them still behave as though there is
nothing they can do to progress in Middle City.

More black people should take advantage of the things we have in
Middle City. But they still act ignorant and I get so mad at times that
I'm tempted to say that if they can't do anything to improve the community then they should stop bringing little innocent children into the
world because it's the children that suffer. . . . We need a change in
attitudes. Just a few weeks ago the recreation department sent some
busses up into the North Quarter to take kids over to the Clear Lake
Park and these busses just stood empty. I went around and asked some
parents why they didn't send their kids on the busses and they told me
they wouldn't let their kids go over to that park because when they was
kids themselves they went and they had trouble over there with white
kids. I told them that was years ago and things is changing but they
wouldn't believe me and so now the recreation department isn't sending
these busses over and I don't blame them—because nobody is using
them. It's just acting ignorant and it's not improving things for ourselves and it makes those of us who been speaking up and getting these
changes look bad.

And it's just like that over and over again. The businessmen and the city government has these summer job programs, to keep the youths in the North Quarter busy, but do you think they really want these jobs? No, they rather be hanging around, doing nothing—just spending their time testing each other. . . . And then there's this business with the police and fire department tests. I spoke up to have the tests looked into—you know, to see if they were discriminating . . . but some of these people, they already got their minds made up: they know for sure it's discriminating and they's got to have a new test. But that's just being ignorant again. Anyone who is aspiring to better himself has to learn and study. There are people and agencies who will help a person who has a thwarted education. . . . Now, are we really helping ourselves by lowering our standards for policemen and firemen? Are we really getting ahead when we get a unqualified black policeman? I'm not saying that these people who are acting so ignorant now couldn't be qualified— some of 'em I'm sure could do it—but they have to learn, they have to make the effort. . . . I was in the air force for twenty-four years before I retired. I learned that you got to perform, you got to be right there and ready when the man with the brass says he got a job for you to do. If you can't perform you don't last—I don't care who you are.

So I think we got to get some new attitudes around here. We got problems sure. No man knows that better than I do. But we also got opportunities and we got to start taking advantage of them. . . . We got to do two things. First we got to make sure that we get good services. Like, for example, right now we got to get some of these welfare programs run better and under one organization. You know, it's a funny thing how too much of something can be just as bad as too little of it. Well, right now we got too many agencies, each one expecting the others to take care of the problem and so's the people with the problem wind up not getting it taken care of. So we need better coordination. But too, we got to stop being too proud to take advantage of the help they offer and help ourselves with the help that's offered. We got to stop saying that's no good or this's no good because it's a white program or because it's the "establishment." As long as we keep on doing that we just going to continue to be just ignorant and unqualified and then we got no gripe about not getting things! . . . I'm kinda on a tightrope, you know. Some of these ignorant types get themselves rolling and they call me "tom" or "oreo." But I don't pay that much mind because that's the same people who'll be yelling ten years from now because they haven't accomplished anything. I may be a "tom" to them but that

won't change the fact that if you're ready and able you won't have to
stay back any more—even if you're black.

☆

People think that George Sellers is going to be the mayor of Middle
City one of these days, but George Sellers eschews any political ambitions. He is, he likes to tell people, not even a registered member of a
political party. Moreover, while recognizing the importance of local government, he finds its pace too slow and its operations too cumbersome.
George Sellers likes to see things accomplished by highly motivated
people working on their own, free of the entanglements of governmental
red-tape. So, the opinions of other people to the contrary, you have to
take George Sellers seriously when he says he has no political ambitions.
He is an active man in civic affairs—as he puts it, he "has a compulsion
to be involved"—but in his view government is not where the action is:

When you can get a group of highly motivated and capable men
together—I guess you might call it the "power structure"—and they're
willing to take some risks on a project, the project can be accomplished
in relatively short order. On the other hand, when you have to have
government involvement the whole business can drag on for years. Just
look at the difference between the Sangomen Center project and the
urban renewal proposal. . . . I was hired as the executive secretary for the
chamber of commerce the same year that planning for the Sangomen
Center shopping mall got under way. Well, without any government
interference and with the efforts of local business the center became
operational in no more than five years. That same year urban renewal
was proposed and we're just now getting to the point where we have
a workable plan. Nothing to this day has been built and we still need
to be renewed. . . .

I don't want to be overly critical; it's just that when government on
any level gets involved you've got to go slowly—too slowly for my taste.
You've got to do everything publicly and that gives every Tom, Dick,
and Harry who may not even know anything about what needs to be
done the right to put his fifty cents in for or against different parts
of the plan. And by the time you take account of everybody's opinion
and meet the requirements set down by bureaucrats who have nothing
better to do than dream up requirements, years pass and you haven't
accomplished nearly as much as you should have. When you do it
through free enterprise, you get those individuals who know what they're

doing, who know what they want, involved—and only those individuals —and you can proceed because you have capable people, people who have a track record of achievement doing the things that have to be done. . . . Maybe I'm biased because this is a community with lots of talented people—it's a community where, as they say, the action is—but I think success breeds success and when you get successful individuals involved and let them do things their way without interference you are just naturally going to benefit. You don't want to put a straightjacket on success, you want to give it room to repeat itself. . . .

I'm a great believer in the individual who has developed his competence and who has self-discipline. I'm a great believer in what such people can accomplish. I don't want to blow my own horn but I think that this belief comes from my own experience. I didn't get to this point the easy way. I had my share of setbacks. I didn't graduate from the university until I was thirty-six years old, mostly because I was one of the "lucky ones" who wound up serving in both World War II and the Korean War. I got out of the army and I had to go to work because even with the G.I. Bill there were just things my family needed and I wasn't able to afford. And just as I'm getting on my feet and planning for the future—whammo—the Koreans start having their little party and I'm back in the service again. So I didn't get to go to college until after the Korean War. But I went because I knew I just had to develop myself if I was ever going to get anywhere. I could have just said, well, those are the breaks and I'm too old now to be going to college; and lots of people would probably have said that. And I wouldn't really blame them if they did because I know that there are differences in abilities and discipline. But I was brought up in a very strong WASP family with a very strong-willed mother and father. And even though we lived in very modest circumstances I just knew that by dint of hard work and, you know, honesty you could get to the top.

I even think that those years in the service turned out to be beneficial because it taught me something about standards. You knew just which way you would have to go and what you had to do to be successful and you knew if you did not do these things that certain things would accrue to you that were not going to be pleasant. It was simple but important. I learned that you get what you deserve. So I learned and I developed and it took discipline but it paid off because I think really successful people like Arnie Taplin—the late Arnie Taplin—and Bert Green recognized this discipline in me when they brought me in as executive secretary for the chamber. I know this sounds like I'm blowing my own horn and I don't want to sound like I'm the most successful person in the world—and I don't think you can go around feeling superior to people just because they may be less talented and less prepared than you are. As long as they do the best with whatever the good Lord sought to give them that's okay with me; but I think my experience bears out my belief in the individual who has had the self-discipline to develop his competence. . . .

I think all this is behind my interest in the junior college. I got involved on the steering committee because this is a chance to develop career education for people who are less talented, less gifted, but who have enough self-discipline to make the most of what they've got. Middle City needs this kind of institution. There are more jobs here than people who want to work—that's a bad choice of words—I really mean there are more jobs than there are people qualified to fill them. We always hear from General Electric and the farm equipment companies that they need supervisory help but they can't get it around here. So if we have technical career courses at the junior college we'll be able to supply these firms with the personnel they need and those people who are successful in these courses will get ahead even though they don't have the kind of talent to get them through the university. I think, by the way, that this will be the salvation of the low-income groups around here. Their big need is skills and those who have the discipline to get them will find that the doors will open up to them and a lot of problems will be solved. Of course there'll always be some discrimination; that's in the hearts of some people and there's nothing much you can do about that. But for a lot of people it isn't prejudice that's the problem; it's simply that they don't want much to do with people who don't seem able to make their own way, people who don't seem to be productive. Well, if some of these people get themselves trained nobody's going to object to them and also they're going to have the money they need to come into some of the nicer neighborhoods in town. I'm pretty optimistic about all this because as I said my own experience leads me to believe in the individual. Middle City is really a good place to live— it's exciting, it's dynamic, and if you've got that self-discipline you can go as far here as your gifts will take you. . . .

Middle City has tested the faith of the Reverend Thomas Ross. For this young, somewhat modish Congregational minister, a ten-year tour of duty as a university chaplain, now coming to an end, has been a

period of great expectations unrealized, a period in which highly principled social activism has wrought but little. Tom Ross expected that
poverty could be measurably reduced in Middle City, and it hasn't been;
he believed that Middle City could become a model community in race
relations, and it is as yet far from that; and so as he is about to leave he
wrestles with increasing doubt about the ultimate efficacy of liberal social action, and he strains to maintain the optimism which in the past
his Christian faith so readily inspired:

We could have accomplished so much here—and, I don't know,
maybe a lot will still be accomplished here—but right now I'd have to
say that we haven't done the things that could and should have been
done. It would be easy to put the blame on the conservative tone of
this community; you could say, "What would you expect to happen in
a city where you have a lot of midwestern Republicans who don't even
like to admit there's a poverty problem and when they do admit it they
just naturally conclude that the poor people have brought it on themselves." It would be easy to say that, you know—and there's even some
truth in it—but it's not the whole truth. The whole truth, I hate to say,
is a lot more uncomplimentary to us all. I'm afraid it's not just the
conservatives in this town who deserve the blame for our lack of
progress. . . .

You take the white liberals who went into the North Quarter. I'm
sure they had the best intentions but they looked around and they saw
that they were so much better educated than the people there that they
just naturally wanted to run things; they wanted to take the lead and
people, you know, resent that. This is really true with the university
people who think that their professions entitle them to lead the poor.
You know this guy Kaplan, this Dr. Kaplan in the ed school who got
O.E.O. money to work with the parents of pre-schoolers—you know, to
stimulate them so that in turn they would stimulate their children who
are in the Head Start program? Well, I know that he's literally worked
his butt off with this program and I'm sure he wanted to see good
things happen up there—but he just goes in there with his own people
from the university to run things; he puts one of his students in charge
and he just ignores the possibility that there are people already in the
community who could do a good job with it—a better job, because they
don't get up and leave when the semester is over or they graduate. So
it doesn't matter how hard he worked and how good his intentions were
—he just couldn't be very successful doing it that way. . . .

And then we had those professional liberal types—you know, the ones that work up there in the regional office of o.e.o. Well, they came down here—spent a couple of days driving around the community—and then they let everyone know that our local program just wasn't up to snuff. They hadn't really studied it; they really didn't know the people who were involved; but they just knew, they assumed that if the poor people were trying to run their own antipoverty program, that it just couldn't be any good. They just assumed that if you're poor you really don't know very much about what needs to be done to get rid of your poverty. . . .

I know that what I'm going to say next is going to sound strange, particularly because of what I just said about the professional liberals who just assume that the poor can't do anything for themselves. It's going to sound like I agree with them and I want to say that in principle I don't, but it is also true that in this case—that in Middle City, not, you understand, necessarily in other cities, but in this city—the poor people haven't really done much to help themselves. I really feel badly about this. I guess I feel worse about this than anything else I've seen around here in the time that I've been involved, because I really admire some of these people . . . like Bo Jones and Richie and Bobby Lee— they're really beautiful!—but I have to say that they really haven't done the right things. It's almost as though—and I'm still trying to understand this—it's almost as though for some perverse reason they don't want to succeed.

First of all they just can't seem to get together. They each have their own small group and instead of working together they take some perverse pleasure in going around and discrediting each other. You know, when Bo Jones put this group together—you know the Brothers—I really thought they might be getting it together; but then just a few days after the group was formed I ran into Ritchie and he tells me that he's not going to have anything to do with the Brothers, because he says they're too middle class and everybody up there knows that they're just in it for themselves. And that's just the way it's been over and over again. They just seem to refuse to do those things that really have a chance for success. . . . Just last year the church had a community organization training program up in Chicago and I got Richie and Bobby Lee in. Well, they went up there and a week later they were back saying, "Well, you know those are nice people up there, very nice people, but they don't know anything at all about the problems we have around here." They don't know anything about the problems we have around here! Good God, you'd think we were on another planet! Of course they know about the problems we have. They're the same problems that exist in any community where you have more than just a few poor people. Of course they know about our problems. But for some reason Bobby Lee and Richie can't see that. So they come back down here without using an important opportunity to learn some things about putting things together in a successful way. I didn't understand it then and to this day I still don't really understand it. . . .

In the end I guess it's a matter of patience. I keep telling myself you've got to be patient with these people. They've been down so long, they've been pushed around so much, and they've had to live with so much failure all around them that I guess it's just going to take some time before they recognize that they have a chance for success if they'll only start doing the right things. It's a matter of patience. They really don't understand success. I think that maybe they're really afraid of it. You can see it in little things. . . . We hire a receptionist over at the church from the North Quarter. And she really wants the job—she's really eager. But in a few weeks she's coming in late and she's leaving mighty early. So I speak to her and she says she really likes the job but she's having these personal problems. So I say, "Look, you just hang in there. You just keep trying." Well, in another few weeks one of the other women who works at the church discovers that her pocketbook has been cleaned out and it's pretty clear that this first girl has done it. The next day this girl from the North Quarter calls and says she has to quit because her mother is dying down south. Well, I happen to know her pastor and when I see him I ask him about her and whether he knows if her mother has pulled through. And he just looks at me as if to say, boy, have you been taken for a ride! He says that her mother is right here in town and that she hasn't missed a Sunday singing in the church choir for the last five years. Well, you can imagine how I felt. And I really did feel this way for a while. I really felt, what's the use, these people just don't want to progress. But then I realized that this girl's bizarre behavior from the very beginning represented a fear of success. It's foreign to them, it's strange. It's something they don't know and so they're uncomfortable with it just the way you and I would be uncomfortable with anything that was foreign to us. So I realized that you just have to be patient both with the big things and the small things.

You might put it this way. There are two cultures in this city: the culture of success and the culture of failure. Those people who are advantaged—you and I—live in the culture of success. We're used to getting things done and being rewarded when we get them done the right way. It's natural for us and we're comfortable with it. The disadvantaged live in the culture of failure. They're just not used to doing things and being rewarded for doing them. They're used to just the opposite—and it isn't their fault. But you can see how if they go out of their own culture they'd be uncomfortable and fearful. You can see that in spite of what they say they are really afraid of succeeding. So you have to be patient. . . . I'm not really sure of any of this. As I said, it's really perverse and I really don't completely understand it. But it just might be this culture difference and if it is, the only thing we can do is to be patient. . . .

. . . I'm going to run for the school board because a lot of people—my friends and some who just know me from the P.T.A. meetings—a lot of people have asked me to. They're fed up and so am I. There's some people that won't ever be satisfied with what you do for them. They'll always want more. These people could do a lot for their own children—they have the ability, I wouldn't say they don't—but either they are not interested in their children and so they ask other people to do their job for them or they just plain don't want to help them, but they make a lot of noise about the schools and discrimination anyhow.

When Virginia Terrell speaks, some people in Middle City do in fact listen. At fifty she is—plain and simple, with no apologies—a spokeswoman for hardline resistance to black aspirations for change, not, you must understand, because she thinks blacks are inherently inferior, but rather because she believes they only want to better themselves at the expense of the hard-working people in Middle City.

You look at this house—I think you'll agree it's a pretty nice house, well cared for and well built. My husband and I have raised four children in this house and we always could find time to devote to their betterment. We have both worked but we always found time to be involved with our children and the activities that were important to their welfare, like the P.T.A.'s and our church. And there are lots of other people like us who can't understand how people who don't take good care of their children can just go out and demand that the city and especially the schools should do the job for them.

I know these people. I worked trying to help them. I worked for Family Services and I know from first-hand experiences that they just don't care about their children and the kind of environment they live

*in. But they demand. Or somebody like Richie Wilson or Bobby Lee
Jackson demands for them. Actually I doubt if they even know what
those two are up to or if they know I doubt if they really care.*

*We've had a disadvantaged problem for many years. We had the
same problems with people like that when I was in high school. But I
don't know why it should be our problem. We've done the work and so
we've been able to get the things we need for ourselves and our children.
But what can you do for people who just don't care to work, people
who feel that honest labor is somehow beneath their dignity to do? Nobody can tell me there aren't jobs available for those people if they
would just take them. My husband needed to have the cemetery that
he manages mowed so he called up Mr. Carter at that so-called antipoverty agency and he called the employment bureau—but he didn't get
a response from anybody. The wages weren't that high but you would
think that some wage is better than no wage at all. But none of these
people came over. So how do you explain that? I wonder how people
like Bobby Lee and Richie would explain that. . . .*

*You know, you can have all the programs you want for people—you
can tell them we'll train you for jobs, like at the o.i.c.—but I don't
think it'll work because those people just aren't really interested. Everybody wants to have things, to be successful, but not everybody wants to
work and I don't think those who do work should have to give up what
they have worked so hard for, for people who just don't care but who
go around saying it's okay for us not to care because we're disadvantaged. How can they be anything except disadvantaged if they don't
want to work? And that's what they show their children. I just don't
think that's very intelligent. . . .*

Not everyone in Middle City conceives of success and failure, of having
and not having, of inequality, in the way that these citizens apparently
do. But given their relative public prominence—all but two have undertaken public roles requiring the support of significant segments of the
community—it is safe to assume that when they speak, they articulate
views more or less representative of those held by many others in Middle City. And if we pause a bit to reflect upon these views, there can be
little doubt that they are consistent with the individual-as-central sensibility of the culture of inequality.

In almost every instance the moral necessity of personal aspiration is
either explicitly espoused or at the very least strongly implied. Norvell

Grooms tells us of the wonderful things you can do with an education, but, as he says, "You've got to want to do it." Bud Branson wants to "make it" himself, and he'll work hard to see to it "that anybody who wants to do some good will get a chance" in Middle City. Sam Jasper believes that everyone should take care of himself, and he admires handicapped workers who don't want pity, who try to make something of themselves in spite of their handicaps. Mrs. Bennett believes that you don't have to be a failure in Middle City just because your father was one. Leon Neighbors, irrespective of his stand on open housing, is very conscious of the fact that "a poor person has the right to try and earn what the rich person has." Paul Dahlberg is absolutely convinced that "you should rely on yourself to better yourself. . . ." Freeman Willett is critical of his fellow blacks for having an "ignorant attitude," for not realizing that if they're "ready and able" they won't be held back anymore. George Sellers believes that people who want to get to the top can get there by dint of honesty and hard work. In Virginia Terrell's opinion, the ostensible aspirations of the disadvantaged can and should be ignored because they are false, because the disadvantaged do not really aspire to better themselves.

If there is evidence that these Middle City citizens view personal aspiration in a manner consistent with an individualistic culture of inequality, the evidence of the culture's presence is even stronger when we examine their views on the reasons for success and failure. The unredeemed conservatives among them—Jasper, Neighbors, and Terrell—give voice to sentiments which reflect the individual-as-central sensibility in its pure moralistic form. To Sam Jasper, success comes when you look out for yourself, when you exert personal effort. Nobody can guarantee success, particularly when it comes to business. You have to go out and make that success for yourself, just as he has done for over forty years. And if you don't make it on your own, if you don't exert sufficient effort, if you're a failure, then don't expect other people to bail you out. "People," says Sam Jasper, "shouldn't expect handouts. . . . But there's people that do. . . . There's little you can do for anyone and you shouldn't do it unless there's a real need. Every man has to take care of himself. . . ." Leon Neighbors is very sensitive to the need for protection of individual rights, but as far as he is concerned those rights do not include guaranteed access to rewards and services which have not been earned. Says Neighbors, "There is always going to be some inequality between people because people don't earn the same things." According to him, you get what you earn or deserve—the perquisites of success or the disadvantages of failure—and it is simply "incredible" that those who have not earned the privileges of success should feel that they are being deprived of them. Virginia Terrell sees success and failure in terms of right and wrong, and she is enraged that the failures—those who have not done the right things, those who don't seem to care about themselves or their children—appear to feel that *they* have been wronged and that they have something coming to them. "We've done the work," she says, "and so we've been able to get the things we need for ourselves and our children. But what can you do for people who just don't care to work, people who feel that honest labor is somehow beneath their dignity? . . ."

The moderate conservatives among our group of Middle City citizens —Grooms, Branson, Dahlberg, and Sellers—have views of success and failure very similar to those of the unredeemed conservatives. They, too, see success and failure as justly correlated with the quality of an individual's effort to amount to something. They are moderate, however, in the intensity of their moralism and the extent to which they are willing to support efforts calculated to improve an individual's chances for making the most of his or her talents. Norvell Grooms believes that his own biography demonstrates his belief that hard work and application pay off. Success goes to those who want it and really work for it. That is the lesson he has learned and has taught his own children. In particular, he has an abiding faith in the schools as instruments for personal success. People can leave failure behind if they will only interest themselves in education and apply themselves in school. The poor continue to fail because they do not do so, because they don't, as he puts it, "have that yen for education." Bud Branson believes in integration because he sees it as the only way blacks are going to learn what it takes to be success-ful. In his view, integration will bring black failures into contact with white successes, and through this contact the black failures will learn that they will have to work for everything they get: "I think these peo-ple have just got to learn that there's no 'free lunch' . . . and I think they won't learn this until they associate with people who are on a higher level. . . ." Paul Dahlberg believes that people should not be denied anything they have truly earned, but he resists any tendency to give people things they don't deserve. He sees city life as potentially demoralizing, because it leads individuals to be overdependent upon other people and results in a  loss of faith in what individuals can ac-complish for themselves. "Maybe I'm naïve," he says, "but I think you should rely on yourself to better yourself. . . ." George Sellers is a champion of the disciplined individual who learns what has to be done to be successful and then, because he or she has the will to do it, goes out and does it. According to Sellers, it's important to provide people with the means to better themselves—that's why he is so involved with the local junior college—but in the last analysis success will come to those who have the discipline to make the required effort even in the face of real obstacles. Sellers comments of low income groups: "Their big need is skills and those who have the discipline to get them will find that the doors will open up to them and a lot of problems will be solved. Of course there'll always be some discrimination. . . . But for a lot of people it isn't prejudice that's the problem; it's simply that they don't want much to do with people who don't seem able to make their own way, people who don't seem to be productive. . . ."

To the three liberals—Bennett, Willett, and Ross—success and failure can be understood as just deserts, but success and failure are not qualities of will: they are—true to the modified version of the individual-as-central sensibility—qualities of experience. Rita Bennett does appear to see success as a function of personal superiority, speaking with pleasure of Middle City people "who have shown that they really can achieve things in their walks of life." But failure, in her view, is not something one moralizes about. It is merely unfortunate—often a function of incompetence and misperception instead of insufficient effort. And the cycle of failure can be broken if only the disadvantaged who are caught up in it will accept the assistance of those successes who are really willing to help out. She grieves over the fact that they do not appear ready to do so: "It's a shame that the disadvantaged . . . don't seem to know what they want . . . because I really think these people who have a lot of talent and who have shown that they can achieve things . . . can be convinced to extend some help. . . ." Freeman Willett has come to see success and failure as in large measure functions of attitude. He knows that in the past his fellow members of the black community have been held back, but while he realizes that discrimination can still be a problem, he believes that things have been changing and that the time has come for blacks to stop being "ignorant" about the opportunities opening up and the help the successful establishment proffers. Success, in his view, will come to people who manage to get the qualifications necessary for it, and it is time for the blacks to change their attitude so that they can possess these qualifications. "We got to stop," he says, "being too proud to take advantage of the help they offer and help ourselves with the help that's offered." And then there is Tom Ross, who in seeking to re-establish his faith in liberal social action gives voice to an interpretation of success and failure that epitomizes the type of deficiency explanation characteristic of the individual-as-central sensibility in its modified form. For Tom Ross, success and failure are in large measure functions of differential cultural experience. People who succeed live in a culture of success, where they learn that accomplishment will be rewarded: people who fail live in a culture of failure, where they do not have the opportunity to experience this correlation between achievement and reward. In counseling patience (counseling himself, it would seem, as well as others) with the disadvantaged, Tom Ross says: "The disadvantaged live in the culture of failure . . . you can see how if they go out of their own culture they'd be uncomfortable and fearful. You can see that in spite of what they say they are really afraid of succeeding."

There are obvious differences in these views of success and failure: where some moralize, others attempt to explain; where some are punitive, others are, in varying degrees, therapeutic. But like the differences between conservatives and liberals in general, the differences in these views are but variations upon a common apprehension of reality. All of these people, whatever their differences, perceive success and failure and therefore inequalities as functions of individual characteristics. For some, success and failure are the correlates of the individual's characterological make-up; for others, success and failure are correlates of the individual's characteristic competence or incompetence, of his or her experientially acquired psychological state or cultural orientation. With the possible exception of Ross, who explains the existence of a culture of failure among the blacks by reference to discrimination and previous exclusion, and Freeman Willett, who, as a black man, displays some sensitivity to discrimination, none seriously entertains the possibility that success and failure can presently be a function of structurally based distributive inequity. None of them seems aware that apparent success for some and apparent failure for others may be foreordained by inequalities in the opportunities to which they have access.

In short, with the possible exception of Ross and Willett (and given the major thrust of their opinions, it is not beyond reason to discount this possibility), none of these Middle City people appears sensitive to the impact of social structure upon the life chances of an individual. They find society essentially benign. For those who tend toward conservatism, any consideration of the impact of conditions exogenous to the individual appears unimaginable. Those who are predisposed toward

liberalism seem willing to consider such exogenous factors as past experience with discrimination or immersion in a culture of failure but
view these factors as having no more than a peripheral connection to an
opportunity structure in need of reform; and when they get down to
cases, they perceive the "failing" individual as the one who must change,
who must leave the experience of discrimination behind as misleading
in the benign present, who must overcome fears of success generated by a
"culture of failure."

The interpretation of success and failure by these upstanding citizens
of Middle City indicates the forceful presence of the individual-as-central sensibility in both its moralistic and its modified manifestations.
Without suggesting that there are no other modes of interpreting success and failure, of interpreting the existence of inequality, in Middle
City, it should be clear—given that almost every one of these people
appears to receive public support from at least some segment of the
community because of his or her views on success and failure, on the
existence of inequality—that the individual-as-central sensibility must be
reckoned a significant, if not pre-eminent, component in the cultural
amalgam which gives meaning to life in Middle City. It would seem
that in the eyes of many of its residents Middle City is indeed a "good
community for those who are willing to work hard and make good use of
their God-given talents." Those who have success are entitled to have it,
and those who do not have it can get it if they possess the will to per-
severe and to acquire the requisite skills. The issue for many people in
Middle City, it would seem, is not what the structure of opportunity
will allow but what individuals are willing to do to make reality of
their dreams.

## 5

"Those people! They're just no good;
they live off the hard-working people;
they don't care about their families; they're drunk;
they're always causing trouble—
they're getting away with murder. . . ."

Willy Loman is alive—and as well as Willy Loman can be—in Middle City. Like some dybbuk, Willy has taken possession of more than a few Middle City citizens and in doing so has visited upon them the torment caused by the aspiration-achievement disparity.

If you look carefully enough, you can find Willy Loman in the person of Eddie Finn, an electrician who really wants to be an electrical engineer; you can find him in Charlie Mathews, an advertising man and sometime Republican politician whose dreams of high elective office are unrealized. You can find the spirit of Willy Loman dominating the lives of such citizens as Arnold Stallings, the justice of the peace who would like to be a real judge, but can't because he isn't a lawyer; John Manfred, M.D., the health department physician who, now nearing the age of mandatory retirement, would much rather have been on the staff of the prestigious Bard Clinic; John Althaus, for too long assistant to the coordinator of primary grades for the Middle City school system; and the inimitable Sam Jasper himself, who, despite his public prominence, seems forever unsure of the significance of that prominence. And Willy is no sexist; his spirit is just as likely to harass women as men. Selma Johnston, now the tenant relations officer for the public housing authority, suffers mightily because as a business woman she never advanced beyond assistant to the credit manager of a local department store; Renée Sachs, fast approaching middle age, is desperate to be something other than a faculty wife and mother but, despite her "raised consciousness," just doesn't seem to know how; Karen Cole ought to be something more than a secretary, but she is afraid to try for a promotion even as she is frustrated and angered by her fear; and of course liberal Mrs. Bennett—Ph.D. and all—aspired to an academic career but finds herself a middle-aged matron who teaches nothing more than an occasional course at the university.

All of these people and many others like them in Middle City have learned, just as Willy Loman did, that elevated personal aspiration is a moral imperative in American life. Yet, having aspired, they have all failed to realize their aspirations in full; and as a consequence of this disparity between what they want to be and what they actually are, all are confronted by potent threats to their self-worth.

As believers in the "American Way," they are held in thrall by the individual-as-central sensibility of the culture of inequality. They have been free to aspire without limit and they have been led to assume that whatever they reached for would be within their grasp if only their grasp were firm enough, if only they possessed the will to achieve and acquired the competence necessary to serve their aspirations. Having failed to achieve up to their aspirations, they are thus tormented by an incipient sense of personal inadequacy, by a sense that they have perhaps not possessed sufficient character to succeed, or that they have perhaps failed to acquire the requisite competence for the realization of their ambitions.

What do they do about these threats to their self-worth? What do these good Americans do about this sense that whatever they have achieved they have achieved too little, this sense that they may be flawed by characterological infirmity or personal incompetence? How do the Willy Lomans of Middle City try to salvage their senses of self? How do they attempt to manage the aspiration-achievement disparity out of their lives?

If some use is made of the claim of situational impediment (in which the individual asserts for and to her- or himself that the disparity is a result of circumstances beyond control), by all indications the claim is infrequent and as one might expect—given its contradiction of the premises of the individual-as-central sensibility—none too successful. Some Middle City people indicate a sensitivity to its possible use but are moved simultaneously to cast doubt upon its legitimacy. When George Sellers tells us condescendingly that he wouldn't blame people who, having suffered some of the bad breaks he has suffered, stopped trying to get anywhere, he is actually telling us that his refusal to stop trying should be admired and that even a real situational impediment can be overcome by those who have ability and character. Yes, situational impediment might be claimed, but in his eyes not without cost to the person making the claim. Whatever its basis in actual events, its invocation is nevertheless a tacit admission of personal inadequacy. Paul Dahlberg says he can sympathize with people who have been discriminated against—he recognizes that some people have been impeded by circumstances beyond their control—but he is unwilling to legitimize discrimination as an excuse for failure. For Paul Dahlberg, whatever has happened has happened and people of real character do not let externally imposed misfortune bring them down. People of substance go on and do their best to overcome impediments that others place in their way. Sam Jasper tells us that physical illness and handicap are about the only situational impediments a person can legitimately claim. He is willing to assist those who are thus afflicted, but for Sam even the claim of physical incapacity is of limited legitimacy as a justification for the disparity between aspirations and achievements: the person of character will strive to overcome incapacity, whatever the obstacles to success.

As might be expected, the very strength of the individual-as-central sensibility in Middle City makes effective use of the situational impediment all but impossible among the whites. By virtue of their relatively advantaged position within the community (it must be remembered that most think of themselves as middle class, even when they are not), they are unlikely to have experienced impeding circumstances—short of severe illness and physical incapacitation—of such undeniable consequence as to render persuasive any claim they might make. It is important to remember that any strategy for managing the aspiration-achievement disparity out of existence can only be successful when the claims or behaviors it inspires are confirmed as justified by a group of people significant to the individual using it. Any claim of situational impediment contradicts the premises of the individual-as-central sensibility; therefore, when that sensibility is a significant element in a community's cultural amalgam—as it apparently is in Middle City—there will be few people likely to find such a claim justifiable in any except the most extreme circumstances.

One might expect that, given their disadvantaged status in Middle City, the blacks would be more likely to claim situational impediment (and, one should note, with obvious justification) as a means of coping with the aspiration-achievement disparity. Blacks do make use of this claim, but there are surprising indications that even among the blacks its effective use is more than just a little problematic. It seems that the individual-as-central sensibility is so strong in Middle City that even those people who might, because of their experiences, be expected to reject its tenets or otherwise neutralize its implications do not always do so.

There is certainly enough rhetoric in the black community to support claims inspired by the situational impediment strategy. As in any black community in the United States, there is in Middle City's North Quarter considerable sensitivity to the racial dichotomy, to the experience of exclusion and blocked access based upon racial distinctions. Go to a meeting of the People's Alliance to End Poverty, the Brothers, the NAACP, or even the Urban League and you will hear repeated over and over such statements as: "The white establishment in this town has kept black people down for too long; it's kept them out of the good jobs, the good neighborhoods and the good schools"; "Black people don't have a chance around here, they've never had a chance 'cause the whites have grabbed off all the best jobs and things for themselves"; or "There's plenty of black people with talent in Middle City who could do a lot if they only got the chance, but they don't get a chance at anything except maybe being maids or porters or car washers." Talk to people on the streets or in their homes and you will frequently hear them say: "There's no future for a black man in Middle City. If I stay it's only 'cause my momma's here and she sick so she needs me around"; or "No two ways about it, if you're black you going to starve to death in Middle City. You name me the black lawyers, you name me the black doctors that's been successful in Middle City—only thing that a black man been successful in here is bootleg liquor, and I know cause I been here practically all my life"; or "You know Wesley Jackson? Where he working, man? In a factory for $2.50 an hour—and he a college graduate from right over there at the university"; or "Look at these kids, how they goin' to get ahead? They in that work study program at school but the only jobs they get is in the car-wash . . . and if they not in the work study program then they still don't get to take those courses they need to go to college."

But in spite of the existence of these confirming cues, it is nevertheless risky for blacks to claim the situational impediment because they are liable to find that at least some of those they are closest to—and consequently some of those whose opinions they most value—de-emphasize exclusion and exploitation as externally imposed impediments to personal achievement. It is almost as though these people, while recognizing the existence of exclusion and exploitation, feel that there is some shame or stigma attached to the experience of being excluded and exploited. While in the abstract such injustice is likely to be proclaimed, and while in the abstract such injustice is no doubt a source of considerable resentment, in particular concrete cases involving friends and acquaintances, the importance of exclusion and exploitation may very well be denied. In such instances the blacks of Middle City sound very much like their white counterparts. While granting that exclusion and exploitation are obstacles to personal succcess, they regard it as a mark of exemplary character when an individual overcomes these obstacles and a mark of characterological infirmity when the individual does not. In this light, comments of some North Quarter residents are, I think, quite instructive:

Nobody around here goin' to deny that things is tough, especially for the men. I mean, everyone knows that these men can't get them good jobs, if they can get any jobs at all. . . . But I'll tell you, many of my friends is just disgusted with the way their husbands just be around the house all the time complaining about how bad things is and being mean and all that. Maybe because she been out there in the community working, a woman is not too easily discouraged like a man is. A lot of them look at their husbands and feel he should do better and he shouldn't complain. They feel he's probably no good, he doesn't want anything—he's not looking toward future progress. . . .

or:

There are some people who think we'll never be accepted—on any standards, economic or social or even religious. They're real angry. It's really difficult to get people to see just how angry they are. But most people feel things are really better for us, for most of us, and we get tired of the excuses that some of these people make. My own brother is like that. Just sits around saying how tough things are, but I don't see him trying to do anything. . . . I figure if you don't try, if you give up your ambition, then how can you know that things are really tough? I told him if he got his ass off the front porch he might just find out that we're making progress.

or:

It used to be that people in the North Quarter could get very discouraged. You see, they would get a job—you know, maybe as a stock clerk or somethin' like that—and they would look around and they wouldn't see nobody like them, no black person who was a manager or a owner of somethin' like that. So they would just get discouraged. They couldn't see any progress bein' made. They couldn't see any better future for themselves. . . . Well, there's no person who wants to be a stock clerk all his life, so they would get discouraged and they wouldn't even care about the job they had. They'd get fired or just quit and they would go out on the streets and be up to no good. But now things is different. I wouldn't say there's lots of people from around here who got themselves better jobs but there's some—and if you watch the television you can see black folks who has really good jobs. . . . I think this is good. We're all goin' to be better off but right now, it's a funny thing, but it causes some problems that we didn't have when things was really bad. I know some people who having difficulty in their families with their wives and all, because of this. A man, now he can't have no excuse for not doin' well. Before, when everybody was discouraged, his wife would believe him when he didn't have no job or no good job. Now she not so sure—she not so sure he just isn't tryin' hard enough. I know lots of people who say they just having all sorts of problems at home because their women is just after them all the time, wanting them to get more than they got. . . .

Undeniably, there are people in Middle City—black and white—who are able to salvage their self-respect by recourse to claims of situational impediment. Some can do it because their claims are indeed confirmed by people significant to them. Others succeed with such claims perhaps simply because their narcissism renders their need for interpersonal confirmation less potent. Nevertheless, I am convinced that in Middle City the situational impediment strategy for salvaging the self can be used with minimal effectiveness at best. It is clear that even those whose objective circumstances suggest that such claims might be employed to maximal effect (the blacks of the North Quarter) are likely to find the reality otherwise. And if this observation is indeed correct, we should hardly expect that others whose circumstances are less "fortuitous" would find that they can use claims of situational impediment to much positive effect.

It is also unlikely that people in Middle City are able to manage the aspiration-achievement disparity out of existence by frequent recourse to the strategy of lowering personal aspirations to bring them in line with actual achievements. As I have suggested earlier, since the individual-as-central sensibility renders high personal aspiration a moral imperative in American life, scaling down aspirations can only be accomplished without attendant self-deprecation when the confirmed presence of situational impediments allows individuals to conclude that their original aspirations were in fact unrealistic—albeit through no fault of their own. Accordingly, one's self-esteem would suffer if, after aspiring to a career as a concert pianist and having failed to realize that aspiration because of ungenerous critical reaction (the aspiration-achievement disparity), one decided that the most to be hoped for was earning a living giving piano lessons to stubby-fingered children; the scaling down of aspiration in this instance would mean at least the tacit recognition that one had not been so good as one wanted to be. But self-esteem would not suffer if, after aspiring to a concert career, one lowered one's aspirations to piano teaching because of a mildly incapacitating arthritic condition (the situational impediment).

In reality, scaling down one's aspirations to the level of one's achievements is not an independent strategy for neutralizing the threat to self posed by the aspiration-achievement disparity. It is, rather, a strategy ancillary to and dependent upon the claim of situational impediment, and can in fact only be employed to bolster an individual's self-esteem in conjunction with the claim of externally imposed impediment. "Yes," says our piano teacher, "I wanted to be a concert pianist and I would have been one, too, if this arthritis hadn't begun to immobilize my left hand [the claim of situational impediment]; but I didn't give up—I decided that if I couldn't play, I still could teach [scaled-down aspiration], and I'm doing pretty well at it." Scaling down can be used, as in this instance, to overcome bitterness and disappointment which are likely to be the personally discomforting aftereffects of a successful claim of situational impediment. By scaling down aspirations, by denying the appropriateness of the original exalted aspiration—given the existence of impeding circumstance—individuals in fact maximize their self-esteem by fostering the sense that they have actually achieved all that they might be expected to achieve, the scaled-down aspiration now being consonant with the attained level of achievement. Therefore, it should be clear that the minimal successful use of the situational impediment strategy in Middle City implies that the scaling-down strategy is also used but infrequently in that community. At any rate, during the period I was in sustained contact with the community, I did not unearth any material which might suggest a conclusion to the contrary.

As far as I can tell, as a result of my observations of the Middle City experience, the only group within the community whose members might make fairly effective use of the scaling-down strategy are once again the blacks of the North Quarter. It is this population segment which, as I have indicated, is most likely to have effective access to the situational impediment strategy (although, as I have also indicated, this strategy is more problematic for the Middle City blacks than one would first surmise), and it is also this population segment, above all others within the community, which contains within it a visible group over-qualified for the vocational status they have been able to attain. There are, for example, black college graduates who work as clerks and maintenance men at the university, black college graduates who work as mail carriers, and black college graduates who work as typists in the community.[1] Assuming that such people make effective use of claims of situational impediment (discrimination), it is not beyond reason to speculate that at least some of them also make effective use of the scaling-down strategy. Black clerks or typists can say, if they wish to do so, that given the existence of widespread discrimination within the community, any exalted aspirations they might have had were really unrealistic and that consequently what they have achieved is about all that anyone could expect. This, however, is sheer speculation, since there is no material to reveal the occurrence of this thought process.

Counterfeiting success, creating the illusion that you have achieved more than you have, is of considerable significance in Middle City as a strategy for neutralizing the self-deprecating implications of the aspiration-achievement disparity. How successful the counterfeit is in any given case remains to be seen; but it appears that Middle City people frequently use it in their attempts to salvage their self-esteem.

If he were not trying to counterfeit a success he has not in fact achieved, why would Peter Pine, assistant engineer in a small civil engineering firm and father of two school-age children, have purchased two functionally inappropriate automobiles? Does Peter Pine really need his gas-eating, oil-thirsty Olds Cutlass Supreme and his sleek two-seater M.G. roadster? Is the costly Olds—and Peter Pine never lets a chance go by to tell you just how costly it is—really a family car? Does he really need that wire-wheeled rally car to make the two-mile trip to his office and back? Maybe Rita Bennett, Ph.D., who occasionally teaches a course at the university, designed her private recreation area complete with pool, multicolored waterfall, and all the latest and "best-designed" equipment for children because the city's recreation department does not provide such things for the general public; maybe it is a demonstration

---

[1] Such over-qualification is and has been characteristic of the gainfully employed black labor force in virtually every community in the United States.

project for her philosophy of recreation, but Rita Bennett, Ph.D., is more than just a little aware of the admiring exclamations which her project, her possession, elicits from the stream of visitors she welcomes most cheerfully. She may be a Ph.D. who has not been able to become a professor in a community where there are many Ph.D.'s who have managed to become professors, but she is the only Ph.D. who has a recreation area (which she herself designed) worthy of the Garden of the Finzi Continis. Eddie Finn, the electrician who wanted to be an electrical engineer, has a passion for possessions which appear to have no function other than to convey an image of status and material well-being not really achieved. His little house is a veritable clutter of such things as the required statue of a black footman sitting on his very small front lawn, a bar stocked with more liquor and more glasses than could ever be used when the Finns entertain (given the size of their home, they could never invite enough people to use half their glassware), the very latest in hi-fi equipment (even though the Finns, by Eddie's own testimony, rarely have the time to just sit around and listen to music), and even a hand-carved inlaid chess set, prominently displayed, but never used because nobody in the Finn family plays chess. And one has to wonder about John Althaus, the fifty-seven-year-old assistant to the co-ordinator of primary grades in the Middle City school system, who lunches every day at his club—the Middle City Country Club—and who thoroughly enjoys being waited on by its totally black and totally liveried dining room staff.

And then there are the joiners. Middle City abounds in voluntary associations and clubs, from the Heart Association, the Mother's March, Muscular Dystrophy, and so on, to the Lions, the Elks (black and white, separately of course), the Moose, the Eagles, Kiwanis, Exchange, the Knights of Columbus, the Jaycees, and so on. Sam Jasper seems to belong to all or nearly all of them. Is it just because there is so much community service to be done and so much good fellowship to be enjoyed? Perhaps, but you can't listen to Sam talk about himself for any length of time without sensing his desperate need to feel important and his perpetual insecurity about that importance. It doesn't overtax the imagination to conclude that these organizations—whatever else they might be—are for Sam Jasper mere props to be used in creating the illusion (for which Sam himself is the primary audience) that this shopkeeper is in fact a man to be reckoned with. You know that, whatever else he may or may not accomplish, Sam Jasper will continue to find organizations which, in exchange for his unflagging loyalty, will make

him their "man of the year." And if Sam Jasper is the champion joiner
of them all, there are others—journeymen by comparison—whose more
modest careers nevertheless suggest that, like Sam, they are seeking to
salvage their self-esteem by grasping for organizational success: Ken
Barrash, who has been an associate professor for much too long and
who has the habit of joining local urban affair groups (one after another), only to leave them (one after another) when his generous offers
to accept the burdens of their leadership are received with minimal
enthusiasm; Myra Lee Bonds, self-designated psychologist and expert on
minority education (she has no credentials other than a B.A. in psychology), who, after being defeated in a school board election (she received no real support from either the blacks or the whites), proclaims
herself chairperson of the Black Education Study Team (BEST), a group
whose members (besides herself and her husband) are, to say the least,
difficult to locate; Martin Burke-Wyman, who is at once a law school
drop-out (he claims he will return to his studies one of these days),
secretary of the Association of Real Property Owners (ARPO), vice-chair-
man of the Citizens' Tax Committee (CTC), and thirty-second degree
Mason; Bob Pickering, who dreams of owning a chain of fast food emporiums but who in fact manages a local bowling alley and is chairman
of the program committee of the Exchange Club, chairman of the
Jaycees' beauty pageant committee, and vice-commander of the local
American Legion Post.

These and other strategies for counterfeiting success are used by
Middle City residents when they are troubled by the personal implications of the aspiration-achievement disparity.[2] But no matter how successful the use of a counterfeit may be, as indicated previously it can
rarely if ever be completely effective as a means of salvaging the self in
the face of the threats posed by the aspiration-achievement disparity. A
momentary distraction, yes, a periodic escape into the fanciful, perhaps.
But unless the people of Middle City who make use of this strategy

---

[2] While I am certain that the success-counterfeit in which adults identify with
their children is used by at least some people in Middle City, it is a strategy which,
because of its intimate locus in the interaction between parent and child, is difficult
to observe and demonstrate. There are two indirect indications of its use in the
Middle City materials, however. It is implied in Paul Dahlberg's counsel of patience
when he indicates that even if an adult doesn't get what he wants perhaps his children will achieve those things, and is also implied, albeit even less directly, in the
emphasis Virginia Terrell places upon the extent to which she and her husband have
worked for the welfare of their children.

are willing and able to withdraw totally into a world of fantasy, a state which would almost certainly be incapacitating and which would no doubt be viewed by others as bordering on madness, reality and with it the aspiration-achievement disparity must ultimately intrude.

Peter Pine can roar into his parking space in that M.G. roadster; for two miles or so back and forth every day between house and office he can, perhaps, fancy himself the debonair master of all he surveys; but for the eight hours of his working day, he must confront the fact that he is an *assistant* engineer, not much more than a glorified draftsman who surveys only what he is told to survey. After lunching amidst the very comfortable ambience of the Middle City Country Club (the food isn't all that good, but that isn't really what is being paid for), John Althaus must return to the office he has shared for too long with too many grey metal filing cabinets and his boss's secretary. In spite of all the good he claims to do and all the "honors" he receives, Sam Jasper has to spend the better part of each day selling sweat socks, tennis shoes, and bowling balls—and he has been doing this for some forty years. And one has the strong suspicion that a meeting of the Black Education Study Team would only threaten the illusion of an elevated self which Myra Lee Bonds has been striving to create. No, assuming the existence of a threat to the self posed by the aspiration-achievement disparity, it is highly unlikely that the self can be salvaged and the threat removed, either totally or in considerable measure, by recourse to a counterfeit. Mundane reality, it would seem, is just too potent to be finessed unless one manages to avoid it entirely; and that of course means not the salvation of the self but its obliteration.

If the counterfeit, though widely used, is in most instances ineffective, and if the claim of situational impediment together with the scaling down of aspiration is used but minimally and to little positive effect, then how do those in Middle City who are afflicted by the aspiration-achievement disparity manage to contain and diminish its troubling implications? How do they manage to salvage their self-esteem? Do they attempt to save themselves from despair by distinguishing between their successes—however modest—and the "unequivocal failures" of others? Do they make use of the individual-as-central sensibility, the source of their troubled sense of self, to interpret the misfortunes of others as volitional or otherwise based upon personal inadequacy? Do they locate responsibility for apparent failure in the characterological and competence insufficiencies which others are presumed to possess, so that their freedom from such apparent failure can be taken to mean that they possess strength of character and more than a modicum of competence?

The Middle City materials suggest affirmative answers to these questions. There are, it would seem, many people in Middle City in a wide array of social positions who attempt to assuage their doubts about themselves by distinguishing themselves from those whose obvious misfortunes they interpret as indicative of moral infirmity or personal incompetence.

Let us focus on this effort to salvage the self—this effort which, it is safe to say, is tragic in its consequences for both those who author it and those whose lives it discredits.

### "Those People . . ."

There are people in Middle City who never miss an opportunity to remark on the personal inadequacies of the poor and particularly the black poor. The extent to which all these people themselves suffer from a sense of personal inadequacy born of the aspiration-achievement disparity is uncertain, but in a number of instances the association between a threatened self and the propensity for attributing misfeasance and malfeasance to the poor is strong enough to give pause to even the most skeptical reader.

Arnold Stallings has been a justice of the peace for about eighteen years. During that period he has presided over thousands of misdemeanor hearings and set bail for many defendants charged with more serious offenses. Justice of the Peace Stallings, however, wishes he were a real judge—he wishes that he could trade his small hearing room in the city hall annex for a real courtroom complete with elevated bench and well-appointed chambers. He wishes, but he also knows that, because he isn't a lawyer, his wish will never be fulfilled: while it is possible for a non-lawyer to become a judge, it hasn't happened in Middle City since before the turn of the century. Lawyers who know Stallings will tell you that the justice of the peace makes no bones about his unrealized ambition and will also tell you that he is very sensitive about his lack of legal qualifications, that he becomes angry and defensive when an attorney chooses to press a point of law.

Arnold Stallings has been accused of discriminating against black defendants who appear before him. In point of fact, he does not do so. He does, however, treat poor defendants—black and white—in a manner that can best be described as paternalistic. Poor persons of any age appearing before Arnold Stallings can expect to be called by their first names, chided for behaviors which have nothing whatsoever to do with the charges against them, and publicly ridiculed by the justice, who will frequently make sarcastic comments about an impoverished defendant's appearance, work history, and "recreational proclivities." Poor persons appearing before Justice of the Peace Stallings are very soon made to feel that their future depends not so much upon the impersonal and principled workings of the law as upon Stallings's personal sense of rectitude. Impoverished defendants come to court supplicants who, if they own up to the error of their ways, admitting to a more or less general moral lapse, can expect leniency (small fines, short jail terms, low bail, probation). For Arnold Stallings, the poor who appear before him (innocent, we must remember, unless proved guilty) are errant children who must be treated firmly if they do not admit their errors but who may be forgiven if they are properly contrite. In the words of one longtime observer of the justice's courtroom demeanor, ". . . Arnold Stallings has a way of making a man feel like something less than a man."

Says Stallings himself:

*I bet you thought I'd have something to say about Negroes. I've been accused of discriminating against them, you know, and there are a lot of people who are out to get me. But I think that after sitting in my court for over a year you would have to agree that I'm not discriminating against anybody except maybe those who are guilty and you can't blame a judge for doing that. . . . The law says you've got to treat the guilty different from the way you treat the innocent. . . .*

*There's no race problem in Middle City and really, even with all this antipoverty business, there's no poverty problem either. The only big social problem we have—if that's what you want to call it—is with those people who don't give a damn. They don't give a damn about themselves, about their children and about other people. They've just quit on life, they've taken the easy way out. They write a bad check because that's easier than working for a living; they beat on the missus because that's easier than working out their family problems; and they let their kids run wild because that's easier than bringing them up the right way. And sooner or later they wind up in my court and I have to admonish them. But most of them don't learn so I'm not surprised when I see them in trouble again. . . . Now, you can't tell me it's because they're poor! That's what a lot of these do-gooders say but it's backwards. They* don't quit because they're poor—they're poor because they quit, because as I say they don't give a damn. There's your social problem, a whole group of people who think the world owes them something. . . .

Bob Pickering, beauty pageant organizer, emcee of the Exchange Club's weekly programs, and vice-commander of the local Legion post—Bob Pickering, who manages a bowling alley although he aspires to the mantle and fortune of Colonel Sanders (of Kentucky Fried Chicken fame), bought the house next to the one he already owned in order to protect his neighborhood. Says Mr. Pickering:

The way I see it, what I did was to invest in decency. There's all this pressure to rent or sell to the wrong element and I figure if some of the more responsible people in the neighborhood can be in a position to resist this pressure then we can make sure that the neighborhood doesn't go bad. That's why when this house next to mine went on the market, I bought it. If I own it I can rent it to decent people and I certainly won't sell it to any buck who just happened to hit it big playing the numbers. You've got to be very careful or pretty soon this whole neighborhood will be like Pomeroy [a street in the North Quarter notorious for its complement of bars and houses of prostitution]. . . .

I guess you might call me prejudiced. Yes, I'm prejudiced, but I'm proud of it. I'm prejudiced against people who think they have a right to live off the welfare; I'm prejudiced against people who'd just as soon steal as say hello; I'm prejudiced against whores and pimps and people in general who've got no more morality than your average alley cat. That's the kind of people I don't want in this neighborhood and I don't think you'd want them too. . . . I want these streets to stay safe and I don't want any of these bucks threatening my kids or giving the eye to my wife. So if that's being prejudiced then I guess I am, but if that's prejudiced I guess I don't mind. . . . I can't help it if they're colored. I didn't make 'em that way. They made themselves that way and if they want to leave their jungle let them clean themselves up first, let them learn to live like decent people first. And if they don't; let them stay where they are—right in the jungle where they belong. . . .

Selma Johnston is the tenant relations officer for the Middle City Housing Authority. She had hoped for a career in business but took this job when at the age of forty-five she saw that she would probably spend the rest of her working days as an assistant to the credit manager of Reiber's, a local department store. She deals with poor people all the time and, as she puts it, "I'm very friendly to them because that's the only way they'll tell you their problems; and we need to know what's going on in the projects." On the basis of her five years on the job Selma Johnston knows a lot about the poor people of Middle City and she likes to talk about what she knows:

There's some that are very good. They come in and they are very good tenants. Never give you any trouble. And in a few years they've got themselves on their feet, so to speak. They've worked out their problems and they're earning a good living. So they come in and just as nice as they can be they tell you they don't need your help any more and they're moving out. Of course you're sorry to see them go in a way, because they're such good tenants, they've been so cooperative and they've never given you any trouble. But it is rewarding to see how these people have pulled themselves up, how they've been determined to change. . . .

But then there's others who you really wish would go, they've been so much trouble; but you know they won't unless you can find some reason to evict them. They're the ones who, if they can get away with it, will live in the projects all their lives. They won't try to help themselves. They don't care about having a better life so long as they have a roof over their head and enough food to keep them going. They're the type who when their kids get in trouble, when they break the outside lights in the projects or cut the screens or throw garbage around—they're the type who won't cooperate with us or with the juvenile office. They're the type who won't take care of their apartments. So many of them will not fight the roaches! And the roaches can really spread. It gets so bad that you think, well, if they don't start doing what they should be doing those roaches will just carry the entire building away. They're the type of person whose morals you have to keep checking, too. We don't rent to the women with illegitimate children, if it's a continuous thing year after year. We check on their history when they apply. We even check with the police. We don't feel we should take them. We do take someone who has had an illegitimate child and has not had any more and is behaving herself. But you've got to keep checking on them because once they get in they can go right back to the way they used to be. . . . It's when women have one man right after another that they cause trouble. But even when you check on them it's very hard to prove and it's very hard to get them evicted. It's low rent and these people will stay and stay because of these low rents. They're the hard core and there's lots of them and about the only way you can get them out for sure is if they don't pay their rent. But then they can always get the township supervisors or the welfare to do that. So we're stuck with them.

*It's sad, but they will not try—not with the roaches or their children or anything....*

Eddie Finn, the electrician who would rather have been an electrical engineer, the possessor of lawn statuary, unlistened-to hi-fi, and a never-used hand-carved chess set, is upset because his union has been accused of discriminating against blacks who have applied for membership. The fact that there are no black members in his local is no proof, he insists, that they are being discriminated against:

*These soft-brained queers from the university [a university group— Citizens for Justice and Equity—has brought the charges of racism in local building trades unions] don't know what they're talking about. As far as I'm concerned they've got their heads up their asses. They don't know a damn thing! They say we discriminate against the colored but that's a lot of horseshit. They think anybody can be an electrician, but if any one of them came on the job I guarantee you'd have roast queer in five minutes. The first time they tried to work with hot wires they'd turn as black as those friends of theirs who they go around crying about....*

*Being an electrician is no cinch—you've got to know a lot, as much as any electrical engineer or maybe even more, because the electrician is out there on the job and he's got to make decisions which come up that the engineer never thought about. So let's get this straight right away, you don't just walk in off the street and say you're an electrician. No way!*

*That's why we've got this test for people who want to join the union. There's a written part and then you have to come and have an interview. And it's no phony. The written part was put together by a bunch of engineers, so you know it's not a phony deal. Anyhow, there isn't a member of the local who hasn't passed the test and if these colored guys who applied had passed they would have gotten their cards. But they didn't and that's why they're not in the union. . . . When I say they didn't pass, I mean they didn't even come close! I was talking to Chuckie Gallagher, the business agent, and he told me that the best that any of these colored guys got on the written part of the test was a thirty-nine out of a hundred. Thirty-nine! Sweet Jesus, they give you almost that much just for getting your name and address right! So when I hear about how we're discriminating it really pisses me off. The only thing we're doing is making sure that the guys we send out on a job know what the hell they're doing....*

*I wish I could figure the colored out. I wish to hell I could under-*

stand what makes them tick. Why do they think they can just get what they want without working for it? If these guys wanted to be electricians why didn't they go out and learn what you have to know? If you're interested in anything that has to do with electricity you've got to know some math. I grew up in this town and I went to high school with the colored and I'll tell you this, you never saw any of them taking the kind of math courses that would prepare 'em. And something else, you never saw any of them even taking the right vocational education courses. No, they'd just hang around and cut classes, goofing off—being cool, you know, and not making any effort at all. While I was working my ass off studying, the colored would be out there laughing it up. . . . So now they want in but they don't have the skill because they were being cool all their life. Like I say, I wish I could understand how the colored think, why they think that they can do my job—that they're entitled to my job—when they don't know how to do it. Like I said, this business about us discriminating is a lot of horseshit and I hope you print that in your book. . . .

John Althaus, fifty-seven years old, the last fifteen of these spent as assistant to the coordinator (actually to two coordinators in succession) of elementary grades for the Middle City schools, seems to have two problems. The first is personal. He's been an assistant for much too long. The second is public. The poor want to have what he regards as inordinate influence in the determination of policy for the public schools. Says John Althaus:

We've thought long and hard about this. I, myself, have spent hours examining my own attitudes on this matter of the disadvantaged controlling the schools their children go to. I've always believed that you have to acknowledge your own prejudices and so on this issue I wanted to be sure that I wasn't letting any prejudice I might have toward the disadvantaged interfere with my professional judgment. I think I can honestly say—after all this soul-searching—that my feelings on this matter stem from my professional judgment and my professional judgment alone.

First of all, I think those people who are causing all this difficulty really don't understand what the problem is. Now this in itself is not surprising since most of them are disadvantaged themselves and can hardly be expected to understand the intricacies of educational policy. . . . They like to talk about a race problem in the schools or a poverty problem. They like to talk about unequal educational opportunity. They see everything as a matter of groups, as majority versus minority. Well, in my judgment that simply is not the problem. The problem is the need to be sensitive to the individual needs of children, of all the children in the system. We need to develop a program of individualized instruction for these children and therefore this whole question of the disadvantaged controlling their schools is a red herring. . . . Innovations in the direction of individualized instruction can only come from professionals who themselves are sensitive to the individual educational needs which these children present. Now, I said that it's not surprising that these disadvantaged people do not understand the problem; but surprising or not, the fact that they seem incapable of understanding it is proof, to my way of thinking, that they are unqualified to run their schools the way they want to. I think it definitely proves that under no circumstances should they have any more voice in the way we do things than they already have. . . . We already have a parents' advisory council and the disadvantaged are represented on it. What they now want is for that council to have administrative powers; and I think that given the fact that they are unqualified—even more unqualified because they are disadvantaged than most parents—this would be a very big mistake.

Second, I think that you really have to think about what being disadvantaged means. If you're disadvantaged it usually means that you are poorly educated. But more than that it usually means that you don't have the skills to get a good job and that because of this you probably are unemployed or you are working off and on. . . . Now I'm not implying that disadvantaged people can't be good people—I know some very good people, some very devoted parents, who you would probably say are disadvantaged—but I do think that such people are not going to be very good role models for school children and I do think that their ignorance of what it takes to succeed in work would be less than helpful if they were in a position to set educational policy. We all know that the schools are very important when it comes to developing work skills and work habits and I don't think it would be wise to have people running the schools who don't have these skills and habits.

Finally, I don't think these people are really interested in education. They're interested in socialization. I've heard them say that the schools should instill a sense of pride in their children. Well, as far as I'm concerned, the schools can't do that unless a child has a sense of pride that he has developed in his home, in his family. I think it's ironic. Besides asking the schools to do something they can't really do, these people are admitting that they themselves have failed in their roles as parents.

*Now, if this is the case how can we give these people the power to determine what the schools should be doing? How can we do that when they admit that they have failed with their own children? All I can say is that if we did it—if we gave in to their demands—we would be very irresponsible....*

Lest these instances of association between the existence of an aspiration-achievement disparity and the propensity to denigrate the poor or the disinherited blacks be seen as unusual or idiosyncratic, the case for the significance of the association can be rendered even more striking by a relatively brief review of materials presented earlier in this volume (see Chapter Four above). We find Rita Bennett, liberal to the core but with an under-used Ph.D., saying, "It's a shame that the disadvantaged are so disorganized. . . ." We find Leon Neighbors, a lawyer with a very modest practice in comparison to other Middle City barristers, saying: "There are just too many people who think that by the magic of the law you can make everyone equal. . . . I don't think you . . . have the right to say, 'I want this so you give it to me because . . . I'm poor.' . . . A poor person has the right to try and earn what the rich person has but he doesn't have the right to have it just because he wants it. But that's how some people are thinking these days. . . ." We find Virginia Terrell, the sometimes employed caseworker who, with her husband, has done well enough but would clearly like to have done better. Full of righteous indignation, she says: "There's some people that won't ever be satisfied with what you do for them. They'll always want more. These people could do a lot for their children . . . but either they are not interested in their children and so they ask other people to do their job for them or they just plain don't want to help them. . . . I know these people. I worked trying to help them. . . . and I know from first-hand experiences that they just don't care about their children and the kind of environment they live in." And finally we find Sam Jasper, whose threatened self cries out for salvation with, it would seem, his every utterance. "People shouldn't expect handouts," says Jasper. "But there's people that do. . . . there is definitely a certain amount that does expect a handout. . . . the ones that are physically able to work and don't do it, I don't want to subsidize them."

The type of data constituting the Middle City materials does not allow for a specification of the extent to which residents personally troubled by the existence of an aspiration-achievement disparity attempt to salvage their self-esteem by recourse to the denigration of "those people." Such a specification would require sample statistics which could be used to estimate population parameters, and the Middle City materials simply do not yield such statistics. Nevertheless, in these illustrations the association between the existence of such a deficit and the propensity to denigrate cannot be denied; and if the argument that those thus afflicted will in fact use denigration to distinguish between their own modest "success" and the "unequivocal failures" of others cannot be proved, a prima facie empirical case has at least been made for its validity.

The illustrative materials very clearly demonstrate the logic of the argument. In each instance commonplace personal circumstances are transformed into achievements deemed worthy of respect because there are "those people," "those others" who, with the same opportunities, have failed of their own volition or incompetence to make these circumstances their own. For Justice of the Peace Arnold Stallings, conventional morality and the ordinary pursuits necessary to get by without running afoul of the law (his morality and his pursuits) become praiseworthy because there are those people who "don't give a damn," who get into trouble because they have "quit on life," because they have taken the "easy way out." For Bob Pickering, common decency (his common decency) becomes uncommon because there is always that "wrong element" with "no more morality than your average alley cat," that element which refuses to live decently, which at the first opportunity will victimize the "right element" with its criminal lasciviousness. For Selma Johnston, just not being poor is an achievement worthy of respect because being poor is clearly an indicator of lassitude and moral infirmity. The public housing poor, she declares, "don't care about having a better life. . . . They're the type of person whose morals you have to keep checking. . . ." For Eddie Finn, being an electrician is exalted because there are others—the black candidates for membership in his union—who have failed to demonstrate the competence that he assumes an electrician must possess. Furthermore, in his view the blacks do not have the competence because they have shown no interest in the hard work (his hard work) necessary to its possession. For John Althaus, the mere possession of educational competence and the absence of a "disadvantaged" status are personally elevating, because of the ignorance (he's not ignorant) and poor judgment (they don't agree with him, so their judgment cannot be good) which the disadvantaged manifest. Rita Bennett, whatever else may be said of her, is not "disorganized" as the disadvantaged are. Leon Neighbors, however modest his law practice, possesses a superior moral sense because, unlike "some people" (the poor), he knows you can't have things you don't deserve. Virginia Terrell can celebrate her own superiority because, while she and others like her have striven to be good parents, there are "those people" who, although they "could do a lot for their children," have steadfastly refused to do anything for them. And, of course, whatever insecurities haunt the ubiquitous Sam Jasper, he at least doesn't expect "handouts"—he doesn't expect something for nothing, as some people do.

In each of these instances, the poor and the blacks are viewed as having had opportunities to do the right thing which they have been unable or unwilling to use. "Those people" could have been like us if they had tried harder, if they had worked harder, if they had gained the competence we have gained. The "fact" that there are identifiable groups in Middle City who have not been able to do what is necessary makes *doing what is necessary* more than just a commonplace. The existence of ostensible failures allows these otherwise ordinary citizens of Middle City to find value in their threatened selves. If others have failed volitionally, have manifested a crippling incompetence, have given in to their baser instincts, so too might these good citizens have done such things. But they have not! That they are not poor, not disadvantaged, proves (a proof premised upon the individual-as-central sensibility) that they have not, and therefore whatever success they have achieved—no matter how it compares with their aspirations—becomes, at least in their eyes, praiseworthy, praiseworthy because the existence of the immoral and incompetent poor, the failures, indicates that they, the successful, like these others, might have achieved much, much less.

What is involved here is a psycho-cultural syllogism which may be characterized as follows:

*Premise* In American society reward is justly correlated with effort and competence. The standing and material perquisites a person enjoys are functions of the quality of the efforts that person has undertaken to better his or her circumstances.

*Ostensible Facts* There are identifiable groups of people of low standing, possessing few if any material perquisites. Whatever standing I do or do not enjoy, whatever material perquisites I do or do not possess, whatever I have achieved relative to what I hoped to achieve, I am not among those whose standing is low, those who are bereft of material perquisites.

*Interpretation of the Ostensible Facts in Light of the Premise*   Those whose standing is low, whose material circumstances are problematic, have made insufficient effort to better themselves. They have been less than assiduous, or less than competent. As I am not among them, it is clear that my efforts to better myself should be deemed effective and competent.

*Conclusion*   I am, because of the quality of my efforts (in terms both of morality and of competence), a person of merit.

For those in Middle City who make use of this syllogism, the existence of the disinherited—black and white—is crucial. One might even say that if the disinherited did not exist they would have to be invented. The disinherited are crucial because, given the premise inherent in the individual-as-central sensibility, their existence can be taken to mean that my ordinary achievement has not been achieved by everyone, and therefore I am not as ordinary as I might seem. The presence of the disinherited can be taken to mean that at the very least I have overcome the moral lassitude and ineptitude that others have failed to overcome. The more visible these people, these contemptible people, these pitiable people, the better; the more troublesome their poverty, their educational failings, their moral torpor, the better. The greater their number and the more apparent their failure, the easier it would appear for any of us to have ended in disrepute as they have. And quite obviously, the easier or the more probable the slide into disrepute, the more uncommon and praiseworthy are my efforts, my successful efforts, to avoid so doleful a fate. Take away the disinherited, render them invisible, and I am indeed in trouble. Without their presence I cannot easily distinguish my achievements from the achievements of others. Everyone, it seems, has accomplished as much as I have, and some—perhaps many—have achieved more. Take away the disinherited, whose gross failures render my modest successes consequential, and my modest successes are no longer consequential or praiseworthy. One can hardly be praised for doing what is necessary if everyone does what is necessary. Take away the disinherited and I am left with the troubling legacy of Willy Loman— I am left with the individual-as-central sensibility and the unrelieved threat to my self-esteem which is born of it.

# 6

## Keeping the Poor in Their Place:
## A Problem Made Necessary

★

Earlier in this book I argued that one major implication of the American culture of inequality is that it virtually mandates the highly visible existence of major social problems such as poverty, the racial dichotomy, educational failure, and crime. I suggested that as long as our imaginations and psyches are held in thrall by the culture's main tenet—the individual-as-central sensibility (in both its moralistic and modified forms)—we will continue to rely upon the apparently unequivocal failures of others for reassurance that we ourselves have not failed; and consequently we will make policy choices and continue practices which, contrary to their ostensible remedial purposes, actually function to sustain those social problems which spawn the illusion of massive failure in others.

Having illustrated the necessity of the "disreputable," "indecent," and even "criminal" poor (black and white) in Middle City, having indicated how comforting their presence is to those who are threatened by the terrifying shade of Willy Loman, I should like to conclude our Middle City odyssey by drawing the reader's attention to some of the ways in which the problem of poverty is sustained by the policies and practices of those who have an ostensible responsibility for reducing its impact upon the community.[1]

In surveying Middle City one searches in vain for policy and practice which promise a significant reduction in the incidence of poverty. However discomforting poverty may be to some, however much a problem some may presume it to be, its continued existence within the commu-

[1] I am focusing on poverty here because in some ways it is an "umbrella" problem under which many of the problems of race, educational failure and crime may be grouped.

nity is necessary to the continued visibility of "those people" whose moral infirmity and demonstrable incompetence—whose unequivocal failure—is a comfort to those who are burdened with doubts about their personal value. What one finds instead is a record of response to poverty which can be characterized as contributing to its maintenance and which can be seen as often eliciting from the poor those behaviors which bring them into public disrepute.

If people go to the township supervisor's temporary welfare office seeking short-term financial assistance, they are apt to be confronted by an official miserliness resulting from the supervisor's mistrust of and contempt for the poor. They will have to contend with the likes of supervisor Joe Dalton, who is certain that "you can't give out money to these people because you never know how they're gonna spend it," who maintains, "They come in here sayin' that they need money for food and the next thing you know they're out there spending it at Westie's [an after hours bar in the North Quarter]," and who in conjunction with his fellow supervisors consequently makes a policy of his mistrust. "We don't give out money any more," he says. "We just give them this chit for a food order or the rent or the utilities and they give it to the folks they deal with who know that we'll be good for it. . . ." Poor persons seeking help will have to contend with Miss Mary Cloud, the sixty-year-old welfare assistant who, while sizing up the applicants, harbors the assumption that unless she guards against it, they will perpetrate frauds against the interests and taxes of the good hard-working people of Middle City. They will have to convince her not only that they are really in need but also that they are worthy of any assistance they might receive—no mean task, because Mary Cloud believes, as she puts it, that "welfare has become a way of life with many of the people who come in here—and the type who come in here . . . well, I don't think they can take responsibility on their own. And they're dishonest. You should hear what some of them will tell you! You know they're not telling you the truth; they stand there and tell you one story after another. You know they are—but to them they're not doing anything wrong. . . ."

People are not going to get on their feet or get a new start with the help of the township supervisors, not, it seems, if the supervisors can help it. The poverty-stricken will receive some help, to be sure, but just enough help to maintain their forlorn existence—enough perhaps to meet a rent payment, to purchase a little food, to pay the month's utility bill—but no more.

We can take it as a virtual given that no family on AFDC is going to receive enough assistance to escape the poverty which brought it to the Department of Public Aid in the first place.[2] An AFDC family in Middle City will—as it would in most American communities—receive just enough to allow its continued poverty-stricken existence. But beyond the financial insufficiency of the program is the demoralization it breeds, demoralization which itself constitutes an impediment to the struggle against poverty and which often appears to elicit, in the manner of a self-fulfilling prophecy, those characteristics that seem to mark the poor as immoral or incompetent.

Applicants for AFDC in Middle City have to confront implicit agency suspicions about their honesty. They are subject to thorough questioning about any possible assets they might have. Do the applicants have any insurance, any property—even a burial plot? The message may be implicit, but it is no less clear for that: a profession of need by a poor person cannot be taken at face value. In fact, the poor person may not be poor after all. The profession of need may be a con; the claim of poverty may be a mask for nefarious intent, the kind of immorality which moves some people to want something for nothing. (You can't be too careful about those burial plots!)

Once accepted for assistance, poor persons must accept a definition of themselves as incompetent, as individuals whose inability to cope with the demands of contemporary life has resulted in their sorry dependent state. If those who claim poverty are really poor, then, as far as the personnel of Middle City's Department of Public Aid are concerned, money won't solve their problems; they need care, the kind of care which will enable them to overcome the incompetence which is, without doubt, the source of their poverty.

"I'm convinced," maintains Mary Elizabeth Ritter, the department's director, "that just giving people financial aid—particularly in the AFDC cases—is not going to help them very much. Most people would not be on welfare if they could carry through on their own. . . . Because of this I encourage our workers to get involved with our clients . . . and if the client is lacking in certain skills I think the worker has to try to make sure that she develops them. That's why we have the high school

2 The Department of Public Aid should be distinguished from the township supervisors' temporary relief. The township supervisors manage a program using local funds; the Department of Public Aid, the welfare department, administers programs deriving from the federal/state partnership.

equivalency program, the group counseling sessions and the homemaking skills program. . . ."

Risa Erving, a casework supervisor, is sure that "the department's emphasis just has to be rehabilitation. We don't want these people to be a continuing burden to the taxpayers. There are some people who have been living out of the public trough for too long and we're trying to get away from that. We're trying to educate them so that they do not have to ask for help. . . ."

For Stephen Reilly, one of the agency's more aggressive caseworkers, it is a matter of skills: "Some people," he argues, "just won't have the skills that this economy needs. There'll always be some without them and there'll always be some who can't see the necessity of getting them. We've got to remember when you're poor you think day to day; you don't think in terms of next month or next year. . . ."

Welfare recipients, whether or not they really need extra economic assistance (a matter which should be determined empirically on a case-to-case basis—but is not), get it. And like the inmates in the mental hospital who, as a matter of survival in that total institution, learn to conform to an imposed definition of themselves as "sick," welfare recipients in Middle City learn that even though the welfare workers' imposed definition of them as incompetent may be inaccurate, it is best to conform to it—if only to insure the continuation of the minimal economic support which the workers provide and which they so desperately need. One caseworker comments: "Some caseworkers believe that if you withhold or threaten to withhold checks you can get people to accept social services. . . . We've done it a lot with the adult education and the group counselling." When confronted with having their welfare checks cut off if they do not go to the Adult Education Center or the group counselling sessions, what else can the clients do except go and in doing so apparently admit, if tacitly, the personal inadequacy presumed by the caseworkers? And if for some reason (economically irrational pride?) the client refuses to be coerced, the outcome is pretty much the same, although more extreme; the recalcitrant client is viewed either as too incompetent to perceive his or her incapacity as the source of poverty, or as one of those malingerers who somehow managed to slip by the eligibility investigation. "There are some," Stephen Reilly maintains, "who you're not going to help, even if you're a dictator and threaten to cut off their checks. You just can't help them because with all their excuses they won't be helped. I can't tell you why but I've learned from bitter experience that there's nothing you can do about it—except maybe keep the pressure on."

Given these attitudes and the resulting programs, can we really expect that public assistance will reduce poverty in Middle City? Can the experience of being on welfare—of confronting a priori mistrust and condescension—be anything except demoralizing and alienating? On what grounds should we conclude that the welfare response in Middle City is anything but poverty-sustaining; that, financially insufficient and informed by the individual-as-central sensibility of the culture of inequality, it does anything except keep the community's visible poor in their place?

There are three public housing projects intended for low-income families in Middle City. Two are almost all black and the other is virtually all white. They are hardly garden spots. Garbage is usually strewn around; windows and door screens are broken in profusion; the trim on the buildings could use a good coat of paint; and the brick facades are marred by the graffiti of frustration and anger. Anyone walking through these projects would probably say something like, "My God, how can people live this way? How can they take what looks like perfectly adequate housing and turn it into a slum?" And that, it would appear, is precisely the reaction desired by the Middle City Housing Authority!

To put it very simply, if starkly, housing authority personnel seem to do everything in their power to ensure that these projects will give the appearance they do; they seem, so the record indicates, to manage these projects in such a manner as to render them physically explicit symbols of the failure of the poor who live in them. Starting with the assumption that only the unworthy have to live in public housing, they do everything they can to make their assumption appear correct.

If the garbage is strewn around in these projects, how should it be otherwise when the garbage is collected but once a week?[3] If garbage is a problem in these projects, it is a problem wished upon the tenants by a director of public housing who can dismiss their request for an extra weekly collection with the observation, "If the tenants have too much

---

3 Collecting trash once a week may be adequate if housing units are equipped with disposals to handle organic food leftovers and unconsumed wastes. A disposal is a luxury item and is of course not found in Middle City's housing for the poor.

garbage they can eat it"! If the garbage in turn attracts roaches and other vermin, whose fault is that? And whose fault is it that requests for exterminators are rarely if ever honored with dispatch? Why, we may ask, is the need for routine repairs in these projects largely ignored by the authority?

There is, it would appear, poor management on the part of the housing authority, but can the authority really be blamed for all the breakage and the rude graffiti which molest the facades of these buildings? Shouldn't the tenants have to take responsibility for this destruction? Superficially, it of course appears that they must. But even if the tenants or their children are immediately responsible, a careful reading of the relations between the tenants and those who manage the projects makes such destructive acts explicable and perhaps even justifiable as expressions of anger and frustration—anger and frustration that are reactions to the contempt in which the tenants are held by those who act in the name of the housing authority.

If the tenants request better service (better sanitation, repairs, and so on), not only are they refused but, because members of the housing authority's staff assume their unworthiness, they are refused in such a manner as to make it very plain that even if the request is objectively justified it will not be honored because the tenants do not deserve better service. You can eat the excess garbage, they are told; and as far as repairs are concerned—well, where do they think they live, in some luxury apartment? Not only do they have to continue living in filth, not only do they have to put up with peeling paint, warped doors, broken windows, and the like, but they must as well endure the insult of the housing authority's studied inattentiveness to these conditions. If in these circumstances some react by defacing their surroundings—by lashing out at the most immediate manifestation of the hated authority—it should not be surprising. Indeed, the absence of such a reaction would be much more surprising!

But even if the garbage were collected and the necessary repairs made, the tenants would have grounds for the anger which manifests itself in extensive breakage and the ugly graffiti. From the time they apply for an apartment in one of the projects to the time they give that apartment up (if they are ever able to), they are treated as though they were morally unfit, as though they were people who, unless closely watched, would take any opportunity to violate the norms of common decency and perhaps the law as well.

Selma Johnston, the tenant relations officer, checks with the police to

make sure that unwed mothers who apply for housing (and the authority is quite wary about renting to such women) have never been charged
with prostitution. Too many of the tenants, she maintains, "are the type
. . . whose morals you have to keep checking. . . ." Don Fogel, the assistant director for operations and security, true to Miss Johnston's
dictum, keeps a close watch on the morals and behavior of the tenants,
frequently encouraging them to inform on one another. Fogel is a man
who doesn't discourage easily, but although he "knows" that evil lurks
in those projects he hasn't had very much success in ferreting it out. As
he tells it: "I've asked the families to report on things that might be
causing problems—like more than one family living in an apartment or
if there's a lot of strange men hanging around an apartment or even if
there's fighting going on. But they won't cooperate. I know things like
that happen but they won't tell me. The only time I ever find out about
it is when I call somebody in and read them the riot act. . . ." The
project tenants stand doubly condemned: not only do they commit
offenses against decency, they have the audacity to refuse to bring these
offenses to Fogel's attention, unless of course he coerces them into doing so.

There is little the tenants can do about their situation. They have
a tenants' council, but its efforts to secure more equitable treatment
are largely ignored by the housing authority. After all, if the tenants are
immoral, why should their representatives be taken seriously? All they
want is more freedom to do things offensive to the good people of Middle City, things which may even be in violation of the law. Any protest
the council might bring against the tactics of Selma Johnston and Don
Fogel is itself likely to be interpreted as signifying immorality. Any protest against those who act in the spirit of righteousness must of course
be nefarious, and it would be nothing less than a surrender to evil if
the authority responded positively to it.

There is little the tenants can do to change things, and if some
should react to their impotence in this situation by destroying and defacing the housing authority's property, it is understandable. If you
mistreat me and I am unable to get you to stop, if you have all the
power and I have none, if you ignore my every entreaty, if you characterize my just protest as inspired by immoral intent—then I may decide
that the only option remaining to me is an attack upon something
presumably valuable to you; and whatever the cost to me I am likely to
make use of it. It is therefore fair to conclude that if the tenants in
Middle City's low-income housing must bear the *immediate* respon-

sibility for vandalizing the projects, the housing authority and its representatives must bear the *ultimate* responsibility for this destructive behavior.

In theory, low-income housing is supposed to provide adequate shelter and a wholesome environment for the poor. Such housing is supposed to provide the poor with an alternative to the decay and the depravity of the slum. It is supposed to be a response to poverty which maximizes the potential for escaping its destructive implications. In Middle City the theory is violated. The shelter is inadequate and the environment is anything but wholesome. The potential for escaping the cruel implications of poverty is minimized, and the poor who live in such housing are made to appear all the more disreputable for doing so. If, in theory, low-income housing is a weapon in the antipoverty arsenal, its real manifestation in Middle City makes of it a mechanism for the maintenance of poverty and for the maximization of the disrepute which, because of the individual-as-central sensibility, the public associates with it. It would seem that Middle City's public housing authority serves very well the need for unequivocal failures spawned by the culture of inequality— very well indeed!

☆

Poor children do not fare too well in Middle City's "pace-setter school system,"[4] but it is not for lack of attention. On the contrary, it is the attention, manifested as concern for the so-called culturally disadvantaged and their problems, which seems to do more harm than good to the children of the poor and which consequently enhances their potential for failure.

In grade school, "culturally disadvantaged" children are exposed to teachers who certainly know what to expect of them. The teachers have all attended the school system's in-service training sessions, where they have been taught that disadvantaged children tend to be both hyperactive and lethargic, where they have been taught that disadvantaged children may not be interested in learning because they come from homes in which the benefits of education are not fully appreciated, where they have been taught that disadvantaged children are likely to present behavior problems because they are influenced by a subculture in which physical aggression and violence are commonplace. The teach-

---

[4] The National Education Association has used this designation for those systems which it regards as progressive and innovative.

ers of the "disadvantaged" are indeed well prepared for them—well prepared, that is, to expect the worst from them. As one disenchanted teacher, a black woman with some twenty-five years experience in the Middle City schools, puts it: "Some of these teachers are so up-tight because of the foolishness that the special ed people have been putting out, that every time one of these kids coughs they think he's hyperactive and every time one kid pushes another kid they think they've got a barroom brawl on their hands. . . ." One can only wonder about the effects of this type of attention. If our disenchanted teacher is even half right, there are a lot of children in Middle City—poor children—who will learn very early to dislike school intensely and who, for that reason alone, will probably manifest those learning problems which are supposed to characterize the disadvantaged.

In the junior and senior high schools there is no dearth of attention, manifested in special programs for the "disadvantaged," but one must wonder about the impact of these programs as well: they in fact segregate "disadvantaged" students from their fellows and in doing so cause their stigmatization and exclusion from the normal range of school activities. As one guidance counselor observes: "I know these kids have special needs but sometimes I wonder if we're really doing them a favor by putting them in these classes. They really are isolated and even if we give the classes nice sounding names—like the exploration class or the cooperative education class—the other kids know that they're the classes for the dummies, for the kids who can't do algebra and the things they're able to do. . . ." One has to wonder about programs which make virtual prisoners of those disadvantaged students placed in them: "Once you're in, you're in for keeps," notes a vocational rehabilitation teacher. "Sometimes you come across a kid who you think should be in the regular classes but unless you're absolutely sure about it and unless you keep banging on doors around here that kid is not going to be moved out of the program. . . ."

The efficacy of these programs is also in question when many of those who staff them are predisposed to expect very little from their students and their students' parents. One wonders what kind of job is being done by the exploration class teacher in the junior high school who maintains: "There isn't much we can do when there's no direction in the lower-class home. I've got kids in my class who are contemptuous of school and there's nobody at home who's going to tell 'em that they're wrong . . ." or by the high school's cooperative education teacher who can say with assurance: "These youngsters are low achievers and they always have been, right from the first grade on up. Just look at their cumulative records and you'll see what we've got to work with. The best that we can do is teach them something about work—you know, appearance, reliability and things like that. . . ." And you've got to question the job being done by the remedial English teacher who is convinced that there isn't much she can accomplish because her students and their parents don't really care at all: "You can show these kids and their folks what's right," she says, "and they'll say, 'Yes, that's right,' but they really don't care about what you're saying because education doesn't rank very high in the culture of poverty."

Most questionable of all are special educational efforts in behalf of the disadvantaged which in the name of realism make a policy of racial discrimination. You have to be more than just a little uneasy when, for example, the director of the pre-vocational programs in one of Middle City's two senior high schools tells you: "We've got to be realistic in what we do. It just doesn't make any sense to prepare youngsters for jobs they won't be able to get. I don't care how many black kids want to be carpenters, it just doesn't pay to train 'em for that because they're not going to get into the union. . . . You put a black kid in a vocational program which is beyond his reach and you're not doing him any favor. All you're doing is misleading him and creating a situation in which he's going to wind up angry. The quickest way to start a revolution in this country is to lead people to believe they're going to get something which you know they're not going to get. . . ."

If these comments characterize the special attention brought to bear by Middle City's secondary schools on the needs of the "disadvantaged" —the children of the poor—then we should not be surprised when one astute school administrator worries aloud about the lack of success which seems also characteristic of these programs: "Whatever we're doing, it's not working. The kids are rebellious and the teachers don't seem to know what to do about it. The teachers lash out at the hard core and that just makes them worse. I think a lot of the disadvantaged are angry and mistrustful and we've got a polarized situation—the teachers on one side and the kids in the special programs on the other. . . ."

Perhaps the children of Middle City's poor would have trouble in the schools under any circumstances. Maybe they are hyperactive and lethargic, uninterested in learning, and much too aggressive. Maybe, but no one in the Middle City schools has really taken the trouble to find out. Middle City's educators—acting in accordance with the deficiency explanations which are part and parcel of the culture of inequality—have simply assumed the truth of these characterizations of the disadvantaged, and having made these assumptions have directed their professional efforts on behalf of the children of the poor in such a way as to elicit behaviors which appear, in the manner of a self-fulfilling prophecy, to validate their original assumptions. If the reaction of the grade school teachers causes these children to dislike school, then it would indeed be surprising if they do not develop "learning problems." If their dislike for school is then reinforced by secondary school programs which isolate them and hold them up to the ridicule of their peers, it would be unrealistic to expect them to respond positively and to surmount their "learning difficulties." If they are locked into programs and classes which they do not like, why should they or their parents display an abiding interest in what the schools have to offer? If, being black, they are discriminated against in the name of "realism" why should they be anything except mistrustful? And if as a result of all they have experienced they are rebellious, what else should anyone expect?

Perhaps the children of Middle City's poor would display these problems if the schools did something other than what they are doing. Perhaps they would fail educationally in the face of any effort the schools might make in their behalf. Perhaps the source of their problems is their family backgrounds or their immersion in an impeding culture of poverty. Perhaps! But one thing is certain: the present direction of the school system's efforts cannot help but elicit these very problems.

It is not possible, given the limitations of the Middle City materials, to ascertain the extent to which teachers and administrators in the system are themselves motivated by a need for failure in others when they contribute to what can only be called the *construction* of that failure. It would of course be surprising indeed if some of the teachers in Middle City did not suffer the same torments and harbor the same doubts about their self-worth as do many of their fellow citizens. And we do have the example of John Althaus, the assistant to the coordinator of primary grades, who comforts himself by distinguishing between his commonplace competence and the apparent incompetence of those "disadvantaged" parents who are pressing for a greater voice in the determination of public school policy (see pp. 149–51 above).

But whether or not the educators construct the failures of their "disadvantaged" students because they themselves are driven to do so is not really the central issue here—any more than it is when we consider the practices and policies of those who administer public welfare or public housing in Middle City. What is central is that educational policy and pedagogical practice emerge in such a manner as to construct the very problems and failures which the children of the poor are supposed to manifest because of the presumed deficiency of their backgrounds. What is central is that those whose responsibility it is to educate the children of the poor do, for the most part, accept as inviolable truths those culturally inspired deficiency explanations which presume that poverty is a function of incompetence. What is central is their continuing commitment to policies and practices inspired by these deficiency explanations even when such policies do not appear to accomplish their proclaimed goals. And finally, what is central is the tacit approval that this commitment receives from the lay public served by the schools. To be sure, there have been criticisms and protests, but these have come from a small minority—from those who have been trying to mobilize the poor and from some of those "university radicals." For the most part, however, the people of Middle City have been content to let the educators do their job—at least where the poor alone are concerned (in stark contradistinction to their vocal opposition to a school desegregation plan which went into effect several years ago)—to let them continue to do things which appear to insure the unequivocal educational failures of many of the poor within their midst. They are, one would have to conclude, well served by the educators' construction of such failure. The poor will continue to be "incompetent," their poverty will therefore continue to be "justified," and those who need to do so will continue to salvage their self-esteem by convincing themselves that although they too might have failed to get an education, that although they too might have succumbed to educational incompetence, they did not and have not and can, as a consequence, count themselves relatively successful.

Poverty and criminality are equated in Middle City. The police arrest the poor (and the black poor in particular, since they are the most visible) for alleged offenses which when committed by the non-poor rarely if ever lead to arrest: playing poker, disorderly conduct, drinking too much, battery. There is an arrangement between the police and the prosecutor's office whereby the latter, at the request of the former, is only too happy to trump up the *right* charges against a poor defendant after an arrest has been made. An ineffective public defender believes that 90 percent of his indigent clients are guilty of the charges against them, believes that they are prone to criminal acts because they just do not know any better, and believes that his office is a manifestation of special treatment for the poor because they do not have to pay for his services. His prejudices make it probable that there will be a high percentage of guilty outcomes for his clients; in addition, he is underpaid, he has the services of only a half-time investigator, and he is allowed to engage in temporally unlimited private practice. Finally, the addresses of the accused are published in the local newspaper, so that the good decent people of the community know that a high percentage of those charged with crimes live in the ghetto or in one of the poor white enclaves.

All these circumstances insure the public's awareness of the "high crime rate" among the poor, even if that "high crime rate" has to a considerable degree been constructed or fabricated by the criminal justice system. These circumstances, in fact, predispose the poor to criminal behavior, if only because the inequity built into the criminal justice system has alienated them from the "right" and the "good" which the law in its presumed majesty defends. The equation of poverty with nefarious interest—of poverty with crime—would thus seem to be assured in Middle City.

But surely, you say, this is an exaggeration; surely there cannot be such blatant prejudice and injustice in any community. Unfortunately, such injustice does exist in Middle City and no doubt elsewhere as well. Harold Herman, Middle City's assistant prosecutor, is quite instructive on this matter of injustice (although unintentionally so): "The whole time I've been in the prosecutor's office," says Herman, "I can't think of many people that's been involved in a criminal charge that I would even put in the lower middle class. Almost without exception they've been lower class. . . ." At the same time he tells us: ". . . you wouldn't believe the number of times that the police call and say, 'We got Joe Doe in jail and this is what happened and what can we charge him with?' and you say, 'Well, hell, I don't see anything there you can charge him with.' And they say, 'Well, we've got him so you'd better think of something.' So you do. You know there's always something you can charge him with—like being disorderly or something like that. . . . This is something you know you can't avoid because the police see a situation and they have to make a judgment when they think something is going on. . . ."

Harold Herman tells us these things without guilt, without seeing injustice in what he has said, without appreciating that his collaboration with the police amounts to nothing short of a conspiracy to deprive the poor (they are by his testimony almost the only ones charged) of their civil rights, and without appreciating that such collaboration must undermine the respect of the poor for the law and those who are sworn to uphold it. Harold Herman can violate his oath of office with impunity because in his view the poor, by virtue of their poverty, must be guilty of something, even if in any specific instance guilt cannot be proved. Assuming that, as he puts it, the poor "live with violence, they grow up with it and they have no sense of right and wrong," he conspires to "prove" these assumptions valid.

What happens to the poor after they have been accused (and very often falsely accused, if we take prosecutor Herman's word for it)? To whom can they turn? It is the public defender's office to which they must turn, where they will have to depend upon the efforts of Denny Waterman, who, by his own testimony, is less than likely to be willing or able to give them his best effort: "There are all kinds of frustrations in this job," says the public defender, "all kinds. First off, I sometimes wonder why I'm doing what I'm doing when 90 percent of the people I have to represent are probably guilty. I wonder what I'm trying to do getting people we've identified as troublemakers off with probation or a thirty-day sentence. Second, I can't do my job right. It's just me and the part-time investigator and I can't get any more help from the city council or the county supervisors. They don't really understand why they should use tax money to defend people, especially if they're guilty—and I can't say as I really blame them.

"And then I don't get any cooperation or appreciation from the people I'm defending. Public defender people will not keep appointments. They won't take me seriously. They don't realize what they're getting. They don't appreciate it and I think they go away without learning much of a lesson. If they had to pay their own lawyer, well then just maybe they'd get into less trouble. But as it is there's old Denny Waterman just waiting to get them off the hook. . . . Those are just some of the frustrations. But it's what you've got to expect when you deal with people with the kind of backgrounds these people have. It's what you expect when people come from homes that are crummy—where the parents do not teach the kids, do not imbue them with ambition or pride and just generally let them run wild. They get away with murder and they grow up thinking that's life. . . ."

Yes, there's old Denny Waterman waiting to get off the hook those ungrateful, immoral poor folks who are probably guilty—even though they have often been falsely accused—but of course since there are so many who are in trouble and since "old Denny Waterman" couldn't make effective investigations into their cases even if he wanted to, a lot of these folks have to plead guilty and take a little punishment in the process. Falsely accused or not, they must be guilty of something—they are, after all, poor, and they do grow up "getting away with murder."

Injustice *does* exist in Middle City (see also pp. 145–46 above), and through it, poverty and criminality are made almost synonymous. The most unequivocal failure of all—moral failure as marked by criminal licentiousness—is tailored for the poor; and garbed as they are in this raiment of disrepute they are a comfort to those people who will never be arrested, charged, or convicted of anything. Injustice does exist in Middle City and it makes the persistence of poverty all the more likely. If the poor are moral failures, poverty is plainly and simply their just desert. If the poor are moral failures, they cannot be trusted with any save the least responsible and therefore the least remunerative jobs. There is no reason to take their complaints seriously or to honor their petitions for redress. There is no justification for special efforts in their behalf. The poor become pariahs, and because they are pariahs the neglect sustaining their poverty appears justified. It is truly a magic circle! The poor can be mistreated by the police and the courts because poverty makes them guilty (just as Kafka's Joseph K. is guilty in *The Trial*). Their guilt is in turn publicly certified by the community's criminal justice system—by the law in all its austere majesty—and this treatment proves to many that the poor deserve the poverty which renders them guilty to begin with. It is a social tautology whose existence, rarely challenged by any except Middle City's "unrealistic do-gooders," is best understood in terms of the collective need for failure in others spawned by the culture of inequality.

That poverty is necessary in Middle City—that the response to its existence is, as it has been, to insure its continued existence—is nowhere more evident than in the record of the community's participation in the now defunct War on Poverty. As we have seen, it wasn't much of a war; at best it would have succeeded but minimally. But in Middle City, even this chance for minimal success was undermined by the machinations of the community's political system. The record of those machinations is far too extensive to be presented here in detail, but its most important aspects should be illustrated, not only for what they say about how the war was fought on the Middle City front, but for what they indicate about the general necessity of poverty maintenance within this American community. What transpired when the Middle City political establishment was called upon to facilitate the efforts of local poverty warriors is dramatized below.

☆

The city council chamber is packed to overflowing. All nine council members, including the mayor (who is a voting member of the council), are present. The audience seems to be constituted of several different groups. There is a group of well-dressed, prosperous-looking adults, both white and black; a group of adults in work clothes, most of whom are black; a group who by age and style (long hair, bell-bottoms, and ersatz work clothes) appear to be college students; and a relatively large contingent of black teenagers.

The meeting begins with the passage of a number of pay-orders on municipal contracts. As this business is transacted, the audience is quiet and inattentive. Some people are reading newspapers or books; some seem to be studying notes; but most are just sitting, apparently bored, glancing here and there and occasionally waving to friends or acquaintances spied in the hall. As the council moves on to its next order of business—a zoning easement requested by a local supermarket—one senses some restiveness in the audience. There are murmurs, the general noise level is somewhat higher, and people are leaving their seats although not apparently going anywhere. After about fifteen minutes of debate by the council the zoning matter is disposed of. Ignoring the now obvious restiveness of the audience, the council turns its attention to a proposal which would set aside two days, one in January and the other in June, as business appreciation days. Several of the council members request recognition, and the first is about to speak when a well-dressed black man in the audience steps up to a lectern facing the semi-circle of desks behind which the council members are seated.

"Mr. Mayor," he says in a loud voice, which is nevertheless barely audible because the microphone on the lectern has not been turned on, "Mr. Mayor, these people have come here this evening on a very important matter and I think the city council should . . ."

Before he can finish his sentence the mayor raps his gavel and, speaking into a microphone that *is* turned on, says, "Al, you know you're out of order. Audience participation is scheduled for later in this meeting."

The black man responds, "Mr. Mayor, I may be out of order but this whole meeting is out of order. . . ."

The mayor raps his gavel again and, visibly annoyed, says, "Al, you haven't been recognized to speak—you're interrupting the orderly business of this meeting. . . ."

At this point someone in the audience yells out, "Let him speak, he's got a right—this is still a free country—even here in Middle City."

The mayor, his usually pallid face now beet red, bangs his gavel several times. "I will not have any of that," he says. "Nobody is telling Al Baxter he can't speak. He'll have his chance but not until we get to the point on our agenda which calls for audience participation." A collective groan rises from the audience. The mayor continues, "I know Al here is representing the Urban League on something you all think is very important—the antipoverty business; but this council has other important business to take up as well and we're going to stick to our agenda and nobody is going to turn this meeting into a three-ring circus."

Again a collective groan rises from the audience. A disembodied voice lacerates from somewhere in the crowd: "If this isn't no circus how come we got a bunch of clowns sitting up there?"

The audience breaks into laughter and applause. The mayor raps his gavel and is about to speak once again when a member of the council interjects: "I know Al Baxter is out of order but I don't think we should let this get out of hand. These good people have come here with something they believe to be very important on their minds and while I don't think we should change our agenda I do think we should give Al a few minutes to say his piece. I think if we do so we'll have less delay than if we continue wrangling."

The audience applauds and the mayor speaks once again. "Okay, all right, he can speak now. But if he does he'll have to wait until everybody else has spoken in the audience participation before he can speak again. . . . The chair recognizes Al Baxter of the Urban League for three minutes and no more than three minutes!"

The black man at the lectern begins to speak: "A few minutes ago" he pauses, taps the microphone which is still not on, and says, "Mr. Mayor, I wonder if you could find it within your civil power to get this microphone turned on. I realize there's a lot of black folks here tonight and I can understand how you might not want to give them a live microphone—seeing as how they're liable to burst into song at any time—but

Mr. Mayor, this black man at least ain't got no voice and lawdy me I don't know why—but he ain't got no rhythm either! So if you use your power to turn on this microphone I promise I won't sing . . ."

Those in the audience who have been able to hear these remarks laugh and the mayor interjects, "Al, there's no need for that kind of remark. The microphone wasn't turned on because we're not in the audience participation—but I'll have it turned on. Now you've got less than three minutes and if you want to be a comedian you just remember that you're wasting your own time. . . ."

The black man begins to speak again: "A few minutes ago I said that this whole meeting was out of order and as sure as I'm standing here right now, it is! This council is supposed to respond to the needs of the people of Middle City—all the people—not just the downtown crowd and the country club crowd . . . but for eight weeks now right up to this very minute you've been ignoring the needs of the poor people. That's why this meeting is out of order and that's why every council meeting in the last eight weeks has been out of order.

"The Green Amendment mandates a one-third representation of city government [5] on local Economic Opportunity Councils. Our local E.O.C. can't do anything until it gets municipal representation. It can't pass its budget for the coming year. It can't hire a new neighborhood centers' director. And it can't submit proposals for new programs to the federal government. It can't do these necessary things because without municipal representation it's not legally constituted. . . .

"For the last eight weeks we have been asking the city to appoint its representatives. First we asked the mayor but he said he didn't have the power to make these appointments, that the city council would have to do it. So we asked you to make the appointments, to put it on your agenda. We know this is an urgent matter and you know it, too. There are deadlines which E.O.C. has to meet or it will virtually go out of business. And it can't legally meet those deadlines unless it has municipal representation. For the last seven weeks you have refused to put these appointments on your agenda and when we've asked why, all you keep saying is that it takes time because you want to be sure you have the right people. Well, if that's true how come none of you has taken the time to consult with the poor people to see who they think these right people are?

"No, we don't believe you—we believe that you would just as soon

[5] Local officials or those they designated to represent them.

see E.O.C. go out of business in Middle City! And what's more I think that this is proved by what's happening here tonight. You finally put it on the agenda, but you put it last. You say it's more important to decide whether or not another supermarket should be built than to do what is necessary to keep the E.O.C. going. You say it's more important to decide on business appreciation days, whatever they're supposed to be. And if we look down the rest of the agenda what do we see? Before we get to the E.O.C. appointments you're going to discuss the appointment of a task force to study outdoor advertising and you're going to discuss an increase in the city's contribution to the county fair budget! Very important!—clearly more important to you than the E.O.C. and what it might be able to do for the poor people of this community.

"I'm not a militant. I represent an organization which stands for the widest cooperation in solving our problems. But what's been going on here makes me sick. And let me tell you one more thing. Unless you change the agenda, unless you show some fairness in your response to the needs of the poor people in Middle City, we're goin' to have not only a long hot summer but a pretty warm spring also. Don't fool yourselves, Middle City can burn just as easily as the next city. . . ."

At this point the speaker sits down and the audience applauds, stamps its feet, and whistles in appreciation. The mayor raps his gavel several times, and the councilman who had requested that Al Baxter be allowed to speak signals for recognition. Getting it, he says: "We've all heard Al Baxter now and I'm glad we did. But I'd like to go on record as saying that he is wrong on every point and he is particularly off base on his last point. You can't threaten the city, Al. You can't get us to do what you want us to do by threats. It won't work. In fact it makes everything worse. If there was any possibility that we might change the order of tonight's agenda let me tell you that your last remarks—your threat—has destroyed that possibility. I request . . ."

From his seat Al Baxter interjects: "I wasn't threatening anybody. I was just telling it like it is. You've got to realize that your acts have consequences. You've . . ."

The councilman, speaking emphatically into his microphone, continues: "Your honor, I believe I had the floor, and I respectfully request that we proceed with our agenda for this meeting."

The audience, now very distraught, boos this last statement. Some people jump to their feet and begin to harangue the council.

"I've had enough of this. We goin' to burn this whole town down if that's what it takes. . . ."

"If you won't do your duty how do you expect us to feel about this damn city? . . ."

"You ain't goin' to do no business until you do the business you supposed to be doing. . . ."

"We ain't going to be treated like we was dirt under your feet. This here's no plantation and you can't act like we was in Mississippi. . . ."

The mayor raps his gavel and shouts into his microphone: "I'm telling you all just once to sit down and be orderly. I'm not going to tolerate this kind of behavior. Sit down and wait your turn to be heard or I am going to have the police chief remove you from this chamber. . . ."

A number of the older, better dressed people get up and motion to those who have been standing and haranguing the council to restrain themselves. Al Baxter comes forward to the lectern once again and speaks to the audience: "Folks, it won't do us any good to get thrown out of here. We know we're right and so do these *honorable* people sitting up here. If they want to stick to their agenda that's their right, but we're gonna stay right here—all night if that's what's necessary—and we're gonna see to it that these *honorable* people do their duty. So let's be cool. It's only going to hurt us if we get thrown out or if they refuse to go on with the meeting. So let's cool it. Let's stay here and make sure that the job gets done." Most of the standees sit down. Some leave the council chambers, and it is clear that the council will be able to continue its meeting according to its own predisposition.

And so it does. For the next one hour and ten minutes the nine members of the council discuss the business appreciation proposal (they support it unanimously), debate the necessity of an outside advertising task force (determining by a vote of six to three that such a task force is necessary, even though the dissenters suggest that it might very well interfere with the inherent right of every American to advertise anything —anywhere), and debate whether the city should increase its financial contribution to the county fair (leaving this issue unresolved, as the emerging consensus is that the proposal needs more study). There are no further outbursts from the audience. People drift in and out of the chamber and no one, it seems, is particularly attentive to the council's proceedings. When finally the mayor calls the council's attention to the last item on the agenda—the appointment of municipal representatives to the Economic Opportunity Council—a number of people leave the chamber, apparently to round up those who have drifted off into the halls. In a minute or so the chamber is once again packed with an audience now silent in intent expectancy.

The mayor addresses the council: "As you know, federal law requires that local antipoverty agencies have to have one third of their governing boards made up of representatives of local government. I asked the committee on city commissions to recommend ten people to act as our representatives, and I would like to have a vote of approval on this slate. Since as it is all too painfully clear this matter is very important to some people I will allow audience participation, but not until the list of nominations has been read and not until those members of the council who wish to have had a chance to comment on the list. Will the city clerk please read the list."

The clerk intones: "Mr. Lewis Barker, president of the First Savings and Loan [a member of the public safety commission]; Mr. Andrew Drew of Drew, McCallum and Short, attorneys at law [a member of the school board]; Mr. Gregory Pfizer of Lincoln Real Estate [a member of the civil service commission]; Reverend Mark Gallico of the First Presbyterian Church [a member of the human relations commission]; Mrs. Doris Simpson, assistant administrator of the Middle City Hospital [a member of the park board]; Mr. Harold Herman, assistant state's attorney; Mrs. Alice Freund, housewife [a member of the school board]; Mr. Clifford Wexler, owner of Wexler's Pontiac and Chevrolet [a member of the planning commission]; Dr. John Staufer, physician [a member of the board of health]; Mr. Harvey Clinton, advertising manager for the Middle City Citizen [a member of the civil service commission]." As the clerk reads the names, people in the audience write them down. Some murmuring and a few groans of disapproval greet the list.

The mayor asks for comments from the council. The first council member to speak is our old friend, Sam Jasper: "I want to say that this is a good group of people that's on that list. You've got a lot of good business and civic-minded people and I'm sure they'll represent the hard-working taxpayers on this so-called antipoverty agency. There's a lot of waste of the taxpayer's dollar . . ." The audience groans. "I see some of the people that's here tonight don't like what I just said—but it's true. How can you expect people who can't manage their own money to take good care of the taxpayer's money?"

Somebody in the audience yells out: "C'mon, Sam, how many times are we goin' to have to listen to you make your speech about sin? This ain't no Sunday school, man!"

The mayor pounds his gavel and Jasper continues: "Maybe if you went to Sunday school more often I wouldn't have to make this speech and maybe we wouldn't be having what you all like to call a poverty problem!" The audience groans again. "But anyway—these good business people that's on the list will be able to shape up the E.O.C. so that the taxpayers will get real value for their dollar and so I think we should approve this list unanimously!"

A second council member, Bill Percy (whom some suspect of being a member of the John Birch Society), speaks: "Earlier tonight when our meeting was disrupted I heard somebody say that if we didn't act on these municipal representatives the E.O.C. would have to go out of business. As far as I'm concerned that would be just fine—because we don't need it and it gives a lot of people an excuse for not living up to their obligations."

From the audience someone yells out: "The Third Reich lives again. Seig Heil, Percy!"

The mayor bangs his gavel and says, "If these interruptions don't stop I'm going to have the chief of police start removing people."

Percy continues: "That's all right, Mr. Mayor. What else can you expect from people who don't contribute anything to this community? The only time we see this behavior is when we're dealing with the so-called poverty problem or the so-called race problem and I think that should tell us something. It should tell us that it's just a waste to support the E.O.C. because all it does is encourage the irresponsible elements to continue their irresponsibility." The audience groans. "I'm going to vote against these nominations even though everybody on the list is a fine person. I'm going to vote against them because I really would like to see the E.O.C. go out of business. I think it's high time we took a stand in this community against gold-bricking. . . ."

Dave Davidson, a member of the Urban Co-Ordinating Council (a group of local businessmen ostensibly in favor of moderate reform in race relations and poverty in Middle City) and a "liberal" on the city council, speaks: "First, I'd like to respond to Bill Percy by saying that I personally resent the fact that he has called the poor people in this community lazy and irresponsible . . ."

Percy interrupts: "I didn't call the poor people irresponsible, just those who want the E.O.C. as an excuse."

"Well, whether you wanted to or not," says Davidson, "you certainly left the impression that you were doing that and I think there is no place for that kind of smear in our deliberations. I think, Bill, an apology is in order. . . . Second, I'd like to go on record as supporting the people who are on the list. There are some other people I might have preferred but I can live with the people on the list and I hope that the people in the audience—even if they prefer others—will welcome the participation of these nominees. After all, these people don't have to take on this job; they are involved in lots of other things and they won't be getting paid for the time they spend on the E.O.C. governing board. They have agreed to take on this assignment because they believe in Middle City and they believe in the future of all the people who are part of Middle City. . . . So I hope their willingness to participate will be appreciated.

"I would also like to associate myself with something that Sam Jasper said—even though I usually disagree with him. These people *do* have a good business sense and that should be helpful to the E.O.C. The people from the federal O.E.O. have said that there is some waste in Middle City's program and I don't think we should ignore that. I'm sure that these people with all the business experience that they've had will be able to help the E.O.C. to be less wasteful and concentrate on providing training for poor people so that they will be better prepared to contribute to the future of Middle City and to their own future as well."

Another council member speaks: "I move the endorsement of this list of nominees."

The mayor responds: "I accept the motion to endorse these nominations but we did promise that there would be audience participation on this so I think we should go ahead and open the floor to the audience before we vote. I will recognize anyone in the audience who wants to speak on this matter—but please confine yourselves to three minutes apiece."

A number of people in the audience rise and come forward to the speaker's lectern. The first to speak is a middle-class black man, Bo Jones, who represents the Brothers, a group of young black men who have involved themselves in a number of antipoverty projects: "Dave Davidson is angry with Bill Percy because he thinks he insulted the poor people of Middle City. Thank you, Mr. Davidson, for your touching concern—but I'm afraid it's not enough. This whole procedure is an insult to the poor people of Middle City and Bill Percy is just a little more honest about his feelings than the rest of you. . . .

"First we wait eight weeks for you to take action. The whole antipoverty program comes to a standstill because you don't think it's important to act quickly. You don't listen to us when we tell you it's urgent. Then we have to wait here tonight until you finish your *important* business. And to top everything off you nominate a bunch of people who have about as much sensitivity to the needs of poor people as Mao Tse-tung would have to the needs of the Rockefellers!

"There's not one black person on your list. There's not one person who has ever lived in the North Quarter or out in the Addition [a poor white enclave]. Even worse, there's people on your list who have a bad record when it comes to dealing with poor people and black people. . . . How come Gregory Pfizer is on your list when his real estate company won't sell houses to black people unless they're in the ghetto? How come he's on the list when just a few months ago he was in this chamber arguing against a fair housing ordinance? How come Doris Simpson is on the list when she was the cause of racial strife at the hospital— firing a black trainee without any good reason? And how about Harold Herman, he's a real champion of poor people, isn't he? Harold Herman has been prosecuting poor folks for years so I guess he really knows a lot about them and the things they need!

"Nobody has asked us for names of people we think should be appointed. Nobody has asked us what we think of the names you all have been considering. And now after eight weeks you come up with a list of people who can't possibly understand what the E.O.C. needs to do. We don't care how much business experience these folks have— that doesn't qualify them as experts on poverty. Mr. Davidson, it doesn't matter too much whether you apologize for Percy because this whole procedure insults poor people and hurts them. . . . All I can say is you all better think twice before you vote on these names—because if you put them on the E.O.C. we won't be responsible for the consequences. . . ."

As Bo Jones finishes, the audience applauds loudly while the members of the council look on impassively. The Reverend Tom Ross, a white member of the E.O.C. board, speaks next: "I'm not going to speak for very long, but I do have a few things that I have to say to you gentlemen. . . . What has happened here this evening is very sad and very un-Christian. Gentlemen, you have treated these people, your constituents, as though they are pariahs, as though by petitioning you on behalf of the E.O.C. they have committed some sin for which they must repent before you will treat them with the dignity they deserve. You have treated them as though poverty itself is a sin. . . .

"I feel no anger toward you for what you have done. I'm sure you are not aware of the hurt you have caused. But I am saddened by what has occurred and my confidence in Middle City's future is shaken. I hope that you will take at least a little time to reflect on your behavior—on what it means not only for these people here but for everybody in Middle City. . . .

"The people you want to appoint to the E.O.C. board are for the most part good people—but none of them is experienced when it comes to the needs of the poor. How can they be helpful if they are ignorant of poverty's travail? How can they understand hunger if they have never been hungry? How can they empathize with hopelessness if they have never suffered that condition? In God's name, how will they help to elevate the spirit of the poor if profit and good management techniques mean more to them than God's grace and God's justice? . . . You have not seen fit up until now to consult with the poor and their friends on these nominations. I hope you will reconsider the course you have taken and listen to us now! I plead with you and I appeal to the Christianity which is within you to at least consider the possibility of replacing some of your nominees with the following people: Nelson Franks, director of the Children and Family Services Agency; Al Baxter, director of the Middle City Urban League; Willie Lee Washington, relocation officer for urban renewal; Cynthia Bloom, a member of the League of Women Voters; and Angelo Miletti, a professor of political science at the university. Please reconsider your nominations. . . . I cannot help but feel that the future of Middle City may depend upon it. Thank you, gentlemen, and may God's peace be yours."

Before the next speaker can begin, Councilman Sam Jasper interjects: "Reverend Ross, I'd like to tell you something that I hope you won't forget. I'm just shocked that a minister like yourself would come in here and call people un-Christian just because they won't do what you want them to do. I think it's a disgrace. You're supposed to set an example for the young people. You're the chaplain over there at the university. . . . Well, if this is the kind of example you set it's no wonder that we have so much trouble with the young people that's listening to you. . . . How can you accuse these people of not being interested in God's grace? One of them's even a minister and the others are all members of a church. . . . I'm just flabbergasted at what you said, just flabbergasted. If you are such a good Christian how could you say what you said? I mean . . ."

The mayor interrupts: "Sam, I couldn't agree with you more, but time is running on and we've got to finish this agenda tonight, so why don't we let the audience continue with its speeches?"

Sam Jasper nods in agreement but he keeps whispering to the councilman seated beside him. As he whispers he seems to be shaking his head in disbelief. The mayor calls on the next speaker, a black teenager, who identifies himself as Clifford Robinson, president of the local youth chapter of the NAACP. "I'm not like Reverend Ross 'cause I got a lot to say. . . . And I ain't goin' to be referrin' to no gentlemen up here 'cause there ain't no sense in talking bout somethin' you can't see. . . . I *do* see nine clowns though, nine clowns who still think white is right, who still sayin' if you're black stay back. . . . Now these clowns up here in whiteface, well, they think they very funny but they so stupid they don't realize that nobody laughin' any more—that the audience is tired of the show—that they getting ready to give them the hook! . . . Now, I want to tell you what these old worn-out dumb clowns still think is funny. . . . They think it's funny when poor folks ain't even got a right to have a program which the government says they supposed to have! They think it's real funny to keep poor folks waiting for eight weeks and when they finally get around to taking up the poor folks' business, they think it's a real rib-splitter to keep 'em waiting until they decide a lot funky things like whether or not they goin' to appreciate business or whether or not they goin' to give more money to the county fair so that the pigs is goin' to be housed better. . . . They really think that routine is still funny and they be laughin' so hard at their own jokes that they just don't notice that the only people that is laughin' is them. . . .

"Well, you clowns, show time is over—and if you too stubborn and stupid to get the message we gonna burn your tent down. We're tired of your circus make believe. We' serious, you clowns—and if you don't get serious too the tent has got to burn, 'cause we ain't got no alternative. . . . Now you can go ahead and put those people on the anti-poverty board. . . . You can do it—but if you do don't think we just goin' to sit back and take it. Don't you think that, 'cause we ain't. We goin' to make them the most expensive appointments you ever made. We goin' to . . ."

Councilman Bill Percy, rage and contempt showing in his face, interrupts: "Mr. Mayor, this isn't audience participation; this is . . ."

But Clifford Robinson ignores Percy's interruption and keeps talking. In fact, in order to be heard over the irate councilman, he shouts: "We goin' to teach you that when we're serious you got to stop clownin' around and be serious too or else it's goin' to cost you . . ."

Amidst the cacophony caused by two speakers yelling at once the mayor bangs his gavel yet another time in what is becoming an exceedingly long evening. He asks, "Clifford, are you finished with your remarks?"

Robinson replies: "Well, I got a lot more to say, Richard [the mayor's name is Richard Schneider], but since there's lots of folks who may be wanting to say somethin' I guess I can save it for another time; 'cause the way you clowns operate, I'm sure they'll be another time."

The mayor recognizes the next speaker from the audience, only to have Bill Percy interject: "Mr. Mayor, I demand the right to speak. As a member of the council I'm not about to sit here and be threatened. This is the third time in this meeting that the council and the city have been threatened. I don't hear people presenting their views; I hear extortion, coercion in front of a few hundred witnesses. I think we've got a case against these people if we wanted to push it. We could have 'em arrested for the things they have been saying here tonight. . . ."

Someone in the audience yells out, "They ought to arrest you—you fascist—for slander . . ."

The gavel is rapped as if on cue, although it is a perfunctory rap, and Percy continues: "This may be the way things are done up in the North Quarter but it doesn't impress me or scare me; it just tees me off, and I'm not going to sit here and let a bunch of people who can't run their own lives run this city. I'm leaving, but before I go I'd like to point out, Mr. Mayor, that everything that these people have done and said here tonight proves that we don't have a poverty problem; we've got a *criminal problem*. . . . And we don't need any E.O.C. unless we can turn it into a law enforcement agency."

Percy gets up and leaves the chamber to an accompaniment of catcalls from the audience. At this point another council member, Joe Simms, breaks in: "I'm not leaving this meeting, but I feel the same way Bill Percy does. Audience participation is supposed to be constructive, but all I hear is insults and threats. I don't see why we have to put up with any more of this, Mr. Mayor. Unless there's people in the audience who have something constructive to contribute I think we should vote on the motion before us."

The mayor responds with more than a hint of weariness in his voice: "I know how you feel, Joe, but we did agree to let people have their say on this issue. I hope"—he addresses the audience—"that nobody will get up just to hear himself talk. If you don't have anything to add to what has already been said I hope you restrain yourselves. It's a quarter to eleven and we would like to finish our business as soon as possible."

This remark does not, however, deter those in the audience who have lined up to speak. For the next three quarters of an hour each in turn steps up to the microphone to excoriate the council for its insensitivity to the needs of the poor. Some speakers offer names as alternatives to the slate under consideration. Others content themselves with invective and with harsh warnings to the effect that if the council goes ahead with its slate of nominees the consequences for Middle City will be dire indeed. The council, minus Bill Percy, sits impassively through it all. No one responds, apparently for fear that any response will only prolong the proceedings. Sam Jasper, of all the council members, seems to be paying the most attention to the speakers. He scowls at times, reddens, and sometimes, hand over the microphone, whispers to the councilman on his right—but he says nothing for public consumption.

When the last speaker from the audience concludes her remarks the mayor asks the city clerk to read the names of the nominees and to restate the motion for endorsement, and then asks the council if there are amendments to the list or to the motion. Seeing that there are none, he calls for a vote. The nominees are endorsed by a vote of 8 to 0 (Bill Percy, having earlier absented himself, does not vote), and the Middle City Economic Opportunity Council has its complement of municipal representatives.

There are, surprisingly, no outbursts from the audience. It is as though, having had their say, the people in the audience have spent their anger, at least for the time being. It is now midnight and the audience, like the council, seems to want to go home. As the council moves to adjourn, the audience files out into the night. Policy has been made and acted upon. The city fathers have determined that the best way to fight poverty is to fight the poor.

It is important to understand what it is that we have just witnessed. If inroads against poverty in any community depend upon the cooperation of the non-poor with the poor, the Middle City council did in fact perform in a manner counterproductive to a campaign against poverty. The entire nomination process must be seen as counterproductive in that it alienated the poor from the city fathers and their choices for the Economic Opportunity Council.

Certainly such alienation had to be the effect of ignoring the sense of urgency which the representatives of the poor had communicated. Why, we may ask, did it take eight weeks to make these nominations in spite of the entreaties from the poor to the effect that immediate action was necessary? [6] Certainly the failure of the city fathers to consult with the poor on a list of appropriate nominees could not have failed to generate a feeling among them that the council was not acting in good faith. And when the council ordered its agenda in such a manner as to communicate the low priority it gave to the matter of the nominations, it virtually insured that the poor would respond with an anger born of justifiable mistrust. The entire nominating process accomplished nothing except to cast into extreme doubt the council's desire to fight poverty in Middle City.

What we have witnessed, moreover, is the playing out of a self-fulfilling prophecy: poor people were provoked into behaviors that appeared to confirm the disrepute in which they were held at the outset by at least some members of the city council. By ignoring the urgency of their petition the council signified to the poor its low esteem for them. And when the poor and their spokesmen responded with a vehemence born of frustration, disrupting the orderly process of the council meeting and threatening dire consequences, some councilmen at least used this understandable reaction as proof that the poor, unlike other petitioners, were unworthy. "Good people" do not of course show disrespect for their elected representatives, and they certainly do not threaten to burn the city down if they do not get their way: thus was the prophecy fulfilled and the assumption of disrepute "proved" valid.

What we have witnessed in the deliberations of the Middle City city council is a process which sustained the community's poverty problem even as its ostensible purpose was to remedy that problem. Instead of strengthening the Economic Opportunity Council's efforts by acting with dispatch to appoint municipal representatives sensitive to the needs

---

[6] In reality, the situation was not as urgent as the poor believed it to be. The Green Amendment did not in fact insist upon the extension of municipal participation in antipoverty agencies; it merely mandated that municipalities might exercise the option of increased participation. In all probability the e.o.c. in Middle City could have continued to function even if the city government refused to designate representatives to its board. What is important in this instance is not what the Green Amendment actually mandated but what the people of Middle City and the poor people in particular believed it mandated. They believed that extended municipal participation was necessary and that delay in insuring such participation threatened the viability of the e.o.c.

of the poor, the city fathers in their delay and in the character of the appointments they did make acted to confound and impede these efforts; and by clothing the poor in disrepute (the self-fulfilling prophecy), the council created a justification for continued insensitivity to their just petitions. Under the guise of a war on poverty, it would seem that the city fathers were in fact engaging in a war against the poor. Far from ameliorating Middle City's poverty problem, what we have witnessed could only maintain and intensify it.

☆

And so we search in vain for responses—past and present—which might contribute to a significant reduction of poverty and its socially damaging consequences in Middle City. What we find instead is a record of policy and practice, based upon assumptions inhering in the *individualism* of the culture of inequality, which largely assures poverty's existence: a record of policy and practice in welfare, housing, education, the administration of justice, and even that great crusade to end poverty in our time, the War on Poverty, which locks the poor into a state of perpetual economic hardship even as it marks them with the disrepute which appears to justify their condition.

Perhaps this record of poverty maintenance has little to do with attempts by many of Middle City's good and decent—albeit very ordinary —people to salvage their self-esteem by distinguishing their commonplace worthiness from the "unequivocal failures" of others; perhaps it has little to do with their personal desperation as they confront who they are in light of who they want to be; perhaps it has little to do with the threat to self posed by the aspiration-achievement disparity. But the fit between what one would expect (assuming the existence of a need to salvage the self by making the commonplace praiseworthy in contradistinction to the moral infirmity and incompetence of others) and what the record indicates is so strikingly good that I, for one, am forced to conclude that the maintenance of poverty in Middle City is—over and above all else—a function of the collective need to sustain a visible population of pariahs whose very existence is reassuring to those who need to distinguish themselves from apparent failures.

The poor are conspired against—not consciously, of course—but the culture of inequality (the same culture which drives many of us to the brink of despair because, accepting its individualistic thrust, we cannot easily reconcile the disparity between our ambitions and our achievements) renders, again by virtue of its individualistic thrust, such a conspiracy all but inevitable. It creates the need (the aspiration-achievement disparity) and it provides the means (the individualistic interpretation of success and failure), and so the conspiracy is entered into over and over again by otherwise good and decent people, the kind of people who live next door, who live in your own home.

Our Middle City sojourn is over. The illustration of the culture of inequality and its implications for the way Americans live their lives is thus concluded. It remains for the reader to determine whether the prima facie case made for the existence of such a culture in the first part of this book has been strengthened or weakened by the presentation of the Middle City materials. I believe that the Middle City materials speak strongly to the potency of the individual-as-central sensibility, to the hegemony of individualistic interpretations of success and failure, to the widespread existence of the aspiration-achievement disparity, to the threat to self it imposes, and consequently to the reality of a salvation strategy necessitating the maintenance of the disinherited and their problems. I believe that the case of Middle City, socially and culturally similar to numerous American communities, shows in sharp relief how the presumption of equal opportunity leads many people to justify the existence of social and economic inequality by reference to assumed unequal personal endowments of character and competence. Conversely, I believe that the case of Middle City reveals the insignificance of those interpretations of inequality that hold it primarily a function of enforced exclusion and discrimination. While its existence cannot be proved, there is, in my view, every indication that the posited culture of inequality is indeed at work in Middle City, making life barely tolerable for the disinherited poor and seriously troubling many of their more "fortunate" fellow citizens—those good average folks who struggle against Willy Loman's fate.

# EPILOGUE

# Some Thoughts on What Will Probably Happen to Us

The culture of inequality, it would appear, makes victims of all but a few of us. It victimizes the disinherited by mandating the persistence of their lowly estate. It victimizes many of the rest of us by threatening our sense of self-worth, forcing us into a demeaning struggle against a specter of self-denigration which threatens us with despair. The culture of inequality victimizes nearly all of us by rendering the theoretically soluble problems of poverty, race, educational failure, and crime effectively insoluable. In short, it minimizes the human serviceability of American society and makes life within it far more troubling than it ought to be.

If this state of affairs indeed exists, there is one final question that demands our attention: *What, if anything, can we do and are we likely to do about this culture so that we may live free of its pernicious implications?* Let us consider the possibilities. Having confronted the way we are and have been, in the preceding chapters of this book, let us conclude by confronting the way we are likely to become.

I, for one, would be very much comforted if I could believe that there is something which might be done to break the hegemony of the culture of inequality as we experience it. I would be comforted if I could believe that by conscious effort we might destroy the individual-as-central sensibility and the necessity of invidious distinction which it implies; that we might replace it with another sensibility, one that would allow men and women to find value in themselves whatever the personal distinction they aspire to and achieve. If such were possible I would have grounds for considerable optimism about the American future. I could envision a society in which the aspiration-achievement disparity would not threaten, a society in which the attribution of moral failure and incompetence to others would no longer be necessary, a society, therefore, in which the problems of poverty, race, educational failure, and crime would be amenable to solution. It is unlikely that such a society would be completely equalitarian: there is no human society completely free of social and economic distinctions; but, free of the individual-as-central sensibility, it could be a society in which such distinctions would no longer be taken as indicative of differences in personal value and its subjective correlate, self-esteem. It could be a society in which useful work well wrought by a statesman, an artist, a mechanic, a homemaker, a teacher, or a porter would, assuming sufficient economic recompense, be its own reward, as men and women would pride themselves in their contribution to the commonweal. It could be a society in which an economics of collective welfare would replace an economics of individual acquisitiveness because individual self-esteem would cease its dependency upon the acquisition of differential rewards.

If the contemplation of such a revolutionized future were more than a utopian dream it would certainly be comforting, but I fear (and I am sure that most readers will agree) that such contemplation is in fact almost wholly utopian and therefore hardly comforting at all. In fact, it would not surprise me if, even after all that has been said about the victimizing implications of the culture of inequality, some readers, still under its influence, were to find such contemplation not only utopian but repugnant as well. Yes, they might very well say, everyone would like life to be better, less arduous, less taxing psychologically; yes, it would be good to reduce poverty, bring about racial amity, increase literacy, and retard the incidence of crime; but who wants to live in a society where individual initiative goes unrewarded and perhaps even unrecognized—who wants to live in a society where all people are more or less the same, where the individual has nothing to surmount, where there are no personal risks? It might be more peaceful, but it would—shades of 1984 and *Animal Farm*—be boring and unfair; and, what is more, while it might suit the mediocrities, it would be a society bereft of the freedom to be great!

It matters little that my contemplation of a more humanly serviceable future implies none of these things. It matters little that a cultural sensibility allowing and even encouraging men and women of every station to value themselves for the contributions they make to the commonweal does not, by any stretch of the imagination, necessitate the neglect of individual initiative, an emphasis on mediocre sameness, and limitations on great undertakings. It matters little that this sensibility would be destructive not of individual differences but only of that pernicious conception of these differences which renders them specious indicators of personal value.

None of this matters very much, because the meanings of the extant culture of inequality seem so natural, so much a part of the American Way, that any alternative to this culture must, in the eyes of the many who are dominated by it, appear antagonistic to the very core of their existence. None of this matters very much, because in its hegemony the extant culture renders any and all alternatives alien and therefore repugnant.

It is for this reason that I cannot be very sanguine about my contemplation of an American future governed by a more humane cultural sensibility, a sensibility that would reduce the extent of social and economic inequality by rendering social and economic differentiation relatively insignificant as a measure of personal value. My contemplation of such a future is utopian not because it is unrealistic in principle, but because it is unrealistic given the limits imposed on the American imagination by the individual-as-central sensibility.

That this sensibility victimizes most of us—that it minimizes the human serviceability of American society—can, I believe, be argued with considerable force. But irrespective of this argument and the fact that many Americans are very troubled by the quality of their lives, most Americans are simply unself-conscious in their allegiance to this sensibility and are therefore not likely to undertake the cultural revolution which would lead to its replacement by something that would better serve them. Most Americans, as I have already observed in these pages (see pp. 17–19 above), have no conscious sense of a culture establishing a system of meaning according to which they construct their appreciation of success and failure, create their views on the personal meaningfulness of inequality, and derive their psychology of self-esteem. Their views are their views. They do not perceive them as derivative. Their views, so they believe, are informed only by their experience, not imposed by something which social scientists call a culture, by something which precedes their experience and to a considerable degree creates that experience. For most Americans, the trouble which I have argued is a function of the culturally induced aspiration-achievement disparity is not that at all; it is merely personal, a function of biographical circumstance. They do not perceive their biographies in cultural context, and consequently even their troubles will not move them to attempt the reconstruction of that culture which in fact serves them so poorly.

Thus I cannot take comfort in the belief that we will do something to free ourselves from the pernicious influence of the culture of inequality. In theory it is possible, but in practice the hegemony of that culture and the consequent naturalness—the taken-for-grantedness—of its tenets make the likelihood that we will reconstruct it minimal indeed.

What then is likely to happen? If conscious effort to make a cultural revolution will probably not be forthcoming, may it not be possible that unplanned change—the drift of events ungoverned by conscious intent—will result in the demise of our culture of inequality? Is it not possible that the culture may fall prey to its own dialectic, that paradoxically it contains the seeds of its own destruction? There is, it would seem, some reason to believe that the culture of inequality is not inherently stable, that in its hegemony it will generate events and circumstances likely to lead to its modification. But whether these events and circumstances portend its destruction and replacement by a culture which promises to be more life-enhancing is open to considerable doubt, and there is, I believe, reason to suggest that the resulting modification will in fact render us even more troubled than we presently are.

Because the culture of inequality mandates the existence of visible failure and therefore the persistence of major social problems in our midst—because it necessitates the continuing victimization of the disinherited—we are caught up in what may be termed a *calculus of estrangement*. This calculus, it seems to me, will lead to a modification of the culture which is at its source, but in a manner which will further minimize the human serviceability of American society. And the calculus is already set in dialectical motion.

Needing the disinherited, we respond to problems associated with their existence in ways which while frequently promising alleviation actually contribute to their persistence. We do not of course consciously enter into what looks very much like a conspiracy against the disinherited—consciousness of what we are doing would, given our equalitarian notion of fair play, make such a conspiracy all but impossible—but operating according to the individual-as-central sensibility we do respond to these problems in ways which have little or no positive effect. If the problem is poverty, we set about to reform the poor; we do not seriously entertain the possibility of income redistribution and other remedies for economic exploitation. If the problem is race, we may make a few passes at legal redress, but for the most part we bracket race with poverty and concentrate on reforming the blacks (just as we have concentrated on reforming their white brethren in poverty), largely to the exclusion of serious efforts to eliminate those exclusionary practices which make poverty their destiny. If the problem is educational failure, we do little except to emphasize special education and to blame such failure on the backgrounds of those who fail; we certainly do not attempt extensive reform of those school systems which often appear inadequate. If the problem is crime, we excoriate the criminal, engaging in rhetorical overkill, but we do little to rationalize the criminal justice system and even less to reform those social conditions, such as poverty and discriminatory exclusion, which are without doubt criminogenic.

When our response to these problems appears to accomplish very little—when, as they must, these problems remain with us—we do not as a rule question what we have been doing, but consonant with the individual-as-central sensibility we hold the disinherited responsible for the persistence of their difficulties. We have tried to help them but *they* have not responded. To the moralists among us—the so-called conservatives whose accounting of failure is pure social darwinism unaffected by the liberal penchant for deficiency explanations (failure viewed as a function of incompetence culturally or psychologically determined), this "failure to respond" is only what we should have expected. The disinherited, after all, are morally culpable, morally unfit, so why should anyone expect them to collaborate in the remedy of problems clearly of their own making. They do not have the moral capacity to change! To the "do-gooders" among us—the liberals, whose accounting for failure relies heavily upon deficiency explanations and who consequently are predisposed to "help" the disinherited rid themselves of incompetencies generating the problems in question—the failure of the benighted to respond to their helpfulness—to respond to such programs as welfare, the War on Poverty, compensatory education, and the like—is disconcerting and ultimately alienating. The liberal "helpers," having begun with a conception of the disinherited as people who *would* be competent if they *could* be competent, now read their apparent unresponsiveness as suggesting that perhaps their original assumption was wrong, that perhaps the disinherited cannot be helped because they will not be helped, that perhaps it isn't incompetence mandating their fate but rather, as the conservatives maintain, moral infirmity which best explains their troubled condition. To the extent that the liberals become disenchanted, they join the conservative moralists in their rejection of ameliorative programs premised on the deficiency explanations they formerly accepted as valid beyond any reasonable doubt.

These reactions are not without considerable impact upon the disinherited themselves. Many are simply demoralized by the apparent perpetuity of their trouble. Others, willing to believe that the programs of the liberals might really change their situation, are sorely disappointed when things are little altered. Some, feeling betrayed by those who have promised so much and delivered so little, become increasingly militant, joining in organized and sometimes violent rejections of the society which has so badly used them. Some develop an intense cynicism which moves them to use the liberals' efforts for their own and often illegal purposes (the many instances of financial abuse in local antipoverty programs are cases in point). Some come to harbor an inchoate anger that finds periodic expression in apparently senseless violence—which in reality is not senseless at all.

The liberals, already doubting the validity of those deficiency explanations which once were an article of faith, are in turn devastated by what they perceive as the reprehensible ingratitude of the disinherited. Not only have the disinherited failed to respond to the best liberal efforts to improve them (and thereby to render some of our most significant social problems less severe), but they have had the audacity to blame those who have been trying to help them for this failure. Hurt and threatened by the anger, militance, and cynicism of the disinherited, the liberals admit to error, but not with the kind of *mea culpa* that would cast into doubt a cultural sensibility holding individuals solely accountable for their failures and that, by so doing, would portend a new and promising approach to the problems of poverty, race, educational failure, and crime. Instead, they admit error which ironically portends increased investment in that sensibility and which therefore promises nothing in the way of the social reform necessary to the relief of these problems.

The liberals admit that they have been wrong in attributing the troubles of the disinherited to deficiencies which the disinherited would indeed choose to remedy. The "experience" of the liberals in trying to correct these presumed deficiencies has taught them that even though such deficiencies do exist they do not constitute the root cause of those problems characteristic of the disinherited—or, as they are wont to call them, the disadvantaged. The root cause, they now maintain, in grudging agreement with the conservative moralists, is the moral and characterological infirmity of the disinherited or disadvantaged. The liberals admit the error of putting too much faith in deficiency explanations, but, dominated as their imaginations are by the individual-as-central sensibility, the only alternative that makes any sense to them is the moralistic interpretation of failure so long espoused by the conservatives. Where once this sensibility had a dual manifestation, in the pure moralism of the conservatives on the one hand and the deficiency explanations of the liberals on the other, it comes to have but one manifestation: the moralistic account of success and failure, the moralistic justification of inequality.

If the anger, militance, and cynicism of the disinherited confirm the liberals' doubts and convert them into moralists, this conversion in turn only increases the anger, militance, and cynicism of the disinherited. From their point of view, those who professed friendship and sympathy have now shown their true colors. The sympathy must appear to have been false, the professions of friendship nothing short of hypocritical. Those among the disinherited who may have been willing to give the liberals the benefit of the doubt, those who may have been willing to excuse the inadequacy of their efforts as good-faith inadequacy, are no longer willing to do so. Those whose anger merely smoldered are now inflamed with rage; those who merely flirted with militance are now convinced of its necessity; those who might have been saved from cynicism are now encrusted in it. For the moralists, both long standing and newly converted, this quantum increase in the alienation of the disinherited is but further evidence of their reprehensible character, further evidence that they are the problem and that their lowly estate is but the just desert of their moral default. The calculus, at this point, will have run its dialectical course. The estrangement between the good solid citizens and the disinherited will be complete and very probably irreversible.

If such a calculus in fact does unfold as I have just projected, the culture of inequality will indeed change, but it will change in a way promising an increasingly troubled existence for most of us. If the calculus of estrangement runs its projected course, the character of the individual-as-central sensibility will become increasingly one-dimensional. Success and failure, together with inequalities of perquisite and status, will be seen more and more as the just correlates of individual morality and immorality. Whereas in the present success and failure are interpreted by some (the liberals) as functions of competence on the one hand and incompetence on the other, if the calculus runs its course the pure moralistic interpretation espoused by the conservatives will become virtually the only credible manifestation of the individual-as-central sensibility. The liberals, despairing at the hostility of the disinherited, will have been won over to the moralism of the conservatives, and their present construction of the sensibility, their present emphasis on competence and deficiency explanations for incompetence, will have been discredited and relegated to history.

Such a characterization, should it emerge as I suspect it will, would only intensify those conditions which even now so sorely trouble us. Most importantly, it would exacerbate the threat posed by the aspiration-achievement disparity, particularly for those people who presently embrace the liberal or competence version of the individual-as-central sensibility.

It is true that the aspiration-achievement disparity already poses a threat to almost all of us, but in the present the meaning and intensity of that threat is likely to vary according to the version of the individual-as-central sensibility we embrace. If we accept the liberal/competence version, the threat posed by the realization that we have not achieved (or are not achieving) all that we had expected to achieve is certainly troubling, but it is not a threat which leads us to question whether or not we possess the character we should; it is not a threat which calls our moral fitness into question. We are troubled because we believe ourselves less proficient than we ought to be in those tasks which if competently performed would bring us the esteem we seek, but we do not view ourselves as having failed to do what is morally right. The would-be virtuoso who is a piano teacher, embracing the competence version, is threatened by the ineptness of stubby fingers but not by any perceived flaw in character. The pianist senses a failure to challenge the eminence of Horowitz or Richter as the result not of insufficient effort but rather of insufficient talent. Subscribing to the competence version, the insurance man who is not the physician he wanted to be, because his grades weren't good enough to get into medical school, is threatened by what he perceives as his lack of ability, but he doesn't sense that his failure to realize his ambition is the result of personal weakness. Embracing the competence version of the sensibility, the longtime assistant bank manager who aspired to a career in high finance is uneasy about an inability to move up but doesn't perceive this inability as the result of characterological flaws noticed by superiors.

If, however, we subscribe to the conservative/moralistic version, the threat posed to our sense of self by an awareness of the disparity between our aspirations and our achievements is troubling precisely because it undermines our confidence in the moral rectitude of our lives. If, consonant with this moralistic position, we believe that success comes to those who make strenuous efforts and that failure is justly correlated with insufficient effort, indolence, and sloth, then any sense that we have failed to live up to our aspirations must be accompanied by intimations of characterological infirmity and moral laxity.

We sense that our failure to achieve our aspirations is the result not of insufficient talent (indeed, that possibility is not even considered) but rather of insufficient effort and personal indolence. Subscribing to the moralistic version, the failed virtuoso senses a lack of the character necessary to practice hard enough to succeed; the insurance salesman and would-be physician senses that he did not have what it takes to study hard enough to get into medical school; and the assistant bank manager who wished to be a financial mogul suspects that superiors have indeed discovered a lack of personal drive, that quality of exceptional effort so necessary to success in the board room.

Because the meaning of the threat posed by the aspiration-achievement disparity varies according to the version of the sensibility we embrace, so too does the *intensity* or seriousness of the threat. Some may wish to challenge this observation, but it seems to me that while the threat posed to those who subscribe to the competence version is bad enough, the threat posed to those who accept the moralistic version is worse by far. The suspicion that you have failed to achieve all that you wanted because you have lacked the skill or competence necessary for success threatens but one component (albeit an important one) of your sense of self—your sense of mastery. The suspicion that you have failed to achieve all that you wanted because you have been morally lax, lacking sufficient character to make the necessary effort to succeed, must however be reckoned a threat to the concept of your total self. There may be shame in thinking yourself incompetent, particularly if you believe yourself incompetent at endeavors significant to the identity you wanted, but such shame cannot compare to the shame accompanying a sense of moral or characterological insufficiency.

To possess character in full measure is in most instances to live in a manner consonant with the moral precepts of the community—to demonstrate these precepts in your daily life and therefore to command respect for *all* that you are. To lack character is in most instances to live in a manner at odds with the moral precepts of the community and therefore to be held in general disrepute, eliciting scorn for all that you are. Where failure born of incompetence may at times be pitiable, failure born of characterological insufficiency must always be contemptible. Incompetence may mean failure and inferiority and is of course painful, but it is a limited liability: it affects only the mastery component of self. Characterological insufficiency, denoting as it does the moral isolation of the total self, is a generalized liability and as such is by far the worse of the two.

If the distinction I have just made is valid, it is fair to conclude that in our present circumstances those who confront the aspiration-achievement disparity from the moralistic perspective suffer a more intense threat to their senses of self than do those who confront the disparity from the competence perspective. The sense that you are not all that you might be because you lack competence is simply not as troubling as the sense that you are not all that you might be because you lack character.

With this point of view in mind, it is easy to comprehend how a narrowing of the individual-as-central sensibility to a single manifestation characterized by the moralistic interpretation of success and failure would exacerbate the threat posed by the aspiration-achievement disparity. First, the conversion of the disenchanted liberals to the moralistic view would not mean simply that they would interpret more harshly the condition of the disinherited; it would mean as well, necessarily, a harsher interpretation of their own perceived shortcomings. Where now such shortcomings intimate personal incompetence, if the calculus of estrangement were to run its course they would come to intimate personal immorality. Second, because the existing debate between conservatives and liberals over the meaning of success and failure would cease with the triumph of the conservatives, the naturalness or "taken-for-grantedness" of the moralistic perspective would be intensified even for those who presently subscribe to it. As long as the debate continues, as long as there is a legitimate alternative (the competence version) to the moralistic version of the individual-as-central sensibility,[1] those who subscribe to the moralistic version cannot escape awareness that not everyone agrees with them; they must deal with criticisms of their beliefs and must therefore be at least a little self-conscious about them. As long as their beliefs are not shared universally, they must have some small awareness of them as beliefs, in contradistinction

---

[1] As far as present day moralists are concerned, the competence version may be an error, but it is a conceivable or legitimate error; see pp. 12–14 above

to moral principles from which dissent is quite inconceivable. With the cessation of debate and the almost universal adoption of the moralistic version, such awareness would disappear. With no legitimate challenge to its validity, the moralistic version of the individual-as-central sensibility, having become the only viable version, would take on the aura of inviolable precept. Taken for granted to a fuller extent than ever before, its impact upon our lives would thus be intensified. There would be no doubt about the immorality of failure, and therefore the threat posed by personal failure as manifested in the aspiration-achievement disparity would be even more marked than it is now.

Taken together, the extension of moralism and its intensification can only mean a future even more troubled than our present, which, as we all know, already has a surfeit of trouble. If the calculus of estrangement runs its course, the moralistic version of the individual-as-central sensibility will no doubt be the *only* version of that sensibility, and because it will have no significant competition, its impact upon our lives will be far more intense than it is now. If the calculus runs its course, there can be but little doubt that we will experience a future in which more people will be more seriously threatened than ever before by a perception of the disparity between their aspirations and their achievements. If many of us are presently tormented by fears of personal inadequacy, that torment will become even more excruciating in the future. If now, in the midst of all our pleasures and all the appurtenances of the good life, many of us are bereft of a sense of well-being and personal fulfillment, that sense will become only more elusive in the future. If today many of us need the apparently unequivocal failures of others as we attempt to salvage our sense of personal value, the future, ominously laden with moral approbrium, will only render that need more intense.

All this would be bad enough, but if this unfortunate prophecy indeed foretells the future, we are likely to confront *social* difficulties of even greater magnitude. The intensification of the threat to self resulting from the triumph of moralism must mean a consequent intensification of the need for failure in others, which in turn can only mean that the disinherited among us will be "kept in their place" to an even greater extent than at present. If the "good solid citizens" are increasingly victimized by a cultural sensibility driving them to question their moral value, it can only mean that the disinherited— the poor, the racially stigmatized, the uneducated, and those presumed to be criminally deviant—will be cast as psychic hostages with increasing frequency; it can only mean that their present victimization will be increased manifold. Should this situation come to pass, the social problems marring the American present will become even worse in the American future. Invested with an intense moralism, needing the poor and particularly the black poor even more than we do now, we shall surreptitiously do in the future those things which intensify the problems of poverty and race. Justified by our intense moralism, we shall no doubt neglect those with educational problems to an even greater extent than we presently do, and we shall do even less than at present to neutralize the criminogenic conditions in our midst. The disinherited will suffer even more than they do now. The intensification of problems associated with their benighted status will result in a correlative intensification of their misery. To create the illusion that we are angels, we will cast them as devils, and in doing so we shall consign them to a hell on earth.

And if the disinherited rebel—if their suffering becomes so unbearable that, having nothing to lose, they turn against us, their victimizers, en masse—our moralism will justify a repressive response. Because they are unworthy, because they are lawless, we shall police them mercilessly; we shall deny them their rights before the law because even the liberals among us will finally be convinced that there is truth in the conservative rhetoric holding that we worry too much about the rights of criminals and not enough about the rights of the good, hard-working, law-abiding people. If they rebel, we shall have the motivation and the strength to restore social order, but it will be order without social consensus and therefore order without social peace. We may "keep the disinherited in their place" by repressive measures which we believe justified, but we shall also live in fear of them. If because of our need for hostages against intimations of moral worthlessness we make enemies of the disinherited amongst us, if we use repressive measures to keep them in their place, we shall have good reason to fear them. They will hate us and should we relax our defenses even for a little while, some, momentarily free of restraint, will try to do us harm. We shall have social order but the price will be very high indeed. None of us will be free—not the disinherited whose aggressive "licentiousness" will have to be held in check, nor the rest of us, imprisoned as we shall be by our fears.

If the calculus of estrangement runs its projected course, the culture of inequality will have been modified, not for the better, as we might hope, but rather for the worse. It will be a culture which still justifies social and economic inequality by presumed inequalities in personal endowment, but it will do so more vehemently. It will still, and increasingly, make the individual and *only* the individual accountable for his or her social destiny, and in so doing it will victimize most of us—the good solid citizens who will continue to be apprehensive about the value of their personal achievements and the disinherited whose "unequivocal failures" will continue to be demanded by the apprehensiveness of the solid citizens. If the calculus of estrangement runs its course, all that troubles us in the present will trouble us in the future; but because moralism will have triumphed, all our troubles will have been intensified, perhaps to the point where whatever freedom and peace of mind we now possess will have been lost forever.

☆

Some readers, I know, will find my dark contemplation of the future unconvincing. Some, no doubt, will find little reason for my unrelenting pessimism. Some, even those convinced that there is an American culture of inequality minimizing the human serviceability of American society, will argue that conscious intervention can make things better, that the history of the American people with its record of great enterprises, and obstacles surmounted, should lead us to optimism about the future. What I see as failures presaging cultural tragedy they see as correctable imperfections, an awareness of which permits humane cultural reconstruction. What I see as the omega of American ascendency, as the tragic end of the American democratic adventure, they see as the alpha of a new era in which the errors and injustices of the past will be corrected to the benefit of us all.

I hope they are right. I hope that our failures are redeemable, that they are indeed nothing more than correctable imperfections. I hope that an awareness of the culture of inequality and of its major tenet, the individual-as-central sensibility, will lead to a conscious effort to break its hegemony over our imaginations; and that in making such an effort we shall succeed in maximizing the human serviceability of American society. That of course is the reason this book has been written. I hope my critics are right; but I fear that they are wrong.

To join them in their optimism I would have to ignore what I see happening around me. I would have to ignore the fact that proposals for a guaranteed annual income or a negative income tax have come to naught, while calls for ridding the welfare rolls of cheaters or for making welfare recipients work for their dole have been on the rise.[2] I would have to ignore the fact that presumably liberal state governors have adopted the rhetoric of the conservative moralists in apparently successful efforts to reduce the scope of welfare programs in their states. I would have to ignore the general hostility to the poor expressed by otherwise good and decent people, charitable people, people you would want as neighbors. If I were to join in the optimism of my critics I would have to ignore the steady rise of racial antagonism and polarization in our communities. I would have to ignore the report of the United States Community Relations Service, which held that in 1975 many American communities were verging on the brink of racial holocaust. I would have to ignore as well the liberals' growing predisposition to shrug off educational failure as inevitable for some, their growing penchant for seeing the educationally disadvantaged as essentially beyond redemption. I would have to ignore the chorus of complaints emanating from liberal teachers when they work in schools primarily populated by the children of the disinherited: their allusions to being wardens instead of teachers, their sardonic observations to the effect that if the schools do nothing else they at least make the streets safer from eight in the morning until three in the afternoon. Finally, if I were to join in the optimism of my critics, I would have to ignore the fact that the rise in reported criminal incidence has not sparked major reforms of the criminal justice system but has rather intensified an already existing preference for punitiveness. I would have to ignore Supreme Court appointments portending that body's increased conservativism concerning the rights

---

[2] When President Carter calls for welfare reform he asserts that there is a need to reduce the extensive fraud which he claims is characteristic under the present system; and ignoring the fact that most welfare recipients are not employable (they are over sixty-five years old, they are mothers of young children, or they are children themselves), he calls for an extensive reduction in the rolls by developing a job program for recipients. He announces that welfare should be provided for the *really needy*, thus implying that many now receiving benefits are morally suspect because they claim assistance for which they have no justification. Some see in the Carter proposals a call for a guaranteed annual income. In my view his proposals merely call for a guaranteed minimum welfare benefit which, by virtue of federal funding, would insure that eligible welfare recipients would not receive assistance at levels below a pre-set federal standard, irrespective of the state they live in. Unfortunately, as presently projected, the federal minimum would still leave recipients far below a realistic poverty line; and it is hardly likely that state governments which have a history of niggardly welfare payments will supplement the federal contribution in sufficient measure to bring the welfare poor out of poverty.

of the accused. I would have to ignore the increased volubility of politicians—from the small town alderman on up to the president of the United States—about the need for "getting tough" with the criminal element in our midst. I would have to ignore a growing tendency among the good solid citizens in this land of ours to view themselves as a besieged minority surrounded on all sides by those who, out of sheer malevolence, lie in wait, eager to do harm to their persons and property.

If I were to share in the optimism of those who see progress ahead, I would have to ignore indicators which strongly suggest that the calculus of estrangement is in fact running its projected course; I would have to ignore indicators which in many instances suggest that the triumph of moralism is at hand—that the culture of inequality is about to be modified in a manner which can only increase the troubled quality of our lives. To join in their optimism, I would have to ignore too much and, to my sorrow for us all, I cannot do so.

# Index

Achievement, 21, 27, 42–43, 49
AFDC programs, 53 n
Alienation from the American mainstream, 40
Ambition, 13. *See also* Aspiration
American experience, 4, 17–19, 21, 40, 44, 51, 61, 78, 86, 88, 91
Anti-crime response, 78. *See also* Crime
Antipoverty programs, 52, 54, 61, 63. *See also* Poverty; War on Poverty; Welfare
Antipoverty rhetoric, 51
Anxiety, 44
Aspiration, 15, 17, 21, 24–25, 35, 39, 42–43, 45, 50, 126–27, 138, 143. *See also* Ambition
Aspiration-achievement disparity, 15 n, 22–27, 29–37, 39, 44, 46–47, 50, 71, 72 n, 78, 87–88, 133–35, 139–40, 142–44, 151, 184–85, 189, 191, 196–99

Banfield, Edward, 62 n, 71 n, 97 n
Barth, Michael C., 53 n
Bell, Winifred, 53 n
Bendix, Reinhard, 4 n
Berger, Peter, 40 n
Bigotry, 45–46
Bigots, 47
Birmingham, Stephen, 5 n
Blumberg, Abraham, 80 n

Calculus of estrangement, 192–96, 198–201, 203
Capitalism, 15–16, 45

Cargano, George C., 53 n
Carter, Jimmy, 58 n, 202 n
Carter administration, 26 n, 53 n
Carver, Thomas Nixon, 6, 43
Chinoy, Ely, 15 n
Cloward, Richard A., 9 n, 55 n, 56 n
Cohen, Bernard, 77 n
Collectivist ideology, 41. *See also* Marxist ideology
Committee for Economic Development, 53 n
Communists, 41, 42 n
Community studies, 94 n
Compensatory education, 70 n, 193
Conservative moralism, 18
Conservative opinion, 40
Conservatives, 10–11, 13
Consumer behavior, 26 n
Courts, 80–83, 85. *See also* Criminal justice system
Crime, 73–87, 155, 167, 169, 189–90, 193–94. *See also* Anti-crime response
Criminal justice system, 80–81, 85–86, 92. *See also* Courts
Cultural bankruptcy, 50
Cultural criticism, 40
Cultural estrangement, 72
Cultural reconstruction, 201
Cultural revolution, 48, 191–92
Cultural tragedy, 201

Davie, Maurice R., 7 n
Deficiency explanation, 9–10, 12, 56, 69, 71–73, 130, 164, 166, 194–96
Demoralization, 55, 57, 157

Library of Congress Cataloging-in-Publication Data
Lewis, Michael, 1937 (Oct. 2)–
The culture of inequality.
1. United States—Social conditions—1960–
2. Socially handicapped—United States.   3. Equality.
I. Title.
HN65.L443   309.1'73'092   77-24214
ISBN 0-87023-857-4